The Quorum's Child

And the Constitution-Challenging Election of 2020

The Quorum's Child

And the Constitution-Challenging Election of 2020

By J. Fred Singleton

A Pun**4**Fun Publication

Copyright © 2013 by Joseph Frederick Singleton

Copyright Registration#: TXu001861007 / 2013-03-31

This book is a work of fiction. Most of the names, characters, and incidents are the product of the author's imagination. Any resemblance to actual persons, living or dead, is coincidental.

All rights reserved. This book or any portion thereof may not be reproduced or used in any manner whatsoever without the express written permission of the publisher except for the use of brief quotations in a book review.

To contact the author, use the address below or Qschild@gmail.com.

Printed in the United States of America
First Printing, 2016
ISBN 978-0-9977019-0-6 paperback
978-0-9977019-1-3 hardcover
978-0-9977-019-1-3 ebook

Pun**4**Fun Publishing
PO Box 401
Croton Falls, NY 10519-0401

About the Author

I was born Joseph Frederick Singleton, but at an early age my family called me either "Fred" or "Freddie". From the late 1950s through the early 1970s I grew up in Mount Vernon, New York (it borders the Bronx), which at the time was a multi-cultural, great place to live. My parents Joseph and Lucille, a postal executive and insurance underwriter, respectively, provided a loving home for me and my older brother Ken.

Like so many young men of that era, I was drawn to playing baseball and basketball, but in the late fall of my sophomore year I tried out for the Mount Vernon High School indoor track team – a decision which forever changed my life. Inspired by the seniors on the team and by my two coaches Dave Rider and Bob Brooke, two men who are on my personal Mount Rushmore, I instantly loved the sport. By the end of my senior year I was a three-time state champion and national champion in two hurdle races.

Accepting a scholarship to Penn State University, I had four good (not spectacular) years of running, culminating, in 1974, in being a co-captain of Coach Harry Groves' ICAAAA championship team – the first for the Nittany Lions since 1959.

Returning home after graduation, I was hired by the White Plains School District as a history teacher, assigned to the high school's alternative school, the White Plains Community School – a position and location I kept for thirty-six years. I loved being in the classroom and being around my colleagues. In my third year, I was hired as the assistant track coach, where I forged a strong coaching relationship and life-long friendship with Nick Panaro, who had also run for Dave Rider. Presently in my fortieth season of coaching in the district, I am so very thankful for the many thousands of people I have met either in our school district or from other schools– coaches, officials and of course, the athletes.

Today I am retired from the classroom but still teaching on the track. I'm meet director for one of the largest high school track meets in the

United States, the Glenn D. Loucks Games (www.theloucksgames.org). My wife Margo, a hair stylist in Bedford Hills, NY, is the sweetest person in the world – my real soul mate and the most understanding person I've ever met. My daughter Amanda is a teacher in the White Plains area. She remains the source of great pride for me. Finally, my brother Ken, a former major league baseball player (Mets, Expos and Orioles), has been a great inspiration to me and a great big brother.

I hope that you enjoy my view of a presidential election in crisis, and after reading it, I hope that you'll contact your representatives and senators and ask them to amend the Constitution.

J. Fred Singleton

Introduction

In the fall of 2003, as I prepared a lesson for my American History class, I noticed what I considered to be a flaw in one of the Amendments. Pursuing the issue, my Internet inquiries led me to a Yale law professor who informed me that he had recognized the same idea in the 1990s, petitioning Congress to make changes to the Constitution. If Congress didn't listen to him, why would they listen to me? Perhaps if more people were aware of the issue and saw the potential problem, the people on Capitol Hill might have to listen.

If I wrote a novel, I could get the word out to more people, so during the summer of 2004 I started outlining my book. By the next year not much had been done – too much was happening in my life, including my father's poor health. I started to write my thoughts on legal pads, filling up several with the origins of my novel. Dad died in April of 2007.

Sadly, it was my mother's cancer diagnosis which spurred me to write. While taking care of my ailing father, my mother had neglected her own health – developing uterine and ovarian cancers which spread into other areas of her body. I spent time with her in Maryland and when she went to bed at night, I would go to my room and handwrite chapter after chapter.

Despite the fact that I had been with her during her last two months, my mother's April 2011 death hit me hard, harder than I could have imagined. As family and friends arrived for her funeral, internally, I was at a loss, yet often reminded of her words to me a few days before her passing, on a night in mid-April of that year, long after she had gone to bed. I was writing and she shouted out to me in desperation. Rushing to her side, I carried one of my yellow pads with me.

After providing the aid that she requested, she asked me what was on the pad. "Mom, I'm getting close to the end of my book." Her words to me hit me like a ton of bricks, making me realize the finality which was rapidly approaching. "I'll never get to read it, but I am sure it will be good. Finish it. You hear me, finish it."

Having been one who had always listened to my mother (well, almost always), after her death, I returned to New York, with a renewed desire to finish my book. After months of typing the copious writings of my yellow pads, I emerged from my basement office to tell my wife, Margo, that I had finished typing.

The next step would be to find a professional editor, and I was fortunate. The mother of two of my former runners was an editor, and Betsy Rapoport made all of the difference, guiding my entrance into the world of writing.

So, world, here it is. Enjoy my view of the not-too-far-in-the-future election of 2020, a presidential election in crisis. Although its scenario might not play out exactly as I have written, my fear is that in some future election our nation will have to face this issue and not know how to handle it.

America, the solution is outlined here. Hopefully, someone in the future will dust off a copy of my book and present its solutions to Congress.

Mom, enjoy it!

J. Fred Singleton

Dedication

To My Parents Joseph Tyson and Lucille Anna Singleton
For providing me with love and the Spirit to Learn and the Courage to Explore

To My Brother Ken
For being a fine example of celebrity and a finer example of being a big brother

To My Many Relatives and In-laws
For always making me feel special

**To the Educators Who Taught (or tried to teach) Me in the
Mt. Vernon Schools**
Thank you all – especially Mr. D. Rider, Mr. R. Brooke and Mrs. D. Rider.
Also: Ms. Barry, Mr. M. Boyle, Ms. Bridge, Mr. A. Carapella, Mr. T.
Cawley, Miss Chick, Mrs. M. Chiti, F. Condon, J. Coughlin, Ms. C.
Feldman, Miss M. Jones, Mr. I. Kogan, Mr. J. Lee, Ms. Mrs. L. Marks, Mr.
H. Meltzer, F. Pandolfo, Mr. A. Pearlman, I. Peterson, Mrs. B. Rafkin, Mr.
G. Ridenour, Mr. E. Robbins, Mrs. A. Schwartz, Dr. Smith, Mrs. Sobek,
Ms. M. Taylor, R. Thomas, Mr. M. Warren, G. White, and S. Wrubel

To My Colleagues (in the classroom and on the track)
For creating an environment of learning for our youth

To My Students
For listening, learning and sharing

To My Athletes
For the endless number of miles and smiles that you have provided me

To My Friends
For allowing me to be able to call you a friend

And last, but certainly not least,

To My Daughter Amanda
For making me thankful every day for the fact that I am your father.
I am so very proud of you and love you so much.

To My Loving Wife Margo
For being there on July 20, 2001 and forever after.
I love you very, very much.

Thank you, all.

Acknowledgements

Legal/Government Items:

Theresa Maguire
    Pollock & Maguire, LLP
    White Plains, NY 10604

Michael Greenspan
    Greenspan & Greenspan
    White Plains, NY 10601

James Pharris
    Former Deputy Solicitor
    General
    State of Washington

Professor Hugh D. Spitzer
    Affiliate Professor
    University of Washington

Barry Pump
    Office of the Historian
    U.S. House of Representatives

Justice James W. Hubert
    Supreme Court, 9th District
    of New York

Steve Davenport
    Library of Congress
    Reference Librarian/American
    History Specialist
    Washington, DC 20559

Bev Morgan
    Thurston County Superior
    Court

Tracy Lewis
    Mayor's Office, City of
    Bellingham, Washington

Craig Kalkut
    Former Counsel on the U.S.
    Senate Judiciary Committee

Don Ritchie
    Former Historian of the US
    Senate

Akhil Reed Amar
    Sterling Professor of Law and
    Political Science, Yale University

Kimberly C. Sheehan, Esq.
    White Plains, NY

Medical Items:

Dr. Louis McIntyre
Phelps Hospital, Tarrytown,
NY

Dr. Michael Gewitz
Children's Hospital at
Westchester Valhalla, New
York 10595

College Campus Locations:

Kelly Maguire
Loyola University

Matt Soyk
Columbia University

Editorial Help:

Betsy Rapoport
Editor

Stonesong Press
Copy Editing

Janet Warmbir
Copy Editor

Julie Trelstad
Guide to the World of
Publishing

Alexandra Battey
Book Layout

Cover Design:

Jill Singer Graphics
Graphics

Patrick Carlson
Illustration

Chapter 1

The Unexpected

The White House
Saturday, November 16, 2019
9:03 A.M.

As the images CNN had captured of dead bodies floating in the Inner Harbor replayed in his mind, an angry President James Augustus Faulkner impatiently paced the floor of the Oval Office. Remembering the terrorist attack in Baltimore, Maryland, three days ago—the seventh city victimized since his 2017 inauguration—made his sour stomach feel even worse. He turned to the three people seated before him: Elgin Hathaway, the Vice President, Kitty Niles, Secretary of Homeland Security, and Chip Furry, head of the FBI.

"How the hell have you not cracked this yet?" Faulkner shouted. "I'm catching major flak here. Fifteen people dead in the Inner Harbor—all of 'em kids. The press conference two days ago was a disaster. We look like freaking idiots. What have you got?"

"Our bombing experts have determined that the materials used in all of the explosions have come from South Carolina," Niles said. "We've been tracking some radical Southern groups, but so far, nothing solid."

Faulkner turned to Furry. "So what do you recommend?"

Furry sighed. "Baltimore follows the pattern. We're looking at a city or town beginning with 'A' next. In each case the black section of the city was hit."

"The Harbor's not the black section of Baltimore, you idiot!"

"It is when Morgan State, Choppin State, and Bowie State are having coordinated class trips there at the same time—there were almost two thousand students in the area from historically black colleges!"

The president looked at him as if he himself had known that too. "Just testing you, Chip."

The day after Faulkner's inauguration, a bomb had exploded in a predominantly black high school in Springfield, Massachusetts, killing three people. Copies of a letter arrived at the office of every senator and at the White House the next day.

We will strike every city, in order, until the black cloud over our nation is dispelled and our government is once again ruled in purity. S.U.C.C.U.M.B., A.M.E.R.I.C.A., N.O.W., or more shall fall.

~G.O.D.

Then a few days later, a bomb exploded in a black church in Union City, New Jersey—thirty dead. Afterward, in order, bombs in African-American sections of Chicago, Cleveland, Utica, Milwaukee followed—a total of an additional seventy-eight dead. With Baltimore, the death toll was up to 123.

"There's no way to know which 'A' city is the next target," Furry said. "People in those cities are scared out of their minds. We simply don't have the resources to ramp up security in every train or bus station or school, church, and mall. They could strike anywhere from Atlanta to Anchorage."

"I'm guessing not Atlanta," Hathaway said. "G.O.D. is obviously some kind of white supremacist group in the South. The only thing we do know is that Southern towns seem marginally safer."

"Most terrorists' attacks use complete surprise as their main weapon," Niles said. "But these G.O.D. guys are putting it in our faces. They're just sitting back and watching us scramble."

"It looks like all we're doing is sitting back too," Faulkner thundered. "Kitty, Chip, I need more. Report back to me this time tomorrow. That's all for now."

Dejected, the two leaders left the office. Faulkner turned to face Hathaway.

"Look, Elgin, one of the reasons that I put you on the ticket was because of the perception that security was your strong suit. You were the tough New York governor that'd make sure we wouldn't have another Boston like Obama. You've given me next to nothing on this. People are starting to say that I made a mistake in naming you. I'm starting to have second thoughts myself."

Hathaway glowered at him. "You don't think that this is hard on me too? I take all of this personally. Utica was the hometown of my parents, where they grew up. Those were my people, from their neighborhood, and clearly the message was aimed at me. You're threatening my position on the ticket. I have news for you—I'm polling way above you. So tone down the rhetoric, my man, and let me get back to work. I have to help my people."

Faulkner slumped onto the couch, his face suddenly ashen.

Hathaway's face softened. "Jim, what's wrong?"

"I don't know, Elgin," Faulkner said, his voice weary. "I've been feeling like crap lately." He clutched his stomach and shut his eyes. Hathaway moved to put a hand on his shoulder and Faulkner twitched it away. "Just back off and give me some space. In fact, get the hell out of here and do whatever it is that you claim that you do."

Later that morning, Darlene Flowers, the president's executive assistant, buzzed him. "It's time for the ceremony, Mr. President."

"Could the timing be any worse?" Faulkner groaned. Today was the day he and his wife Caroline were scheduled to open the time capsule from the Wilson Administration, buried one hundred years earlier. The press had been hyping the event for weeks, but in light of the Baltimore bombing, the whole thing felt trivial at best.

"I don't know, Mr. President," Darlene said. "Maybe we could use a little distraction from all the bad news lately."

"Maybe you're right," he said.

By 10:55 Faulkner was standing in the Rose Garden, where a small crowd had gathered around a ten-foot ditch and a huge cast iron ball, split in half, its contents arrayed on the canvas beside it beneath a navy blanket. The time capsule, which had been made by the Maryland Ironworks

Company, was in remarkably good shape after its hundred-year interment.

Faulkner put his arm around his wife, Caroline, and gave her cheek a big kiss as the photographers snapped away. The diminutive blonde, from their home state of Oregon, smiled for the photographers before quickly turning her face away.

"Could there be a more beautiful First Lady to grace the Rose Garden on this special day?" Faulkner asked the crowd. "Ladies and gentlemen, thank you for joining Caroline and me on this historic occasion. A hundred years ago today, the president and First Lady created this time capsule containing the wonders of their age, items chosen to reflect their times as well as their aspirations for this great country." Faulkner read the brass-plated inscription on the side of the cast iron ball: "Sealed by First Lady Edith Bolling Wilson—November 16, 1919." Then he added, "President Woodrow Wilson and his wife Edith are two of the most important occupants of this office. It is my pleasure to be the sitting president who has this glorious opportunity to link them and the people of the twenty-first century. The Wilsons placed this chest in the ground a century ago. Let's have a look at the gifts for the ages, from the twenty-eighth president to the forty-fifth."

With a swift motion Faulkner lifted the blanket, revealing dozens of items from the year 1919, most wrapped in white linen cloth. A team of archivists wearing white gloves quickly stepped forward to unwrap the items: a glass-encased copy of the Eighteenth Amendment signed by Wilson, a complete setting of the Wilson china by Lenox—the first china to be embossed with the presidential seal—a baseball autographed by batting champion Ty Cobb, a pair of roller skates, a signed photograph of the members of the US Supreme Court, and several other items, which he held up amid a shower of flashes as photographers snapped away before the treasure trove was sent off to be officially photographed, tagged, and catalogued. At the bottom of the pile was a large sealed metal box, upon which were written the words "FOR PRESIDENTIAL EYES ONLY."

"Open it!" someone from AP yelled. "Yeah, c'mon, Mr. President, let's find out what secrets Wilson's spilling!" shouted someone else in the press scrum.

"Nice try, guys," Faulkner teased. "But I worked hard to get these eyes into the White House. Let's just keep this secret between me and Woodrow."

Back alone at the Oval Office, Faulkner broke the metal seal on the box to examine its contents. Pushing aside some crumpled newspapers, he saw a sealed letter resting on top of a pile of papers. Carefully unfolding the four-page, handwritten letter, Faulkner slowly started to read it.

November 16, 1919

Dear Mr. President,

Please excuse me for not calling you by name, but I have the disadvantage of the time difference between us. I have been lead to believe that the year that this letter is being read will be 2019, about one-fifth of the way into the twenty-first century. Knowing how different life in 1919 is from how it was one hundred years ago when our fifth President James Monroe was in office, I cannot imagine the changes that the years must have brought to our nation and to the world between the time I am writing this letter and the time that you are reading it. President Monroe's world had no electricity, no telephones, no airplanes, and no automobiles and on November 16, 1819, there were only twenty-one states—Alabama joining about a month later to become our twenty-second. Now our world has so many wondrous items that were not even imaginable so long ago.

Our world, thanks to Mr. Edison and Mr. Tesla, is illuminated in a way that has spared us of the darkness of night. Thanks to the miracle of flight, we are able to travel at fast speeds across this vastly expanded nation, one that has us stretching from coast to coast and, with the addition of Arizona, boosting us to forty-eight glorious states, stretching fully from the Atlantic and to the Pacific. At last, our nation is complete.

I envy you for being alive during what I am sure is an age of science, arts, and wonder. I am sure that 1919 America will seem to you as archaic as Monroe's did to us.

I wonder if music has changed much since my day. Are people still flocking to see the movies? My husband and I love the movies, with D. W. Griffith's The Birth of a Nation being our favorite. Is it still remembered as a classic? Does our American society still stand for the same important mores depicted in the movie? Women have just been awarded the right to vote and will do so in next year's election. I am very pleased with this social change and wonder how many other changes to society have transpired during the decades.

With the advantage of your history books, Mr. President, I am certain that you are aware of our current events. We were able to win the terrible War to End All Wars. The president had tried to avoid our intervention into the European conflict, but events dictated that we participate.

Our nation was able to survive the nasty influenza that killed so many. Another item that the history books have allowed you to read about is President Wilson's illness. Perhaps you knew that earlier this year the president was himself victimized by the influenza. He collapsed while in Pueblo, Colorado, and fell extremely ill on October 2nd. I have chosen to keep the full nature of his condition quiet, but I am sure that the people of your generation are well aware of its true circumstance. It is the illness, and its all-consuming nature, which is the final topic of this time-delayed communication. I ask you to please read the following paragraphs very carefully.

After catching the influenza, the president became concerned about his future, frightened that his condition might lead to the same sad fate that had befallen millions of others around the world. I, too, was very worried about him.

He told me that he was in possession of several important secret documents, whose existence was known to only a few, and that these documents were of, what he called, "A very dangerous nature." He warned me that our nation, here in 1919, is ill prepared to cope with the nature of their subject matter. He made me promise that if he were to become gravely ill, that I was to give the documents to the future president rather than to Vice President Thomas Marshall, whom neither the president nor I trust, as we feel that he has desires to see the demise of my husband. It is for that reason that we have kept the vice president from speaking to the president, making it more difficult for him to assume the presidency. Hopefully, we will be able to keep him away until the end of my husband's term.

I have therefore chosen to place these secret documents, whose subject matter I do not know, in this chest, along with this letter, hopeful that the nation in 2019 is better prepared to handle the nature of the circumstances that they present.

Mr. President, my sentiments are with you. I am hopeful that the concerns of this letter are ones that in your far-off future world will be considered to be of a trivial and of a non-threatening nature. Good luck, Sir, and may God be with you.

Sincerely,

Edith Bolling Wilson

Darlene Flowers buzzed the president on the intercom. "Senators Hamilton, Tinnirello, and Ascher are here to see you." Faulkner quickly seized the documents and buried them in the drawer of the Resolute desk.

Rebecca Hamilton (R-MO) was a no-nonsense senator, the Chairperson of the House Committee on Homeland Security as well as the Governmental Affairs Committee. The Granny Clampett look-alike entered the Oval Office with a frown upon her face that could be seen all the way back to her hometown of Independence. In a no-more-pleasant mood were Daniel Tinnirello (R-IN) and Andrew Ascher (R-OK), well-respected veteran senators. As they sat down, Hamilton started immediately, "Mr. President, we have a nation gripped in fear, worried about the next explosion."

Faulkner looked at her coldly and said, "I am aware of the pulse of the people, Senator, and I assure you that I am trying to do everything that I can to calm the people down and to apprehend those who are perpetrating these crimes."

Hamilton lashed back. "It's not enough. Three years ago you were placed on the ticket to make sure that these things didn't happen. And I'm telling you that you'd better get things changed in a hurry."

"Senator, I appreciate you taking the time to see me, but don't come into my office telling me what I 'better' do! I said that I'm working on it and I am."

"Mr. President," Tinnirello said, "The governor of our state, Robert Ryan, is a former law enforcement man who won the state by promising to keep crime down. And he did it, too. During these bombings he has gotten a great deal of national airtime. People are starting to suggest that he'd be a tough opponent in 2020. You have to do something. People like this guy. They're calling him the 'Twenty-first Century JFK'. He looks presidential and, of more importance, he acts presidential."

"And I don't? I have the presidential look and have the house to prove it," said Faulkner with a chuckle.

Hamilton wasn't amused. "You might think that this is funny, Mr. President, but the party is worried about your ability to retain your office next year. I think we have no choice; we have to rethink the 2020 ticket."

"Look," Faulkner sighed, "I get it. And I won't say it hasn't crossed my mind. But how would it look if I dumped the first black vice president? I'd be crucified."

"Not as much as the polls have you crucified right now," said Hamilton, as she handed Faulkner a list. "We and the rest of the party are serious. We have some ideas of who can help you get re-elected. It's not Hathaway."

Reluctantly the president reached for the list and ran his eyes down the names.

"Maria Martinez," he inquired. "Seriously? You'd want me to consider her?"

"Why not?" asked Hamilton. "Arguably she's the strongest candidate on the list. As governor of Florida she's turned around the economics of that state, been tough on crime, and after what happened to us in 2012, we Republicans could use a boost from the Latino community. Our numbers only rose a little in 2016. It's time we had a woman on the ticket."

"Mr. President," Tinnirello said. "Please. Consider the list. We're going to need to make some changes if we want to win next year."

After the senators left the room, Faulkner reflected upon his earlier conversation with Hathaway. Clearly he didn't want to be like President George Herbert Walker Bush, who, as an incumbent, in 1992, was elected out of office by a then-governor Bill Clinton. He slipped the list of candidates into his pocket, and then reached into the desk drawer to pull out two large envelopes labeled "one" and "two."

The first envelope contained a wrinkled handwritten note from Woodrow Wilson himself.

Thursday, March 6, 1913

Mr. President,

I welcome you to office. Let me get right to the matter at hand.

Two days ago I took my oath of office and have already received my first crisis, one totally unexpected despite the fact that it is almost forty-eight years old. Yesterday, on my first full day of office, I received a package from President Taft. Inside was a letter from the former president explaining that the contents of the package had been handed down to every president since Andrew Johnson, I being the latest to receive it. Upon examination, I was shocked at what I read, as its contents describe a position that I cannot espouse, one that clearly strikes at the core of my essence, and at the heart of my soul. I find the legal ramifications presented by the material something I cannot condone and so, I refuse to act upon it.

This lack of action is not unusual for a president, as the legal document's record shows that every president since Andrew Johnson was aware of this law and likewise chose to ignore it. You might question why the American public hasn't challenged Johnson, Taft, or any of the other nine men who have held this highest of office since him. The fact is that the public is unaware of this secret law, which was passed by Congress in 1865. A secret law? As I am sure you know, Mr. President, according to Article 1, Section 5 Clause 3 of the Constitution, Congress may have such secrecy, keeping items away from the public scrutiny.

I Invited Chief Justice White to the Oval Office, figuring that as two southerners—White hailed from Thibodeauxville, Louisiana—we could spend time discussing the ramifications of the law and how I should handle its complicated subject. The Chief Justice explained to me that he had been a senator when he had first heard rumor of the law, admitting that he rejected any notion that such a law could have passed Congress. I told White that, unlike the many presidents who had preceded me into office, I did not want the law to remain ignored—instead, I wanted to expose it to the public and then quickly dismiss it for "its evil intentions." But the Chief Justice feared that the publicizing of the long-forgotten law would result in lawsuits upon which he, as Chief Justice, would have to eventually rule. He confided in me that when he first learned about the law on his second day in office, December 13, 1910, and that he prayed that he would never have to face lawyers who were trying to defend it; fearful that, although in his heart he would want to vote against it, that he might not be able to; his mind might not allow such an act. He pleaded with me to pass it onto the next man in office.

Thus, like my predecessors, I, too, have chosen to ignore this law, instead, passing it on to you. Please read the contents of the other parcel to determine whether you choose to make public the law or, like me and those who preceded me, ignore it.

Sincerely,

Woodrow Wilson

President of the United States

President Wilson himself had intended the contents of the box to pass to his successor, shortly after he left office. Wilson would have never had suspected that his wife had instead chosen to have the materials delivered to a president some hundred years into the future.

Faulkner tore the second envelope open and pulled out a sheaf of yellowing papers. On top was a handwritten note from Senator Charles Sumner, an opponent of slavery and the guardian of rights for the Freedmen. His handwritten message was:

Please be advised that the following is the Law of the United States of America. It was passed by a majority of members from both houses of Congress; a majority of its members being present in each.

It is the intention of Congress to have President Abraham Lincoln sign this legislation and with its passing, allow for a new era to envelope our nation. Its sole intention is for the betterment of Americans—all Americans, regardless of their background.

Charles Sumner

His curiosity now piqued, Faulkner started to read the actual law, his jaw dropping with each word. Finishing, he stood with his hands on his hips, shaking his bowed head. *"How the hell did Congress get away with this?"* he wondered. *"What the hell were they thinking? And what the hell am I supposed to do with this crap?"*

Faulkner realized that he was in the same position as Wilson: called to act upon a law that would certainly harm a region of the nation, a law whose consequences could tear the entire nation apart.

Who else knew about this? He realized that no one on Earth, other than himself, was aware of it. What in God's name should he do?

Chapter 2

The Promise

Interstate 87 near the Fordham Road Exit
Tuesday, May 12, 2020
6:57 A.M.

On Thursday, May 3, 2018, the seventieth anniversary of Douglas Edwards's first CBS regularly scheduled news broadcast[i], for the tenth time on the anniversary of that date, the American Association of Newscasters named their annual list of history's top television journalists, with Leah Manders making her inaugural appearance. From that point forward, her high level of performance made her a mainstay on that list.

And so, since 2018, in national polls of television historians, along with the names of Murrow, Cronkite, Sevareid, Brinkley, Walters, Brokaw, Jennings, Chancellor, and Wallace, the name of the anchor of the GDC Nightly News Leah Manders had appeared on the list of Greatest Newscasters in Television History. The five-year old national network, based in Washington, D.C., had gambled, naming Manders, a popular, long-tenured Atlanta anchorwoman, as the voice of their newly founded network news. After low ratings in her inaugural season, her popularity skyrocketed during the 2016 presidential campaign, as her candid candidate interviews proved to be well-received by a supportive, adoring audience.

However, it was for her coverage of the rash of terrorist attacks that the Angela Bassett look-alike was placed upon the All-Time list. Her heartfelt coverage of the plight of the victims of the various attacks, as well as her criticisms of the Faulkner Administration's handling of the devastating strikes, made her, each evening at 7:00 Eastern Time, a must-watch newscast for millions. Just as Murrow had had his World War II and Cronkite had had his Cold and Vietnam Wars, so, too, did Manders have her galvanizing, signature news event, the Terror Countdown. Even more alluring than her television appearances were her morning commentaries that were heard each day at 7:00 A.M. on GDC Radio, as in each of the fifteen-minute sessions she provided opinions as well as facts to her audience. She was at her most highly acclaimed best as she comforted the millions of Americans who were nervously waiting for the next attack to be launched, while at the same time lambasting the seemingly helpless Faulkner administration. The most alluring portions of her A.M. addresses were her comments supporting the efforts of the first responders throughout the nation, keeping her very popular among working-class Americans.

Listening intently on this particular May morning was lawyer and Adjunct Professor of American History at Columbia University Tyson Joseph, who was commuting from his Mount Kisco, New York, home to the Ivy League school in Manhattan. Although each morning he usually listened to ESPN's *Mike and Mike*, today he was interested in hearing Manders's comments regarding the previous evening's attempted attack on Cornell University in Ithaca, New York, an attack thwarted by a security guard's quick thinking. When the guard, Cortez Hemminger of Cortland, had found a group of explosives that seemed to be set to detonate at that coming Saturday's graduation ceremonies, she'd called the authorities, and the package was quickly disarmed, rightfully earning Hemminger heroine status.

Joseph was a fan of Manders and had appeared on her newscast several times. He listened as she announced, "Ithaca, New York, has become the latest target for the still-unclaimed terrorist attacks upon our nation. Ithaca, New York? A town of approximately 32,000 people was in the crosshairs of these cowardly attacks. Why? Perhaps the aim of the terrorists was to show us that, just as with their attack on Utica, no place in the United States was safe. Who would imagine that cities that size would draw their attention? Now, people in cities of all sizes are on edge.

"Certainly, if nothing else, Ithaca fits the pattern of spelling out the words 'Succumb, America, Now,'" Manders said. "After the November attack in Baltimore last year, here in 2020, we have now had five attempted or successful attacks. As you know, in January, in Akron, Ohio, fifteen people were killed in a parking lot when a car bomb exploded after a rap concert at the JAR – the James A. Rhodes Arena. A week later, at a night club on First Ave., in Minneapolis, during a Motown Revival, eleven people were killed by a fiery explosion as the song 'Heatwave' was being played. Then there another successful bombing, this time on the east side of Erie, Pennsylvania. during a high school basketball game; this one killing a dozen fans."

Manders continued her review. "In April, the Abraham Lincoln Hotel in Redding, Pennsylvania, was rocked as a bomb exploded during a celebration of the one hundred fifty-fifth anniversary of the end of the Civil War. Eight died as a result of the blast and the ensuing fire. And last night we had Ithaca. As the letters are being spelled out, it looks as if the next city on the list will start with the letter 'C.'

"So, Mr. President, what is being done for the people of Corpus Christi and Cheyenne? How about the people of Charlotte and Colorado Springs? There is real fear out here, Mr. President, real fear. Here is what Buddy Turner, mayor of Cincinnati, had to say, 'Our office receives thirty to forty calls each morning and then double that figure each afternoon. All of the callers have one central theme, concern for the safety of themselves and their families. Bus ridership has shrunk. Children are not attending schools. Malls are half-empty. We seem to be at the mercy of some group or some individuals who have created panic in our streets. We have had two 'C' cities hit so far—Chicago and Cleveland. There will be another one soon. Is it Cincinnati's turn? Do our citizens face the same fate that happened to the fine citizens of those two other Midwestern cities?'"

Manders said sternly, "Those words, from Cincinnati mayor Buddy Turner, suggest the helplessness that has engulfed our nation—especially in cities whose names begin with certain letters. On tonight's evening news we will explore potential targets and ways for our citizens to pro-tect themselves. We will have an exclusive interview with Vice President Elgin Hathaway and see what he says about the White House's response to this wave of terror. Join me tonight."

Traffic slowed down in front of Tyson and before he knew it, his car, and dozens of others around him, had slowed to a crawl. Joseph tried to look around the upcoming turn, but all he saw ahead was an endless string of red brake lights. As his car crept forward, moving toward the turn, he looked inside other cars, the eyes of impatient drivers making contact with his.

Finally clearing the bend, he saw what had decelerated his commute on the other side of the guardrail in the northbound lanes: several New York State Trooper cars, four New York City squad cars, and two unmarked cars had surrounded three white vans, the drivers of which he saw on the ground, handcuffed and, apparently, under arrest.

Just like a herd of African wildebeests on the dry Serengeti who had slowed their migration to watch several of its members being overtaken by a pride of lions, so too did the southbound commuters slow to watch the northbound vans that had been apprehended by the police.

"Probably some of those damned terrorists who have been wreaking havoc all over the country," thought Professor Joseph, who was on his way to his classroom in Fayerweather Hall. Quickly dismissing the incident that had slowed him down, the professor chose to concentrate upon the news that he had been listening to since he left home.

With his radio still tuned to station GDC, the storyline was stunning. Earlier that morning, reports had come out of Asia of a strain of influenza that had been resistant to all previous vaccines. Concern was spreading faster than the flu itself, as nations and medical researchers throughout the world joined forces to combat the pandemic episode. "It's the year 2020," one reporter moaned. "Can't we control those things yet?"

Traffic had finally started to move and while passing several slower cars, Joseph tried to figure out which would be worse, dying from the disease or being victim of the rash of terrorist attacks that had plagued the nation. After several minutes of thought, he thought the disease might be a worse way to go, as one might take several days or weeks to succumb.

With the exception of the police raid and the news on the radio, Professor Joseph's morning commute to Columbia University had been a normal one. Interstate 87 had been crowded and after hearing the news, he felt guilty for starting the day in such a great mood. After all, it was the last day of classes; his joy was understandable.

He entered Fayerweather Hall and proceeded to his classroom. He arrived several minutes late, detained first by the poor traffic and then by those curious about his reaction to the morning's news. Despite it being the last day of classes, Professor Joseph was attired as usual, a fine-tailored suit, colorful shirt, and an expensive tie.

"Good morning, everyone," he announced. "I'm sorry I am tardy. I trust we have studied all of the required readings. Today's final exam has no surprises, just the information—and yes, I know there was a great deal of it—that I insisted that you know. Good luck, take your time, and upon completion I will hand each of you an envelope whose contents will have your projected final grade based upon various possible scores that you could obtain on today's exam. If there are no questions, I will hand out the exams. Remember, the present ends with your heartbeat; the future begins with your next breath. Go out and make history, for history's sake. Good luck with your lives. It has been my pleasure teaching this group. So, let's get it on."

With the completion of his words, he received a standing ovation from the students. And why wouldn't he? For years he'd been one of the most popular professors in the History Department. Smiling, he thanked the students and then climbed the short steps to the seating area to hand out the exams.

While the test was being taken, the professor occupied himself with various tasks. The *New York Times* had coverage of the influenza outbreak, as did MSNBC.com on his laptop. But he chose to spend most of his time reading the many brochures he had accumulated regarding his planned June 3rd trip to Nigeria. "I'll finally meet Dr. Adeleke," he thought. "Thirty years of painstaking research and now I'll meet the person who'll take me to the village near Zaria where my family originated."

After many years of expensive and time-consuming genealogical research, the professor had traced his family roots to a small village in the northeastern part of that nation. The upcoming trip had dominated the last few months of his life as he worked out his itinerary and received the necessary health-related shots.

The professor had become lost in thought and, after a little less than an hour, he was startled when a student tapped him on the shoulder.

"Excuse me, Professor Joseph," the student said, "I don't mean to disturb you, but I want to hand in my test."

"I'm sorry. I was daydreaming. Forgive me," said the professor, "I'll take that." While looking through the pile of alphabetically arranged envelopes, he found the envelope marked "Nichols" and said, "You can take this. Please have a great summer." Upon opening the envelope, the student, Consuela Nichols, smiled, knowing that, based on the grading formula that had been provided on the first day of class, a score of forty-five or better on the exam would guarantee her grade of A+. She knew she had aced the test, just like every exam she had ever taken in her life. Consuela shook the professor's hand and exited the classroom, her smiling face etched in the educator's mind.

The pile of envelopes continued to shrink until finally only one student remained. Summer vacation was soon to begin, and the professor sighed with relief as he returned to his brochure. A knock on the classroom door broke his concentration.

"Come in," he exclaimed. The beautiful young woman who entered the room stunned him. Her figure made the Commodores' hit record *Brick House* echo throughout his mind. Her smile lit the room, while her looks opened his eyes. "It's her," he thought. "She's back, and I know what she wants."

"Hello, Professor," she said with glee. "Do you remember me?"

The answer to that question was as obvious as asking a starving man if he wanted a Subway foot-long wedge. "Desiree Dalton, you should be ashamed of yourself. Who wouldn't remember the brightest, loveliest student one has ever had in his classroom." His words to her were not exaggerated; by a slight margin she had been the brightest student he had ever had and there was no contest regarding her rank on the beauty charts. No one was close.

"*What's Going On?*" asked the gleeful Tyson.

Desiree rolled her eyes. "Professor Joseph, 'What's Going On'? *Really?* Please don't tell me that you're still doing that Marvin Gaye-quote thing? If I remember correctly you'd get the titles of several of his songs into almost every conversation."

Joseph beamed at her. "Yes, I'm still doing it. It's my way of paying tribute to America's greatest singer and songwriter. His works demonstrated his concerns for the environment, racial equality, and peace. Why wouldn't I praise him? This year's bunch didn't catch on too quickly; musically I'd have to give them all F's," he said with a chuckle.

"Professor Joseph, you are *so* 1970s! It's the twenty-first century, man! Get with it!"

"Girl, I'm a history teacher," he said with a smile. "I make my living because of the past."

Just then, the last student, Gracie Sansone, approached. "Excuse me Professor Joseph, here is my test." While extending her arm to give him the paper, she added, "By, the way, I'm a huge fan of Marvin Gaye. My father used to play his songs all of the time." With those words, she smiled, waved goodbye, grabbed her envelope, and walked toward the door. Just before exiting, she quickly turned around and said, "Professor Joseph, the only way I can describe my feelings about you is by saying, '*You're a Wonderful One.*' And, you know, that was from Marvin Gaye in 1964!" She blew him a kiss and walked out the door. Turning to Desiree, the professor smiled and whispered, "I'm only kidding about this, but for that last remark I should give her an A for the semester." She winked back.

After several minutes of catching up with each other's lives—it had been two years since Desiree had been a student in the professor's class—she reminded him of a conversation they had had in 2018. "Do you remember your promise?" she asked.

"How could I forget?" he said with a smile, all along being fearful that the topic would surface.

She returned the smile and then added, "Two years ago you told me that I should return to you when I graduate. Then you would fulfill my wish. You said you couldn't act upon it while I was your student, or for that matter, a student here at the university. I understood your words, and although I didn't agree with them, I respected your views. But now in three short days I graduate. So, I'm here to collect."

The smile left his face as the details of the past conversation became clearer in his mind. "Desiree, that conversation was a couple of years ago. You were young and had just gotten over a long period of depression concerning a tragedy in your life. You had lived much of your life without a father and perhaps you saw me fulfilling that important role. You looked to me for help and I made it clear that I would have loved to honor your request. Hell, judging from those pictures you showed me, any man would want to. But I'm still—"

"That wasn't it at all," interrupted Desiree. "I liked what I saw then and I like what I see now. I'm not looking for a new daddy. I'm looking into someone who's into Caribbean cruises, horseback rides on the beach, skiing in Lake Placid. You know, someone who's sexy."

"Okay. That's enough," said an embarrassed Professor Joseph. "I take it that you're still looking for him?"

"I think I have him in view. Heck, I had that thought two years ago."

"And you think that I am that man?"

"Yep," said a smiling Desiree, who then said without hesitation, "You are that man and I have always thought of you as that man. You'd be perfect for—"

"I don't know about perfect, but I appreciate the thought," said the professor sincerely. Looking into her light ebony eyes he said, "I really do."

"Good, I'm glad," she said. "So what do you say about an evening where two consenting adults can get to know each other?"

All that Tyson could utter was, "Well—"

"Professor Joseph," she said with a raised voice, "You are the most popular man on this campus. You are a man who we, your students, trusted to tell us the truth. You promised me a date and I'm here to collect. One night! Dinner, dancing, small talk, and whatever! I promise you that if you don't have the time of your life, you'll never hear from me again. I promise, never again."

"Did you say, 'Whatever'? What do you mean by 'Whatever?'?"

"You know 'Whatever,'" she said with a you-know-what-I'm-talking-about smile.

At that point the professor had to laugh. "Okay, you delivered your argument very well. I know that you'll be destined to be number one in your law school class."

"So, how about it? I'm two years older and I want this more than I did back then. For two years I've seen lonely weekends, holidays with no one to share gifts. I've seen two years of no birthday presents from a special man. I'm tired of it. A date would be the fitting graduation present from the man I most admire."

Although he would never admit it to her, the thought had been in his mind for a long time. But a date? He'd always been concerned with the thoughts of his colleagues in academia. However, she was correct. Graduation was close at hand and she would no longer be a student at Columbia. "Why not?" he thought. "It wouldn't be like she was a student anymore."

"Okay, Desiree, I'll do it. Perhaps when I get back from Africa." After explaining his travel plans to her they agreed that nothing should happen until he returned.

"Professor Joseph, are you sure about this?" she asked with a sheepish grin.

"My dear, nothing would make me happier. I can't wait for this to happen. But, let me ask you a question. What will your family think?"

With a look of certainty, Desiree said, "Please, I've talked about you at home for two years. All of my cousins, aunts, and uncles like the idea and are looking forward to meeting you. A night out with the famous Professor Tyson Joseph! What woman wouldn't want that?"

"And your mother? What does she think about this?"

"At first she was dead set against it. I remember her saying, 'Forget it. He's your teacher!' But two years ago she was in a much different place.

I think, make that I know, she likes the idea now. In fact, she told me so last night. So, here's the phone number. Don't lose it. In fact, let me see you place it in your cell."

"I'll put it in my phone. I'll call. I promise."

"So, it's a done deal?" asked Desiree.

He stepped forward and gave her a reassuring hug, softly kissing her on the cheek. While still embracing her, he sighed. "Fine. If we have your family's blessings, let's do it. I can't wait to fulfill my promise. I will gladly take your mother out for a date, like I said I would. Tell her I'll call her when I get back from Africa."

---

i. Wikipedia Article, "CBS Evening News" July 21, 2013

Chapter 3

The Doctor's in the House

The White House
Washington, D. C.
Friday, July 3, 2020
2:28 A.M. Friday

Seldom during his illustrious career in Washington, D. C., had Doctor Brook T. Rider made house calls. After all, at age sixty-seven, the Jimmy Stewart look-alike was a living legend who had had patients travel to him from all over the world.

His legend had developed as he followed in the footsteps of his father, Bob "Big River" Rider, who, in the 1950s, had carved his niche in Texas history by cruising the Rio Grande in search of poor patients who were in the need of medical aid, usually providing it without charge. During the Eisenhower administration, Big River was the most highly respected doctor west of the Mississippi River. Nicknamed for the Rio Grande, he reached national fame in November 1963 when he, the scheduled emergency room physician at Parkland Hospital, had been forcibly removed by agents of the federal government, who wanted their own doctors to attend to the wounded President John F. Kennedy. The elder Rider made it clear to all that he had been overlooked by what he felt was a medical conspiracy. Most people dismissed his claims, but the statements always resonated with his only child Brook (who had gained his name by literally being a "small river").

By 1982, Brook Rider had established his own practice and had become the most sought-after doctor in Northern Texas. His deepest desire was to prove his beloved father correct, so in 2000, in a much-heralded move, at the age of forty-seven, Brook, his wife Liz, and their son Branch—the smallest river—moved to Washington, D.C. During his twenty-year stay in the nation's capital, he had become a fixture at all major social events, Republican and Democratic alike.

Shortly after his arrival in the nation's capital, one of Rider's first clients was the then-Senator James Augustus Faulkner of Oregon. The men, in addition to their doctor-patient relationship, developed a wonderful friendship. Over the years they shared many laughs as well as many disagreeing words and the occasional vicious argument. However, in the end, they always remained friends, with a bond that many in Washington thought was unique.

Thus, very few were surprised to learn that upon his 2016 election as president, Faulkner reached out to his friend to find out if the doctor would accept the position of Physician to the President. The request was unusual, as typically, the White House doctors are active-duty military officers who don't have to close and then reopen extensive private practices. Also, Rider's practice was as extensive as anyone's in the area.

Yet, to the surprise to many around the Beltway— including the president—Rider agreed to halt his highly successful practice to be able to become Faulkner's personal physician, a position that back in 2016 paid an annual salary of $125,000. The explanation wasn't complicated. Rider, who had invented two popular medical devices, had made millions upon millions of dollars; he didn't need the money. He was still young enough that even if he closed down his practice for four years (he signed on for one term only), he would still have the opportunity to reopen the office and place himself in a position to make the big dollars again.

The less-obvious reason for his acceptance was that Rider had always had in the back of his head the circumstances that had caused his father so much despair—not being able to help a president who was in need. Saying "no" might jeopardize his only opportunity to provide a president with help. That, along with the fact that, by being in the White House, he might be better positioned to uncover some of the facts from 1963 that might cleanse his father's reputation, led Rider to take the job.

Now, in the early morning hours of July 3rd, he received a phone call from his most famous patient, a call that caused the doctor to leave the comfort of his own suite. Doctor Rider ran up the stairs to attend to President Faulkner, angrily glaring at his wristwatch, which read 2:30 A.M. "Probably had too much to drink again," thought the sleep-deprived Rider.

As he arrived at the living quarters the First Lady opened the door and greeted him.

"Caroline, what the hell is going on?" Rider demanded.

"Brook, I'm not sure. He's been vomiting all night and has had terrible abdominal pains. I'm really worried. He's been ill before, but nothing like this."

"How long has he been complaining about the abdomen?"

"I'd say about a week. He hasn't said anything to anyone but me, but now it seems to be getting worse."

"Dammit! A week?" said an angered Rider. "Anything could have happened in a week! You should have told me right away. I took out his appendix, so we know it's not that. But knowing how stubborn he is, he may have grown another one. Still, next time, you have to get him to call me earlier than this."

Pointing to the master bedroom, the doctor asked, "He's in there?"

Caroline's weak nod of confirmation signaled Rider's entry into the adjoining room. The ashen-skinned President laid before him, in bed, propped up with several red, white, and blue pillows. As Brook approached the bed, he thought he'd never seen the president look so ill.

The weakened Faulkner could barely muster enough strength to say, "Brook, thanks for coming."

"You look like crap!"

Faulkner cracked a smile and with a weakened voice replied, "Good. Crap is two steps up from how I felt a couple of hours ago." Pointing to Rider's medical bag, the president added, "I hope you've got something in that bag of yours to make me feel better."

"Caroline says you've been vomiting all night. What did you eat today?"

"Nothing out of the ordinary, steak, baked potato, asparagus, and a salad—no onions—for dinner. No dessert either. I've been trying to lose weight, as you know. And, I know what you're thinking. No, I had nothing to drink. Well, except for cranberry juice."

More questioning revealed that the episode was the third time in two weeks that the president had had a rough night. His abdomen had been sore for a couple of weeks, and for a month he'd been losing weight. Faulkner admitted to sporadic fatigue and bouts of diarrhea and nausea. He'd even resorted to using more makeup to cover his loss of coloring.

"So, Brooksie, what the hell do you think?" asked the president in a quiet voice. "I'm starting to think there's something really wrong."

"Probably nothing a little rest wouldn't cure. Listen, Jimmy, I know you have many stressors in your life. Those terrorist attacks must be driving you crazy. And let's not forget the flu is spreading around the nation, and, you have the upcoming nominating convention, too. Damn, it's a wonder you haven't quit or died of a massive heart attack."

Rider looked down at his feet. "Listen, I'm sorry I haven't been around for a couple of months. Branch's death hit us hard."

Faulkner shook his head. "Jesus, Brooksie, he was just a college kid at a party. Then he looks at some football player's girlfriend and gets pounded for it! I still can't believe it."

"I'm nowhere near being over it, but I'm coping," Rider admitted. "Liz is still a mess. I just got back a few hours ago, and I must say that you don't look good to me. You've lost way too much weight since I've been gone. I didn't get a chance to check the notes from the fill-in doctors. What did they have to say?"

"Okay, they kept their distance, just like I wanted them to do."

Rider handed his friend a few pills. "These should help you sleep. We can look into things in the morning." Trying to conceal his concerns, Brook looked at the president and said, "Listen, Jimmy, I'm going to run some tests, just to be sure. And I don't want to hear you moaning about it, you hear me? I'll fix you up with something for the nausea and the runs, but what you really need is a decent night's sleep."

Faulkner closed his eyes and said, "Fine."

Caroline, who had been by her husband's side, walked the doctor to the door. "Thanks again for coming up so late," she said, kissing him on the cheek.

"If he has any more discomfort, Caroline, no matter what it is, you tell me at once. I don't care how late it is. And I mean, at once!"

"I promise," she told him.

After Brook left, Caroline crawled into bed beside her husband and kissed him goodnight. "Next time I handle things. Is that clear?"

He was able to muster a weak smile as they both readied for sleep.

Chapter 4

The Date

Seneca Avenue
Mount Vernon, New York
Friday, July 3, 2020
8:00 P.M.

At exactly eight o'clock, the doorbell rang and Dominique Dalton, wearing black jeans with a black-sequined top, opened the door to find a short, handsome older man who greeted her by saying, "Good evening, Ms. Dalton, my name is Kingsley, your driver for the night. Professor Joseph awaits you. May I escort you to the vehicle?"

After staring at Kingsley and the automobile for several moments, a slightly embarrassed Dominique said, "Please excuse my manners, Kingsley. Please come in while I finish getting ready."

"No thank you, madam. I'll wait here at the door until you're ready to leave."

"I'll get my purse and I'll be ready in two minutes."

Dominique hurried into the bedroom, grabbed her handbag, and checked the mirror one last time. Looking at her reflection, she said with a smile, "This is about as good as it gets. He better like it, 'cause I know I do."

With bag in hand, she walked to the door, held open by Kingsley, who then walked her down the stairs and to the waiting black Lincoln Town Car.

Kingsley opened the car door and out stepped the most gorgeous man Dominique had ever seen. Desiree's photo had done the man justice. The professor was six foot five inches tall and very well-muscled. His hair was cut short, his eyes were a light hazel-green, and his mustache was well trimmed. His face was round, with a beautiful brown skin tone, accented with a beard that appeared to be a light shadow. He looked to be in his mid-fifties. His loosely fit black slacks didn't hide his athletic build. If his appearance wasn't enough to make her feel like a schoolgirl on her first date, when he opened his mouth to speak, the deep baritone voice was enough to send chills down Dominique's spine.

"Ms. Dalton, you are a vision of loveliness. You look delightful! That black is a great color on you. Desiree was correct; her mother is a very beautiful woman."

"Thank you, Professor, that was—"

"Please, please, call me Tyson," he interrupted with a smile, "Professor is my work name."

"Certainly, Tyson, that was nice of you to say, and I must add that you look charming yourself—that blue jacket is a winner. This automobile is outrageous, and Kingsley was certainly a surprise."

"Kingsley and the car are classics," said the professor with a laugh. "They've both been with me for almost eight years now. So, which would be your dining pleasure for this evening—Italian, Mexican, or something else?"

Thinking for a short moment Dominique answered, "Mexican," although she would have eaten anything with this man. "It's my favorite food."

Lowering the window that separated the couple from their driver, the professor conveyed the choice to Kingsley who responded with, "Very good, Sir." With that, the window was rolled up and the Lincoln sped into the night.

"Have you ever eaten at Las Mananitas in Brewster? It has the finest Mexican food north of Tijuana. Louis, the owner, has done a tremendous job there."

"No, I've only been to Brewster a couple of times, and it was for business. But if we're heading that far north, the food must be very good."

Acknowledging with a nod, the professor hit a button and soft music played in the background. As the car traveled north on the Hutchinson River Parkway and then onto Interstate 684, the couple talked and laughed. Much of the conversation centered upon the professor's trip to Africa, which had been canceled because of an outbreak of influenza there.

"That stinks that you had to cancel the trip. Any plans on going at a different time?"

Tyson nodded. "Of course, there will be opportunities once this flu thing dies down. I'll get there for sure."

"It's scary. I'm afraid that it could hit record levels here," Dominique said. "One of my last acts as superintendent was to set into motion contingency plans for the district if it hits our area. I hope that my successor heeds my warnings."

"I hope so too. I don't think that the public is taking this one seriously. It's eerily similar to the great pandemic of one hundred years ago. Hopefully it won't match it for its potency and death totals. But this talk of disease is for another time. We should be talking about more pleasant items. So, how's retirement? You were the superintendent of the Mount Vernon schools?"

"Yes, this was my sixth year in charge. I have to get used to the idea that I'm not returning to the schools; it seems as if my entire life has revolved around them. But, I'm adjusting. I'm certain, next month, when I don't have to make sure all of the schools are set up, that I'll really appreciate it. But, honestly, it was time for me to go. I had a different vision for the district than did the board. And the head of the board had just gotten two new allies elected, so I knew that things might become difficult for me. Don't get me wrong. I enjoy a good challenge, but they threw a very enticing retirement package at me. It was sort of like the Godfather—they gave me an offer that I couldn't refuse. So, I took the money and ran."

"You know, Dominique, a good fight is one thing, but financial security is another. You did the right thing."

"So you don't think that I sold out for the money?"

"On the contrary, I think you sold into financial security."

Dominique thought that the conversation was very enlightening. Passing Mt. Kisco, in her mind she blew a kiss to her favorite hairstylist, and the best in Westchester, thanking her for rearranging her schedule and her stylish haircut. "Margo, you're the best," she thought to herself.

The trip to Brewster was extremely fast, in part due to the fine driving of Kingsley, but due mostly to the fun the couple was sharing in the back of the car. He had proven to be a great conversationalist, asking all the correct questions and providing all the right answers. She couldn't help but think, "No wonder Desiree and the rest of the students love this man so much."

Once inside the restaurant, Dominique felt that she was in the presence of a rock star. People applauded the arrival of the professor and called out to him.

"Tyson, my man," exclaimed a tanned elderly man at the bar.

"Hey Mr. Joseph, thank you. You're the greatest," said a smiling middle-aged man at the first table.

"Wow," thought Dominique, "Is this a setup or does he get this treatment everywhere?" Her thoughts were interrupted as a beautiful young woman tapped her on the right shoulder and said, "Mrs. Joseph, you are the luckiest woman in the world. I'd kill to be in your shoes." Hopeful that the evening would not take that exact path, Dominique had already felt lucky to be with a charming man like Tyson, when it dawned upon her what all of the fuss had been about. Desiree had told her about one of the professor's cases, one in which he had won millions of dollars for Putnam County plaintiffs who had had their well water poisoned by a local fertilizer plant. Correctly she assumed that these people were some of those who had received payments in the settlement.

Although he had netted a large return from that case, it was a case in 2011 that Joseph, as the lead attorney in one of the century's most important cases, became rich and famous. He represented the plaintiffs in the class action suit against several of the major auto insurance companies. He argued that his clients, all fifteen thousand of them, were poor citizens from the Bronx, Brooklyn and Queens and that each of them had had his or her Fourteenth Amendment equal protection rights violated by the companies. He insisted that the charging of higher rates to them, because of their addresses, was unconstitutional. His argument was that because the insurance companies were regulated by the state government, the companies were subject to the same restrictions that, according to the Fourteenth Amendment, had been placed upon the states. His argument, which equated the similarity of their situation to that of other discriminated groups, notably the handicapped, claimed that discrimination by the companies against his clients unfairly burdened them with higher rates, in effect, handicapping them further.

His investigation of the matter found that New York State Superintendent of Insurance Raquel Benjamin was aware of the inconsistencies and, in effect, covered up the entire incident, allowing the New York State Department of Financial Services to become party to the cover-up. Upon appeal, in a stunning 5–4 decision, a favorable United States Supreme Court, ignoring the years of previous decisions, upheld his view, ordering the companies to "Stop the unfair practice of deliberate discrimination against those who could afford it least. If New York State, or for that matter, any other state, is not allowed to indiscriminately charge different tax rates to citizens from different parts of their states, then companies regulated by the same states, which, after being approved for business by the states, in essence, become de facto arms of the states and should not be allowed to assign differing rates to customers based upon their zip codes. We are ordering states to charge their rate assignments to become uniform across the state—lowering the rates of some of their customers, while raising those of others." For his efforts, Tyson received twenty-five percent of the 1.6 billion-dollar settlement. The notoriety he received flooded his firm's phone lines with potential clients, further assuring him of financial security. As the status of the firm grew, he was able to spend more time in the classroom. Those circumstances, plus his wife's untimely death in 2008, had made Dominique's date one of the nation's most eligible bachelors. In fact, she remembered seeing Tyson featured in many television interviews and reading many articles about the famed professor.

Meanwhile, during the time period of the law firm's growth, Dominique's life had been centered on her late husband Frank, who, on the moonless night of October 27, 2011, had fallen victim to an out-of-control drunk driver. The intoxicated driver's car caused a head-on collision in Mount Vernon. The horrific crash, which killed her husband instantly, claimed the lives of all four of the passengers in the drunkard's automobile. From the moment of Frank's burial, she vowed to keep her life alcohol-free. Her heart had always been filled by him, but, perhaps, it was time to make a little room in there for another.

As she witnessed Tyson's handling of the crowd of admirers, she couldn't help but think how long it had been since she had had a date. Was Tyson the next person to make an entrance into her heart? Then she thought, "Hey, wait a minute. This is our first date, and it's only fifty-five minutes old. Slow down, girl. Slow down."

It took a full four minutes and dozens of handshakes for the couple to reach their seats. "I'm sorry," the apologetic professor said. "That seems to follow me whenever I come here. I guess that's why I stay home most of the time. I hope it didn't bother you too much."

"Tyson, you handled the situation very well, especially the man at the bar who wanted his picture taken with you but had to go to the car to get his teeth. Thank God you waited for him," said an amused Dominique with a chuckle.

The couple, after sharing in the laugh, received their menus and then ordered virgin piña coladas. Tyson suggested that the rest of the evening should be quieter than their entrance. The conversation between the two was free-spirited, flowing from one topic to another, much of it centered on Desiree's future at Georgetown Law School. Dominique expressed pride in her daughter's achievements and her ability to cope with the loss of her father.

"She is a remarkable young lady," commented Tyson. "I could tell that from my time with her in class. I'm sure she will be successful in Washington. I was so sorry to hear about the sad events of her, um, your lives." A short, silent nod of appreciation suggested that the topic of conversation should be changed quickly.

After several questions Tyson was reluctant to talk about his law case winnings, suggesting that he appreciated the fact that the money had allowed him to do good for others.

"Tyson, what were your favorite cases that you worked on?"

"I love working, so any case that I am working on would be among my favorites. But I really enjoyed helping out a teacher, Amanda Hadley, who had won a big payout in the lottery. She had gone to one of the regional claim centers to receive her prize, when she was told that to collect her winnings, she had to be photographed. Then the pictures would be used for promotional reasons. You know, with the three foot check with her name in large letters."

"Yeah, I know what you mean."

"Well, she refused, and as she had a year to collect the prize, she hired me to go after the Lottery rule."

"I missed this case. What happened?"

"I cited the horrible circumstances in Illinois where a meter maid, Gwen Rivers, from Maywood had won two hundred million dollars and was required to have her picture taken. She quit her job and a few days later her photo was blasted all across the state.

"A guy named Mitchell saw the picture and remembered her as the lady who had ticketed his car—a ticket that allowed the local police to connect him with a violent assault. He served his time knowing that the only way that he was caught was because of the ticket. After he got out he kidnapped the five-year-old daughter of the meter maid, and the young girl's body was found three months later.

"I argued that the New York Lottery rule provided opportunity for the same thing to happen in New York. The Court of Appeals ruled in our favor."

"That's a great story. I'm not a big lottery player, but that must be reassuring to those who play and win big."

Suddenly, it dawned upon Tyson and he looked at Dominique with his eyes wide-opened.

"Are you a baseball fan?" the professor quickly asked.

"Hey, who doesn't like a good game of baseball? I'm a big Yankees fan," she proclaimed with pride. "I wanted to go to tomorrow's game. It's Derek Jeter Day, you know. In honor of his induction into the Hall of Fame last year, the Yankees are retiring his number 2 and dedicating a monument to him. They chose to do it on July 4th, as it is the birthday of the late George Steinbrenner and it is the eighty-first anniversary of Lou Gehrig's famous speech."

"Do you want to go with me?" an excited Tyson eagerly asked. "I'm taking a group of kids, and one of them canceled on me. I have an extra ticket, and if you have no plans, I'd love for you to attend the game with us."

"I'd love to go with you. This weekend Desiree is visiting some friends at Georgetown, so I have no obligations."

"Great, you'll enjoy the kids."

"I've always enjoyed being around kids, thus my chosen career."

The topic of the conversation switched to Dominique's life. She told the professor that she had graduated first in her class at Mount Vernon High and that after four years at Harvard, she was again the class valedictorian. "So, I returned to Mount Vernon, taught chemistry, while at night I completed my Master's and Doctorate Degrees at Columbia's Teacher's College."

She was named the Superintendent of the Mount Vernon School District, a position she held until her recent retirement three days earlier. "I know that my departure will leave a void in the system, but to be truthful, I've grown weary of the grind and wanted to concentrate upon my newly found desire to write. Traveling to Africa was another of my goals, and I am envious of your trip.

"So you have traced your roots back to Nigeria? That is great. Like many of our people my efforts were blocked by the slavery period," said Dominique. "My ancestors were from Alabama—the Talladega area. But I couldn't figure out how to traverse that period. How did you manage?"

"Luck and hard work—but mostly luck," he said with a smile. "Like Alex Haley, I had a fortunate set of circumstances that allowed me to trace my father's side back to Africa. While doing work on my mother's side of the family, I, too, however, met a similar fate as yours—blocked by events of the early eighteenth century. But, I'll keep trying."

After eating what Dominique called "the best guacamole I've ever had in my life," Tyson suggested ordering the seafood chimichangas, which, upon eating, Dominique insisted were as delicious as anything she had ever eaten.

Feeling more comfortable with Tyson, when asked by him, Dominique told him about the death of her husband, a topic which she seldom discussed.

"The night he died, he had been home. He opened up a newspaper and saw that it was the last day of the sale at Target on the sixty-inch set that he had had his eye on. So he told me that he was going to go get it.

"On the way home he called to tell me that he had it and that he'd see me in a few minutes. According to the police report, he was near our home when some college guy—drunk as a skunk—turned the corner, drove across the double line, and wiped out that part of my life.

"He was running really late, at least so I thought, and later the knock on the door startled me. 'Did he forget his keys again?' I asked. As I approached the door I wondered why there were two policemen there. Upon learning the nature of their visit, my knees buckled and the sudden despair hurled me to the ground, where I stayed for what seemed an eternity." She wiped away the flow of tears and then said, "He had to get that damned television!"

As Tyson quickly pushed away his chair, in an attempt to comfort her, she feverishly waved him off, "I'm okay. I'm okay. I've had several years, millions of tears, and most importantly, many sets of listening ears to help me get through this. Sorry, it still gets to me."

"Please. I'd like to supply you with another set of ears, if you'd let me."

"Honey, I'm hopeful that my lips and your ears will be able to discuss things for a long time to come."

Smiling, the professor added, "Me too. That would be real nice."

"It's our first date and I'm telling you about my late husband. How romantic is that?"

Tyson reached across the table, signaling for her hands, which Dominique quickly offered, and without missing a beat he said, "Dominique, part of romance is getting to know someone so well that you enjoy listening to them talk about anything, anywhere. And if part of that conversation is painful for them, then you willingly share the pain. For you, I'm a willing participant, and I can't wait to be with you again, which brings me to tomorrow. We'll pick you up in a little different vehicle, a bus."

"I can't wait. The Yankees haven't been that good since Jeter broke his ankle a few years back."

Just then the professor's phone rang. Looking at the caller ID, he asked Dominique to forgive him. "It's Todd at my office. They never call unless it's very important. Do you mind if I take it? I promise to be brief."

Her approval received, the professor said into the phone, "Todd, what's going on?"

"Boss, I just received a call from a Mr. Don Woodman from D.C. He said that it is urgent that you call him."

"From whom? I've never heard of him. What did he want?"

"He said that he found some papers that involve Klyde Joseph. He said they seem to have national implications."

"That's about my great-great-great grandfather. Did he leave me a number?"

"Yes, he did, sir."

"Text it to me, and I'll call him tomorrow. Thank you, and have a great weekend."

Turning back to Dominique he said, "Someone found some papers that have something to do with my great-great-great-grandfather, Klyde."

"And how did the caller know that was your great-great-great-grandfather?"

"He probably read my book, *Joseph and Sons, a Study of the Descents of Squire Joseph*, which details my family tree. I wrote it about four years ago, and it sold at least a dozen copies—he must have been one of the twelve people who bought it," said Tyson with a laugh.

"I remember Desiree telling me about the book. I'm impressed. I'm sure you must have sold at least twenty of them. Sorry, I couldn't resist.

What can you tell me about Squire?”

“Squire was a slave who served in the White House starting in 1809—under President Madison. Prior to that he had helped build the Capitol Building—he did such a great job that his owner, who must have had some connections to the government, sold him, and he became a house servant at the White House. It was there that he really made a name for himself and was promoted to the position of Madison’s personal assistant. It was that promotion that led to our family’s history of White House service—many worked inside the Oval Office, including Klyde.

“I can’t wait to see what this Mr. Woodman has found.”

“Perhaps it is something that will supplement your writings.”

“Yes . . . , but the message said something about national implications. I’ll call him after the game. Don’t know what he has, but he’s got me kind of interested.”

With that, he motioned for and quickly received their check. The professor left the required amount of money, along with a very hefty tip. The couple, after waving to more adoring fans, left the restaurant, and with the help of Kingsley, got into the awaiting Lincoln.

Tyson and Dominique continued the conversation, although clearly the professor’s mind was elsewhere. Even the Marvin Gaye music didn’t seem to interest him.

“Please excuse my lack of communication. I have been thinking about Klyde and what information might be out there.”

“Don’t worry about it. I’m curious too.”

As those words were spoken Kingsley pulled up to Dominique’s house. She asked Tyson if he wanted to come in, but the lateness of the hour and the early morning errands that he had to do before the game convinced him that he needed to get some sleep.

Disappointed, but understanding, Dominique thanked him. “Tyson, it was a wonderful evening; I had a great time. Thank you so very much.”

“I enjoyed it too. I can’t wait to see you tomorrow.”

Tyson hugged her and kissed her on the cheek. As their eyes met, they shared a smile and before either could blink, their lips met for a brief, but substantial, kiss. Although the kiss was short, the energy that surged within Dominique could have lit a small city for a week and a half.

As Tyson walked down her steps, Dominique watched his every move, aware that the next day's date would not be their last. She chuckled at her thought. "Now that's a professor who's in a class by himself."

Chapter 5

The Short Stop

Yankee Stadium
Bronx, New York
Saturday, July 4, 2020
1:57 P.M.

The overcapacity crowd at Yankee Stadium was as energized as most on hand could remember. As each old-timer walked or jogged onto the field, the spectators cheered loudly. Even former Red Sox slugger David Ortiz was shown the proper appreciation. When Hall-of-Famer Cal Ripken was introduced, the crowd stood and applauded for several moments, shouting, in unison over and over again, "Rip-Ken. Rip-Ken. Rip-Ken…" The spirit of the spectators was so positive that even a video of Alex Rodriquez received some favorable applause, seemingly forgiving him, to some degree, for his years of alleged use of performance-enhancing drugs, exorbitant pay checks, and his one-year suspension.

And why wouldn't those in attendance be in a great mood? It was Derek Jeter Day. The crowd erupted as Bernie Williams and Mariano Rivera emerged from the dugout together and were introduced by co-announcer Ken Singleton. When Singleton's longtime announcing partner Michael Kay called for Joe Torre to come onto the field, Dominique, along with thousands of other fans rose to their feet and started shouting, "Tor-ree, Tor-ree"—in honor of the Hall of Fame manager's successful string of championships.

All of the kids had seen Jeter at the end of his career, missing some of his finest moments, from his younger years. But they cheered for each of the highlights flashed upon the scoreboard. There were many: The Mr. November World Series home run against the Diamondbacks, the Flip against the A's, the Dive into the stands against the Red Sox, the home run off David Price for hit number 3,000. Yes, Tyson knew that he had done well, as all of the members of his group, including Dominique, were having a great time. But sadly, despite their surroundings, Tyson had the same lost look in his eyes that he had on the trip home from Brewster the night before. Even after what she had assumed had been a good night's sleep, she knew that the professor was still pondering what information this Mr. Woodman might have.

At 2:05 Jeter stepped out of the dugout to a standing ovation that, some claimed, could have been heard all the way to Cooperstown. Meanwhile, at the same moment, some two hundred forty miles away, a seemingly healthier President and Caroline greeted Dr. Rider. Both Jeter and Faulkner were appreciative of their respective audiences, although Jeter's outnumbered the president's by more than forty thousand. Both men found themselves in situations with which they were very comfort-able; Jeter standing at home plate and Faulkner standing in the Oval Office. Despite their locations, in what one might call "comfort zones," each man's present role was unfamiliar. Jeter usually addressed the crowd with his bat, glove, and legs, not with the microphone that had been handed to him by Singleton. Faulkner, when he was in the Oval Office, usually found himself in position to be dictating policy and having his statements being the focal point of the conversation. Today those roles were in the hands of Dr. Rider.

Jeter spoke for two minutes; the crowd listening to each word. Upon the conclusion of his speech, Jeter was his usual stoic self, smiling and shaking hands. Rider's speech, slightly longer, wrought with emotion, produced few smiles.

A low-key Rider took a final look at his notes, turned to Faulkner and said, "Jim, you'll have to check your itinerary, eliminating some non-vital meetings, because we have to schedule a few more medical tests."

"Brooksie, tell me straight out," said a somber-looking President, whose grip on Caroline's hand intensified three-fold.

"All tests but one are complete, but I've seen enough to make a diagnosis."

"Brook, I know you physicians have a set way of doing things, but stop beating around the bush, will ya?"

"Jim, I've known you and Caroline for many years. I'm sorry to tell you that you have pancreatic cancer, and from all of the tests, it doesn't look promising for you."

Caroline chimed in with, "NO! Are you sure Brook? That's terrible news. What can we do?"

"Unfortunately, I am positive of the results. The tests confirm it."

"How bad?" asked the president.

Bowing his head to the pressure of the situation, the doctor took a deep breath, held his head up and said, "I will have to run a few more tests, but Jim, you're in bad shape, bad enough that I think that you should reconsider running for re-election. You might not have much time left."

"Like hell I will. It's July, I'll make it to the freaking election. And then into my next term. Right?"

"Perhaps, but there is a high percentage that you won't."

A stunned president heard Rider's words, but was lost in thoughts about the future. In a muffled voice he said, "How long do I have to—"

"Live? You want to know how long you have to live," said a saddened Rider. "Probably a few months, at best."

Brook directed the president to check his schedule for the next two days. Hearing that there was a July 4th dance that night in Philadelphia, the doctor ordered Faulkner to clear about two hours during the following afternoon. The president agreed and asked if he could make a quick call to his Chief of Staff, William Coughlin.

Speaking softly but deliberately into the phone, the president told Coughlin, "Will, I'm looking at tomorrow's schedule. I have to clear a couple of things. In fact, clear everything after I return from the Jefferson Memorial."

"But the people are going to be very disappointed."

Listening to Coughlin's response, the president said, "Just send Hathaway and I'll explain later."

After slamming down the phone, he turned back to Rider. "We're set."

"Good, tomorrow I'll do the last of the tests and we will see just how far this has metastasized. We will make things as comfortable as we can for you."

"Gee thanks. I'm going to get through this—you just watch."

Turning toward her husband, the sobbing First Lady said, "Thanks, Brook. We'll see you tomorrow."

After the doctor left she turned to her husband. "You know, he's a good man. We should be thankful that we have him. Perhaps you should listen to him about the election."

"Were you freaking listening? I'm running—case closed."

Chapter 6

The Accident

Gramatan Ave.
Mount Vernon, New York
Saturday, July 4, 2020
6:45 P.M.

After Kingsley stopped the bus at Mount Vernon's Hartley Park and emptied his passengers, the teenagers hugged the professor and Dominique, thanking them for a tremendous afternoon. Each of the Mount Vernon youths had gotten to know a rival from Yonkers and, of course, there was the baseball game. Being a witness to Derek Jeter Day and a Yankee victory (the team had won 9–7 with a pinch-hit home run in the bottom of the twelfth inning) made each of the teenagers forget about the problems in their respective lives. Well, at least for a day.

Kingsley returned the bus to the depot, where he hopped into his own car to travel home. Knowing that the professor was going to be out of town for several days meant a vacation, of sorts, for him, so he was heading to Lake George to go fishing.

Tyson, in a better mood than before, began to drive Dominique to her house. Their time alone in his car had been upbeat, and she was anticipating arriving home to entertain the professor. But as the car turned a sharp corner, so too did the lighthearted conversation.

"Dominique," said a serious-sounding Tyson, "I've had a delightful time with you. I'm hopeful for more days and evenings like we've had. But I have to drop you off and go home and pack my suitcase. I'll be out of town for a few days."

"Business?" asked a disappointed-looking Dominique.

"No, it's not business. It's something totally different—a family matter. Two days from now marks the twelfth anniversary of my late wife's death. As I told you before, she was killed in a car accident by a drunk driver."

"I remember. In fact, Desiree, knowing that we had both lost spouses to drunk-driving accidents, brought us together, aware that we shared that sad distinction. I understand it if you want to be alone. After Frank died I didn't want to talk to anyone. Each October 27th, I feel alone and depressed, knowing it marks the day of the accident."

"It's not that I want to be alone, I have to go to Bar Harbor, Maine, to share the anniversary with my son."

A surprised Dominique said, "Your son? Desiree never told me that you had a son. What's his name, and how old is he?"

"Desiree didn't know. Few people are aware that I have a son. His name is Robert and he's now twenty-seven years old. He was in the car when it was victimized by the drunk driver. Since the accident he's been living in a special care facility that has helped him cope with the trauma of that day. They've kept him alive and have given him some dignity, but he'll never live a normal life. He is a smart kid and knows the anniversary. Each year I'm there to help him get through it. I'm there no matter what. We look forward to our time together."

"Then that's where you should be. How often do you see him?"

"I get there pretty often—every five to six weeks or so, depending on other aspects of my life. Don't take that to mean I put him off. I get there a lot. Once a year, usually in the late summer, I vacation there for two to three weeks. I have a home not too far from his facility, and so I commute from there to see him almost every day. Sometimes though, on shorter visits, I stay in a hotel, which is much closer."

Dominique, looking for the correct way to approach the question gingerly asked, "Does he remember much from the accident? I know my memories from Frank's accident are spotty, so I can imagine it must have been hard for him as a young boy."

Tyson, not trying to dodge the question, but eager to change the topic gave her an answer that he felt would be satisfactory. "He hardly remembers anything—let alone details from the accident."

"Oh, I'm so sorry to hear about that. It must be tough."

"It is."

Tyson pulled up to her house and parking the car realized that he couldn't leave Dominique on such a sad note. He tried to change the subject to a more upbeat topic, but when he was asked to talk about his former wife, he knew the mood was not going to lighten.

"Can we talk about her another night?" begged Tyson. "It's a long story and not a pleasant one."

"Stay for a while. I'm not going to see you for a few days, and I know I'm going to miss you. You don't have to go in the house, just sit here in the car with me for a few more minutes," begged Dominique.

Tyson, knowing he couldn't resist a charming plea like that, unclipped his seatbelt and turned off the engine. "I usually don't like to talk about this, but I've grown to realize that I can't resist you and your requests."

Although Tyson continued to talk, in her mind, Dominique kept repeating his words. "I can't resist you and your requests. I can't resist you and your requests. I can't resist you and your requests," she kept saying to herself, until a soft touch of his hand summoned her back to the conversation.

"Barbara was a good person, but not a good wife. I feel bad talking about her, especially to you. But you asked. We met in California, just outside of L.A. I was visiting a college friend who knew Barbara, and he introduced me to her. We liked each other, but it wasn't until my third visit that we really hit it off. Talk about long distance romances; I was in Westchester and she was, well, out west, in Anaheim.

"We started to see each other, and our three-year courtship saw many frequent flyer miles and long distance phone bills. Finally, she agreed to move to New York, and in a few months we were married. But, after Robert's birth, Barbara lost interest in me. Our marriage suffered greatly, as we were intimate once every two years or so.

"I remained loyal to her but couldn't understand why she had lost interest in me. My long hours of class work started to cause things to unravel. I guess I became more interested in my work, compensating for the loss of attention at home.

"After several years, I became less attentive at a time when she probably needed more attention. Her reaction was to slowly carve me out of her life. It got to the point that when I came home from the office or from class, she wouldn't speak to me. The chasm became so wide that we slept in different parts of the house. We stopped socializing with friends and family. When I found out that she was spending our money foolishly, I hit the roof. What finished us was the fact that I found out that she was sleeping with my neighbor, a woman named Tanya. I moved out," said a sorrowful Tyson. "Her drinking became a problem. I filed for sole custody and won. She was so bitter she threatened to kill herself and Robert."

Dominique saw that his hands were starting to tremble, and his words were coming out more slowly and deliberately. Tyson was uneasy, for sure, but he continued. "Over the phone one night we had a terrible argument, a real beauty of a fight. I told her that she needed help and that I was coming over to retrieve Robert from his weekly visit with her. She told me to 'Kiss off' and that she'd return him four hours later than she was supposed to. After close to two hours, I couldn't wait any longer. I started to drive to Barbara's house. I was stopped at a light on Route 22 in Armonk, when I saw a speeding car going the other way, running the red lights. The car had to be doing seventy miles an hour in a twenty-five miles per hour zone. I quickly realized that it was the car that I had recently purchased for her.

"I made a quick U-turn and tried to catch up to her. It was a couple of miles down the road that I saw it."

At that point Tyson took the handkerchief out of his pocket and started to wipe his tearing eyes. Dominique's reassuring hug and kiss on the cheek provided some comfort, as did her words, "Tyson, you don't have to go on."

"I want to finish."

"But I know how it happened, I remember from the papers and television."

Despite her words, he cleared his throat, took a deep breath and continued. "She ran one more light, one that had a SUV hurrying to make a left as the arrow changed from green to yellow. Barbara had a red light but she sped through it. The crash was horrific, and I was there to see it. The fiery crash killed her instantly. I was able to rush out of my car and quickly get to the burning SUV. Thank God Robert had been in the back seat sleeping."

His head was now hung in a position that suggested guilt. He looked up and cried, "I've never seen anything so bad in my life. Never! Why did I have to demand that she bring him home? Why couldn't I have been more patient?"

His rant continued. "He was trapped in the car for more than two minutes. Imagine being in there, helpless, while watching and smelling your mother's bloody remains roast before you. His oxygen supply was depleted, and the flames approached the backseat and engulfed his clothing. The temperature kept rising, causing his hands to have third degree burns, a result of his having tried to beat back the flames. Then he lost consciousness. I tried to get into the car as fast as I could. It was painful not being able to get inside."

He explained that he had been told that the entire time of Robert's exposure to the fire had been less than three minutes, but to Tyson, it had seemed like hours. Finally, with the help of several others, Robert's limp body was successfully pulled from the charred remains of Barbara's green Chevy SUV. The irony could not be missed; her flaming car had been a Blazer.

"Robert's body was unresponsive and he was hardly breathing. In fact, I remember performing CPR on him. Others helped to keep the blood from oozing out of his body. He lived, but Barbara was killed by a drunk driver—herself."

"Tyson, her drinking was not your fault. Her statement to you hinted that she was suicidal. You were trying to do what you could. Look at it this way: Robert was fortunate that you were there. He is alive because of you."

After several minutes of consoling him, Dominique sensed that he had calmed himself to the point that she could leave. But, after she announced that she was going to head inside, Tyson grabbed her hand

and asked her to stay with him. "Just five more minutes."

The recently retired superintendent knew she didn't have to worry about a morning alarm clock. More important, she wanted to stay. Perhaps she could insist on his coming in for a drink—tea or coffee. She thought about a way to get him inside.

"Tyson, please come inside for a little while. I'll make some tea or coffee for us."

Tyson listened and thought it over for a second. "OK, sounds good, but only for a few minutes. I have a plane to catch in the morning."

Inside her head Dominique gave herself a high five. "Tea or coffee?" she asked.

"I'm a tea man for sure."

Walking into her magnificent colonial house, Tyson looked around the living room, seeing dozens of beautiful family photographs. Several large still-life paintings adorned the walls, and a closer look revealed that Dominique had been the artist of each. One photo, a mother-daughter composition, was the most eye-catching. Tyson had never seen two more lovely ladies.

On the corner end table, almost altar-like, draped with black cloth, stood a picture of Frank. With the exception of that one corner, the room was well lit and upbeat.

Meanwhile, in the kitchen, Dominique prepared the tea. Tyson's answer of "I'd love to taste the latter," produced a loud laugh in the kitchen, which perplexed him.

Her question had been heard as, "Which would you prefer, lemon or milk?" but had actually had been asked, "Which would you prefer, lemon or milk," followed by a muffled, "Or me?" His response of, "I'd love to taste the latter," tickled her funny bone, but she knew he had actually been referring to the milk.

Her living room was decorated in a modern style, with a white leather sectional dominating the room. Her silver and black wall unit surrounded a large flat screen television.

As she entered the living room carrying a tray with two cups, a tea kettle, a milk dispenser, and cookies, she noticed that Tyson had been reading an article about the recent terrorist attacks. "I didn't get a chance to read today's paper or look at my computer. Where was the attack? And how many casualties?" she asked.

"Chester, Pennsylvania, in a highly populated shopping mall. Dozens died." replied Tyson. "They're getting more brazen with the attacks; fortunately, the death toll was low. I've lost track of how many places have been hit, but I'm sure it's at least a dozen or so. They hit a black club."

"These attacks are getting crazy. I hope Faulkner can get a handle on them soon. I'm worried about traveling."

As they prepared their tea to suit their respective tastes, the two discussed the ramifications for the Faulkner administration, as well as the psychological effect the bombings were having upon the nation. Several minutes passed when Tyson glanced at his watch, saw that it was 10:45, and regretfully announced that he would have to be going. He apologized for making it an early evening.

"Listen, I really have to get going. I haven't packed and I have to be at Westchester Airport for a 6:30 A.M. flight."

"You know, I'm retired now. I could go with you."

"Robert would freak if I brought another woman with me. He's not ready for that."

"I could stay back in the hotel room or at your place."

"I don't know if *I'm* ready for that," he said with a smile, "But after being apart from you for the rest of this weekend, I will be."

"Will you at least think of me?" she asked him.

The smile came off his face and while looking her straight in her watery eyes he said, "Since I first laid eyes on you, I haven't stopped thinking about you. I'll call you when I get to Maine."

With that he took two steps toward her and wrapped his arms around her. She looked up into his eyes, eyes focused on her and her alone, and anticipated their first real kiss. Instead he asked her, "May I kiss you?"

Her nodding head, returned hug and closed eyes signaled "yes." Slowly and respectfully he took his hand and gently pulled her head toward his. She tilted her head and he rotated his so that their mouths would fit together perfectly. In an instant their lips met. As he slowly brought his head back, releasing his hold upon her, he looked at her and asked, "Would you mind if I did that again?" Before she could say yes, she reached for his neck and pulled him in for a second kiss. After the first few moments they each realized that although the kiss had ended, the relationship had really just begun.

As he walked down her steps, Tyson looked back at Dominique, eager to see her smiling face again. Likewise, her mind was on his return to her door, hopeful that it would be soon. Neither was aware of the doors that soon would be opening and closing in front of them.

Chapter 7

The Call

Bar Harbor, Maine
Sunday, July 5, 2020
9:00 A.M.

Tyson's visit with his son Robert started well. As he entered the hospital room, Robert sat up in his bed with a huge grin on his face.

"Hi, Dad," Robert said with words that were slurred and would have been hardly recognizable to anyone except to Robert's nurses and to the professor himself.

"Hi, Robert. How are you feeling today?"

"Dad, I have a headache, but breakfast was good."

The professor smiled and showed him the gifts that he had brought—something that he did every time that he came to Maine. "Robert, if you remember, the last time that I was here you asked for this," said Tyson, as he handed Robert a small gift-wrapped box.

Helping his son unwrap the paper, the professor was delighted to see the joy in Robert's eyes as he unveiled a new camera. "Let me show you how it works."

After several minutes, Robert was taking pictures of everything in the room. After helping him out of the bed, the father and son took a short stroll to the large family room, Robert tethered to the IV pole that supplied his life-supporting medications.

Once in the family room, from the window, Robert was able to take dozens of pictures of the beautifully manicured hospital grounds. After several minutes, Robert told his father that he was tired and wanted to go back to bed, a statement that didn't surprise the professor as it was common to almost every visit that he made.

Walking down the hall and back to the room, Robert was helped back into the bed and smiled at his father. "I love you, Dad. I'm going to sleep now."

"I love you too, Robert. I will see you tonight."

Wiping a tear from his eye, the professor bent down and kissed his son on the forehead. He watched as his only child closed his eyes and quickly drifted off to sleep. He handed the camera to Nurse Patti and asked her to put it in a nearby place because, "As soon as he wakes up, he's going to be looking for it." After watching Robert sleep for two hours, Tyson completed his morning by going to the billing department and paying the bill for the next six months.

As he left the hospital he was greeted by several well-wishers, all of whom were eager to share their wonderful stories about Robert. Tyson was so happy to hear all of the details and thanked all of the staff for the fine service that they had provided for his son.

Tyson, like his son, was tired; he couldn't wait to get back to the hotel. The Bar Harbor Regency Hotel, with its ocean views, had been called by many the city's most exclusive lodging. Although the professor owned a home a little less than an hour away, he often chose to stay at the Regency, especially if his stay was going to be a short one. After his visits with Robert, the professor enjoyed coming back to the hotel and sitting in its outdoor Jacuzzi, as all he wanted to do was to relax.

Later that evening, traveling back to the hospital to have dinner with Robert, Tyson stopped at the front desk to speak to Loretta Harrison, who was in charge of Robert's case.

"Mr. Joseph, thank you for coming in. I wish that I had better news for you. Robert's condition has been declining, and we don't know why. His spirits are down and, frankly, the prognosis isn't good."

Dejected, Tyson longingly asked, "Although it's not easy to hear, I had had several thoughts that he wasn't getting any better. What else can we do for him?"

"For the last week we have provided a maintenance program for him, and he is somewhat responding to it. I'm not saying that he is getting better, because he isn't. But—"

"I want to thank you for everything that you and the staff have done for him. I couldn't imagine what he . . . no . . . make that *we* would have done without you. I have known that I would hear this at some point, just wasn't ready for it now."

"Please understand, I am not speaking of an immediate demise, he will have time. But—"

"I know. I'll enjoy every moment that I have with him."

Leaving Loretta's office, Tyson walked up to Robert's room, seeing him sleeping soundly. Softly, almost stealthily, Tyson walked toward his resting son's bed. Seeing all of the monitors and hearing the sounds that they were making, Tyson's eyes welled up, knowing that his time with Robert was coming to a close.

Wiping his eyes he quietly said, "Robert, I love you and will be here whenever you need me." But Tyson knew that his opportunities to see Robert had dwindled down to a precious few.

Chapter 8

The Second Call

Washington, D. C.
Monday, July 6, 2020
10:17 A.M.

Don Woodman opened his briefcase, revealing a large stack of papers, the size of which caught the professor by surprise.

"You weren't kidding when you said that you had a lot of stuff for me to read. That's pretty impressive."

"No, I wasn't kidding," answered Woodman in a monotone voice. "I don't do a great deal of kidding, Mr. Joseph. Besides, I wouldn't have had you come down on a moment's notice for something insignificant. I told you that the material would be worth the trip and, upon reading it, you will see that I know what I'm talking about."

"So, what do we have here?"

"These are the papers that Klyde left your family. They were hidden in a wall for decades. I only found them because I was renovating the basement and found them hidden in one of the walls. I think it was this stack of papers that led to his untimely death."

"Yeah, as I told you family rumors suggest that the government had something to do with his disappearance in the early twentieth century."

"From what I've read, those rumors are probably true. Your family had stumbled upon something that the government wanted none of the public to know about."

"So what on Earth is it?"

"I only read a few pages, but instantly, I knew that it was substantial. I know from your book that you were his descendant and figured that you should be in possession of the materials.

"It seems that your family had a history of working at the White

House and it was there that generations of your ancestors hand wrote their own history of presidential decisions, especially on one topic. Before you read it, let me comment that I have a profound respect for what your family did, because if these materials had been discovered it would have certainly meant their demise.

"Also, as I give them to you, I'm cutting my ties to these materials, hopeful that you will never reveal how you obtained them. Be mindful that the cautions that were taken in the past should still be followed by you. Confide only in those who you feel you can truly trust. Otherwise, it could cost you, like it probably cost Klyde."

Carefully removing the stack of papers, he placed them on the table, slightly spreading them out. "I took the liberty of making copies of these, in case something happens to the originals. These are the copies. You'll see that the originals are very well preserved, as if your ancestors knew that they wouldn't be read for a while."

Handing Tyson a single page, Woodman said, "This is the best place to start."

Carefully taking the paper, the anxious professor looked at it and read out loud,

"To the future generations of the Family of Squire Joseph, please understand the significance of these materials. Guard them carefully. Klyde."

"Wow," said Tyson. "That's his signature; I'd know it anywhere. See the swirling style in the K."

Woodman, realizing that this was really a private moment for Tyson said, "Professor Joseph, let me leave you alone with your family. Take your time and become familiar with them. Spend as much time as you want here. I have things to do and calls to make."

"Are you sure?" inquired Tyson.

"Of course I am. You'll find this material to be very interesting, I am sure. Holler out if you need me for anything."

Acknowledging that he would, Tyson sat in the comfortable chair and started reading some of the most mind-blowing words that he had ever read. He was amazed by the clarity of thought that had gone into these paragraphs, words that were so revealing that if they had been read by government officials would have led to the arrest of, at least, one of his ancestors.

As he read the pages, Tyson transformed himself into the time period in which they were written, one of extreme prejudice in our nation. He thought of the courageous act that it took for Klyde and other family members to secretly copy the written diary of some of the previous presidents, an act that some might view as treasonous. Yet before him were the journals, mostly from the nineteenth century—an indictment of the secret activities of the White House and Congress. As he read page after page of incriminating sentences, he couldn't help but think of their implications.

After an hour of reading and taking notes, he thought, "What the hell do I do with this stuff?" He called out, "Mr. Woodman, please come in here."

A moment later Woodman arrived, intrigued.

"First of all, I want to thank you for saving these papers and for sharing them with me. They are priceless and certainly something that I will cherish.

"But my problem is what to do with them. They have an importance to more people than just my family. Millions could benefit from what I just spent an hour reading."

"May I interrupt? Of course there is a tremendous amount of value within those pages, but let me warn you that there are many people who might want to keep their message silent. As a lawyer, and I might add, as one of the nation's top lawyers, you certainly see the legal value in the materials. But, so would others. And these people wouldn't want this information in the public domain. Tread carefully, Tyson."

"I guess there's one person with whom I should make contact."

Woodman said, "Elgin Hathaway?"

"Yes, Vice President Elgin Hathaway."

"I forget. What is your connection to the vice president?"

"We went to high school together in White Plains, New York, and were teammates on the track team. In fact, we were on a relay team, the 1600-meter relay that won the state championships. Over the years we've remained very close friends."

"Talk to him often?"

"Our schedules usually allow a call every couple of weeks or so. Because of his position, he's usually the one to call me—it's tough for me to get through to him. But knowing him, I think he'd be very interested in this stuff."

"Once you let him in on this information, he'll have to be even more careful than you."

"I know. I almost hesitate to tell him, but he should know about this."

"I've kept the originals in a safety deposit box. Here's the address and the key. I've already placed your name as one who can gain entry into the box. Now that I've given all of this to you, my connection with this is over. Right?"

"Yes, sir. It's all mine now."

The men talked for another twenty-five minutes before Tyson announced, "If I'm gonna catch that plane I better get out of here."

"Okay, Professor. Just be careful."

Chapter 9

The Diagnosis

The White House
Monday, July 6, 2020
11:15 A.M.

Answering the intercom, President Faulkner shouted, "Send him in. I've been expecting him."

As Dr. Rider walked into the room, he was greeted by a shouting President.

"It's about time you arrived. What the hell kept you? You're ten minutes late. It's not right to keep the President of the United States waiting; especially one who's been anxiously awaiting your arrival."

Correctly sensing the president's mood, Dr. Rider became defensive. "I was here on time, Mr. President. I was detained by your inquisitive staff, who were asking me questions about your health; questions I didn't want to answer. Or for that matter, questions I didn't even want to be asked."

With a hint of sarcasm, the president responded, "Can the President of the United States ask a question of the great Dr. Rider? Is that allowed?"

Disgusted, Rider snapped back, "Look it was your attitude that—"

"You're right. Sorry. I feel like crap. I really don't feel well at all. What's happened to me?"

"Well, Jim, you should feel like crap—you have cancer. As I told you, you have a life-threatening, perhaps life-ending form of pancreatic cancer. I put a fake name on your tests and the other doctors and I agree that someone named Frank Hemingway has cancer. So, as your doctor and friend, I'm here to tell you the bad news. It has metastasized into a few other areas of your body."

The news jolted the president, making him slouch in his chair, assuming a position of defeat. Although anticipated, the news had been sobering.

He looked at Rider and in muted voice asked, "I'm afraid to ask you this, but how long?"

Rider glancing at some notes lifted his head and with a touch of sadness, declared, "You might make Election Day. And if elected, you might, and I mean might, make it to your inauguration. But, for certain, you wouldn't live far into the next term.

"I highly suggest that you drop out of the running. Trying for the next term is like hurrying into the airport to catch a plane that you know is going to crash and burn. Don't do it. Spend your last few months—months that could prove to be painful—with Caroline, chilling out and getting your affairs and the affairs of the nation in order."

"Brook, I appreciate the suggestion, but I am going to run for the next term."

"Are you out of your freaking mind? That's the stupidest thing I've ever heard. Why would you do that to yourself?"

"I have to make it to January 20th and my inauguration for my second term. I can't run the risk of not making it until then."

Rider, looking a bit confused, asked the president, "Jim, your ego has to take a back seat to your health. Think about your health, man. Why are you insisting that you have to get to a second term? I'm telling you that you'll never complete it!"

Angrier than before, Faulkner lashed back, "It's not about my damned ego. That's not what I'm talking about!"

Rider smiled. "*Sure* Jim. It's my suggestion, as your doctor, that you call a press conference and announce that you're out of the race. Then tell the public that you're putting all your support behind Vice President Hathaway."

The emotionally weakened Faulkner sprung up out of his chair and shouted, "That will be the day that I allow *him* to become president!"

"What? For God's sake, he's the vice president. He'd be the one to take over."

"I have my reasons. I don't want that man to become president. There are facts out there that he should never know."

Rider, not sure what the president was suggesting, asked the simple question, "Why not?"

Faulkner sitting down again, took a deep breath and said, "Look Brook, we're close friends. We have shared many things. Perhaps one day I can discuss this with you, but now is not the time. Trust me. Despite the fact that you don't understand, I know what I'm doing. It has to be this way."

The president's statement didn't make anything clearer to the doctor, and Rider still wasn't sure what the president was talking about. "I don't get it. I'm a doctor, Jim, not a politician. As your friend, I might eventually listen, but as your doctor I'm ordering you not to run."

"Stick your stethoscope up your—"

"Hey, watch it, Jim. One of us is going public with this information."

Faulkner looked at his friend and said, "Okay, wait. Suppose I told you that your father's ranch in Texas, the one that he left to your brother . . . suppose I told you that there was a chance that it could be taken away and given to someone that you have never met, someone who has never even seen the ranch. Would that upset you?"

"Hell yeah it would."

"I'm telling you that if I'm not here, there is a possibility that that could happen. Your father's legacy could end up in the hands of someone you've never met in your life."

"Well, I'm still not certain what you're talking about, but I will trust your judgment. So, I'm not sure if that is enough for my support. Jim, as your friend, I will stand behind you, but as your—"

"Spare me that 'As your doctor crap,' will ya? You never told me how to live, so don't assume that you can tell me how to die. Look, Brooksie, as *your* friend, all I'm asking for is for you to let me do it my way. That's all that I'm asking for."

"Jim, it's not going to be a pretty ride, though. Make sure you're buckled in."

Faulkner, with a sly look on his face said, "Thank you, Brook. Help me the best that you can. I appreciate it."

"You'll be in charge for a while, but I can't promise how long."

"I understand. Just keep me as strong as you can."

"I'll do all that I can, my friend. Should I get Caroline in here?"

"No. I'll tell her myself. By the way Hathaway has agreed not to be part of the ticket. He and I talked!"

A shocked Dr. Rider sat back down in his chair. A quizzical look on his face suggested disbelief. He scratched his head, "There's been no mention of this in the press. The convention is coming up soon. When were you going to let the American people know about this?"

"Soon," said Faulkner with a stern voice. "Before the convention, Vice President Hathaway was going to announce that he was leaving the ticket. At that point I would introduce the name of Florida governor Maria Martinez. She will easily win nomination and become the next vice president of the United States. But, I'm telling you this knowing that you'll realize that it's sensitive information, not to be shared."

The still-surprised Doctor Rider nodded his head, "No problem."

Then, after a moment's thought, the disgusted Dr. Rider shook his head and said, "I've got news for you, Jim. I think that before the swallows fly back to Capistrano, she will be the next president of the United States, because, I'm afraid that you will be gone, my friend."

Chapter 10

The Tub

White House
Thursday, August 13, 2020
3:12 P.M.

"I know that you are upset, Elgin, but you won't be the first vice president not to be brought back for a second term. Hell, it seems like FDR had half a dozen or so during his years in office. We've talked about this for three freaking days; I have had it with you and this terrorism thing. By having you leave, the public will have the perception that we are doing more to get a handle on things. And Governor Martinez has been strong on the issue—her state of Florida has worked well with the federal government at shutting down potential cells of terrorists. She's been a great leader in that area. Four years ago you were the pretty boy of the party. Well, you've done little of substance for us since then. And an alleged strength of yours has turned into a perceived weakness of mine. I can't tolerate you dragging me down anymore."

Hathaway tried to respond, "Jim—" he started, but was shouted down by the president.

"I want someone who has a future in the party and Governor Martinez has everyone's eyes open. I have spoken to her, and she has accepted the offer. Plus, you do nothing for me in Florida; she's the freaking governor. You're from New York, a state which four years ago was in play. Now, it appears that it is a state that I am destined to lose. I see no political advantage that you can bring to me or the party in November.

"So during the next few months, just be a good company man and say all of the right things. Tomorrow I will make the announcement myself from Camp David; that way I will spare you the humiliation!"

"Spare me that humiliation crap, you bastard! You never supported me, and now you're hanging all of this terrorism crap on me? You'll pay for this, Jim. Big time, you'll pay for this."

"Hell, I'm already paying for it—paying for having your ass in office with me. You're useless to me and to the entire freaking party."

"Like I said, you'll pay for this. You'll get yours."

"Drop dead and get the hell out of my office."

"I'm not done with you yet."

"Well, I'm freaking done with you and that's all that counts in this office. Now get out."

"You've always had trouble with black people, haven't you? Ever since that brother from Oregon kicked your ass in that election thirty years ago?"

"Only particular blacks—and right now you're one of them."

"I don't think you like any of us; your voting record shows that."

"My record's fine, and in the end it's going to show that I'm replacing your ass with someone who can help me win."

"Your record shows that you were anti–Dr. King and the civil rights movement."

"That was fifty freaking years ago, and I was a young man back then."

"Is this the part of the conversation that you tell me that now some of your best friends are black? Besides, you were a young man in Vietnam when you alienated half of the unit that you commanded."

Pointing his finger in Hathaway's face, the angry president said, "I'm proud of my record in Vietnam—I served this nation well."

Hathaway shouted back, "Your freaking men hated you."

"They didn't understand me."

"How could they? They were from West Philly, Watts, Harlem, Newark, and other black areas. Hell, you're a freaking farm boy from northern Oregon."

"I'm telling you, I got along with them well."

"How could you? The only thing that you grew up with that was black was the farm's cherries."

"Screw you."

"And unlike those cherries, those men wouldn't let you take out their guts and crush them, would they?"

"It was freaking Vietnam, you idiot. Tensions were high—all around, for everyone."

"They hated your guts, and admit it, you hated theirs. Admit it dammit!"

"The only thing that I'll freaking admit to hating was sucking up to the party four years ago and allowing them to talk me into accepting your ass on the ticket."

"Yeah, maybe, but with your reputation as a closet bigot you needed me on that ticket. You'd have lost the election if it wasn't for me. I was the carryover from Obama."

"That's crap."

"Is it? I got the minority vote for you and got your ass elected. We're the Republican Party, you ass. We're the party known for parading out Herman Cain and then sitting back and watching him get his character destroyed."

"That's politics, my brother."

"Take that 'brother' crap and stick it where the sun don't shine."

"Crap? I thought that you nappy—"

"What did you say? You mother—"

The president felt another attack developing. "Get out. Get out now. We'll finish this later. I'm done here, now get out."

Watching Elgin turn and leave the office brought a perverted pleasure to the president—one that made him smile, despite the abdominal pains he was feeling. He then turned back to his desk, packing a few last-minute items that he wanted for the trip. A few hours later Faulkner traveled to Camp David to write his acceptance speech. But Faulkner knew that he was there for more than writing a speech—he was there writing his ticket to re-election. He carefully chose his words, knowing that the nation would be paying close attention to each and every one of them. But Faulkner also had a devious plan that he needed to place into action, the plan that had been put forth by his wife, Caroline.

After several hours in his Camp David office and with the draft of his speech written, Faulkner was set to put into action the plan that he hoped would be able to convince the American people to re-elect him. Soon after picking at his dinner Faulkner announced that he was going to take a bath, as baths had always been a way of life for the president, providing him with an occasional time to escape the entrapments of the office. Caroline announced that she was going to the library to read.

As always Faulkner told his aides that he didn't need any help in the bathroom, choosing to retire there alone. Once he was upstairs, he started running the water in his tub. He used his familiar brand of bubble bath and had the water at the correct temperature that he loved, a temperature that was hotter than most people could tolerate. As he disrobed and stepped into the awaiting bath, he closed his eyes and prayed that his plan would work.

As he lowered his second foot into the water, he looked at his leg, knowing that it would be the last time it would look and feel that way. After fifteen minutes of bathing, the president watched Caroline walk quietly into the bathroom. The nervous president acknowledged her arrival and stood up in the water.

Gazing at his naked, wet body, the First Lady was distracted by the thought of how many other women, since their marriage, had seen him in a similar light. For years she had put up with his philandering as he slept with any and every available woman who smiled at him. She channeled those thoughts to use in her soon-to-happen action, as those thoughts fueled a fire within her, one that had long lied dormant.

Jim noticed that the expression on her face had changed from one of nervousness to one of readiness.

"Just do it," he demanded.

Caroline walked to her travel bag, reached inside and found the hammer that she had placed there. Taking two slow steps toward her awaiting husband, the confident First Lady tightly grasped the instrument and quickly raised it above her shoulder. Envisioning the faces of several of his alleged lovers, her fast downward action forcefully struck the spot that she had read about on the Internet, one inch below the top of the president's bent right knee.

As the tool hit the bone, the president collapsed on the floor, the pain too intense for him to bear. In a heap, he collapsed onto the floor, barely conscious. The First Lady took the weapon with her and, after looking carefully in the hallway and seeing no one there, silently crept back to the library, where everyone thought she had been all along.

It was from the library that Caroline called the president's aide, Paul Anthony Roma, and asked him to check on the president, seeing if he needed anything. "Remind him that that movie we wanted to watch is coming on in a few minutes." As she watched the aide go up the steps, she hoped that the plan would continue smoothly.

When she heard Roma's call out for help, she knew that this part of the plan had been successful. Reacting to the pleas for help, Caroline joined several others as she ran up the steps to see what was wrong. As the bathroom door was now ajar, each of the people were able to see the naked President's quivering body on the floor, surrounded by a large puddle of soapy water.

The Secret Service men were on their walkie-talkies calling for medical attention. Keeping within the plan the First Lady cried uncontrollably. She held her husband's hand, saying to him, "Jim, please wake up. Please Jim, move. I'm begging you, please wake up."

A moment later Dr. Rider joined the group, taking charge and immobilizing the president's right leg by using sheets from the nearby closet to tie it to the left leg. He looked at the crowd of onlookers and said, "Get me some ice immediately! We have to get him to the hospital. Call the ambulance corp. Judging from the swelling, he may have broken his kneecap."

A gurney was brought up and the president was carefully placed upon it. Now awake and with a robe around him, a groggy Faulkner gave Dr. Rider and the others around him a painstaking account of how he was trying to get out of the bathtub, his right foot hitting the top of the tub, causing him to slip and fall.

"What the hell do we do now, Brook?" asked the agonized president. "It hurts like all hell."

"From the feel of it, it looks like you may have broken your patella."

Pushing the doctor's hand away, Faulkner yelled, "Don't touch it again—just freaking fix it."

"Not here. You're going to need surgery."

The entire time he lay in the area, Caroline was torn between the emotions of guilt and pleasure. Certainly she had been successful with her aim, which pleased her. But, despite the dozens of times that his womanizing had hurt her, hurting him was something she had never done before, and that pained her greatly.

After several minutes, which to Faulkner seemed like an eternity, the president was told that it was time for him to be transported to the hospital. Asking for his press secretary, Faulkner responded, "Send Carlos in here immediately."

Two long minutes later, Carlos Agunella knocked on the door and was granted permission to enter. "Mr. President, I was so sorry to hear about your accident. How are you feeling?"

Receiving no response he quickly stated, "My suggestion for the press is . . ."

"I don't give a crap what your suggestion is," said Faulkner angrily. "Here's what you do and make sure you do it right. Full disclosure! You understand the term 'full disclosure'! I'll take a beating about being clumsy; Fallon and Kimmel will crucify me. I want you to put out that next week's acceptance speech is unlikely."

"Yes sir. I'll put that information on the wire. Is there anything else?"

"Yeah. Tell them that my foot got caught on the top of the tub and with my hands holding reading material, I couldn't catch myself. I'm in extreme pain, and Dr. Rider will handle any questions from here."

"Yes, sir. I'll get that out immediately."

As he was loaded into the helicopter, President James Augustus Faulkner held Caroline's hand tightly. He knew she was feeling bad, so once he was secured, he waved his hand, motioning for her to come close.

"I want to whisper in your ear," he said to her. A moment later he said, "You did a great job back there. You know what's at stake and you were excellent. The last people that hit like that were Ted Williams and Stan the Man Musial."

For the first time in more than an hour a smile fell upon Caroline's face. It had really been the first time in several days that she had smiled. The First Lady leaned over and gave the president a huge kiss on the lips, a kiss that said, "I'm sorry."

The helicopter, waiting at the pad, was a loud reminder to the Faulkners that their plan, although successful at first, still had a long way to go. But once the president's gurney was secured for the journey, he felt a little more at ease.

"Caroline, it was worth it, you'll see."

"I'm usually not the person in this relationship who inflicts the pain on the other."

"Even now? Lord, could you for once give it a freaking rest already? Just once."

Upon arrival at the hospital, the president, leaning up from the gurney, was amazed to see the flurry of activity that surrounded him. Dozens of people with walkie-talkies were communicating and trying to get him to the operating room as quickly as possible. A young doctor, Roxanne Okun, greeted the president's emergency party.

"Mr. President, Mrs. Faulkner," she began, "It's my understanding that this injury was from a bathroom accident. I'm sorry to say that there appears to be an injury to your patella or kneecap. They said that you really did a number on it. If it is broken, and x-rays will soon determine that, I'm afraid surgery will be required to correct the situation. And I'm afraid you'll have to rest, missing the rest of the national convention."

The x-ray session lasted only a few minutes, and the president was quickly taken to the operating room, where he was greeted by his team of surgeons, Doctors James O'Toole, Robert Purkey, and James Maloney; the latter tried to comfort Faulkner, "Mr. President, this will be a routine operation."

"Routine my ass," said an angered President. "It's not your knee; it's mine."

"Good point, Sir. But I've done hundreds of these operations. You're in good hands."

"I better be."

After an hour of surgery, O'Toole along with Carlos Agunella addressed the media carefully, explaining the injury's cause and nature. During their forty-five-minute conference the two men answered dozens of questions, the last being answered by O'Toole with these words, "Yes, the president will have a full recovery. I guarantee it, but the convention doesn't look possible."

With those words the press conference ended and the deception had gotten off to a good beginning.

Chapter 11

The Governor's Speech

Republican National Convention
Madison Square Garden
New York, New York
Wednesday, August 26, 2020
10:28 P.M.

After two days of less-than-exciting speeches, the capacity crowd at Madison Square Garden was anticipating a rousing speech from their vice presidential nominee, Maria Martinez. They were not to be disappointed.

As Martinez walked toward the podium, she was greeted by the capacity crowd's lukewarm applause, save for the proud Florida delegation. Martinez, who was beautifully attired in a light red dress, dark jacket, and a white satin blouse, confidently acknowledged her audience and began to speak with Spanish-accented words.

"I am Maria Martinez, and I plan to be your vice president."

Momentarily deviating from her notes she said, "Many of you may not know much about me, so let me tell you just who I am. I grew up in a poor Fort Lauderdale neighborhood that many would say was on the wrong side of the tracks. I was fortunate that our one-bedroom home was located where I was able to view the tracks. Indeed, as a young girl, I often walked down to those tracks, looking far off to the point where they reached the horizon, wondering if they could take me to a faraway place. I knew that sometime in my future, I would follow those tracks to a place that provided many rewards. So, my dreams followed the tracks, toward the horizon, knowing that my future was out there somewhere, far beyond the sight lines of what others called a dilapidated neighborhood.

"I was an inquisitive student, who received good grades, although many regarded the elementary school that I attended as substandard.

My teachers all loved my interest in learning, never being one who was satisfied with the obvious, wanting, instead, to know the reasons why things were like they were and why some other things couldn't be better. My wonderful mother, Isabella, worked with me at night, making sure that I would get all of my homework done. She was there to review my work, despite the fact that she spent thirteen hours a day working at the homes of others."

Clearing her throat, Martinez sensed that the crowd was beginning to come around as her story was receiving more and more applause.

"My mother was proud of me, later saying that one homework assignment, in particular, had brought her to tears. As we sat in our candlelit apartment, we studied the life cycle of the monarch butterfly. After I convinced her that I knew the material frontwards and backwards, I turned to her and told her that I would be like that butterfly, leaving behind a cocoon and one day returning with glory and beauty, rising above the troubled area in which we lived. From that moment on, my mother said that she knew that I would aspire to, and achieve, greatness in life."

Her words created an atmosphere supportive of her candidacy. Inside, Martinez was glowing, knowing that she was winning the hearts of most of those in attendance.

"By eighth grade I had become the leading student in my class and although very financially challenged, I sought to further my education at some of southern Florida's top high schools. My efforts paid off, as I received one of a dozen hardship scholarships for the prestigious Young Women's Preparatory Academy of Miami, the acceptance letter still framed and hanging in my mother's house.

"It was during my four-year stay at the highly acclaimed school that I was able to reach the levels that I had been born to achieve. It was at this institution that I met many of my lifelong friends. Due to hard work, I gained the respect of the entire staff, as by the end of my senior year, my weighted high GPA topped that of all of my classmates, making me, Maria Martinez, the school's valedictorian. At graduation, I brought many in the crowd to tears as I thanked all of those people who had ever attempted to help me, providing a description of the nights, often by candlelight, that I had spent with my mother, who despite working those long hours cleaning the homes of those more affluent, was able to make sure that her 'Little Maria' got her homework done. It is said that my tearful wave to my mother, who was seated in the front row that evening, would forever be etched in the mind of all who were in attendance that May night."

At the Republican convention, Isabella was introduced and received a tremendous ovation from the entire crowd. Maria, who had become the shining star of the party, was gleaming even brighter than her running mate President Faulkner. Maria was aware that it wasn't her time, not quite yet. But the audience's loud ovation made her come to the realization that her day as a presidential candidate could be soon, perhaps as early as 2024.

"After my years at the University of Pennsylvania, I returned to my native Fort Lauderdale and worked in the mayor's office. It was there that I witnessed the needs of so many people who were like me, making me pledge to do whatever I could to help them all. It was seeing an eighty-year-old woman—Mrs. Lugo, yes, I will always remember her name—seeing her go to City Hall and ask for more police presence in her neighborhood because she felt frightened when she pulled her food cart back home from the supermarket. That day was the day that launched my political career. I thought about the manner in which the government had turned its back on her. From that day on, I promised that I would make a difference!"

Maria heard cheers from all corners of the arena. People were on their feet screaming at the top of their lungs. She sensed that they now embraced her for whom she was, "Little Maria," the one who makes a difference.

The speech then centered upon her rise in the party, eventually occupying the office of Mayor of Fort Lauderdale. "My two terms as mayor were some of the most prosperous years for the city, and many have given me credit as being the person most responsible for the large economic growth witnessed by the city and its surrounding suburbs. I thank those who gave me the credit, but much of the credit should also go to the region's hard-working citizens, who dug themselves out of the financial abyss.

"I was then urged by many in the party to seek the governorship, and I accepted the challenge of running the nation's third largest state. My tough stances on crime and terrorism were the reasons why the people of the Sunshine State re-elected me to a second term and why so many have asked me to pursue the position of vice president. I have accepted their requests, and I am here tonight to thank you for believing in me."

Again the Florida delegation rose to their feet, "Martinez" signs and banners proudly displayed.

"Let those individuals who have brought terrorism to the shores of our great nation be aware that the Faulkner-Martinez Administration is here to put them out of business. We will have the support of all Americans, rich or poor; black, white, or brown; Republican or Democrat.

"I vow that I will bring the same strong skills that I brought to Florida to my new position as vice president of the United States—helping President Faulkner achieve what every American from every background wants, an eradication of terrorism from the shores of our fine nation.

"My word is my promise—ask the person sitting there. That's Mrs. Eloise Lugo, the woman whose neighborhood was cleaned up during my administration."

At that point, other delegations had enthusiastically joined the Floridians, cheers echoing throughout the World's Most Famous Arena.

Asking her aides to help her stand from her wheelchair, as she rose to her feet, Mrs. Lugo, aged ninety-six, received a huge round of applause from the capacity crowd.

"My warning goes to those who are hurting Americans—your days are numbered—and I will see to that personally."

She promised those in the audience, those at home and those of the opposing party, that "You will always have good things to say about me, the future vice president of the greatest country in the world, the Land of Opportunity, the United States of America!

"America, please stand with me and support the presidency of James Augustus Faulkner and put us to work for you, let us march to every corner of this great nation, knock on each and every door and tell our friends, neighbors and those who we don't know, that it is our destiny that needs to be fulfilled and that that destiny will be fulfilled by the ticket of Faulkner and Martinez. Let us pray for a full recovery for the president."

After a thunderous ovation she continued, "Like those railroad tracks that I looked down so many years ago, there are opportunities out there that need to be found. Opportunities for you, you, and you! I looked down those tracks, and here before me is my opportunity. Do the same. There, beyond the horizon, there is an America that only James Augustus Faulkner can bring to all of us. Don't let the train leave you at the station. Get on board. Get on board. Get on board."

As she pushed herself away from the podium, the tears flowing from her beautiful face, the crowd cheered in unison, "Get on board. Get on board. Get on board," their cheers making it impossible for her to leave the stage for close to ten minutes. Her frantic waves tired her arms, the repetitive motion causing her to drop them to her sides. But only for a moment did her arms stay down, as she raised them again to wave to her supporters.

As she scanned the crowd she saw that almost every person was on his or her feet, including Mrs. Lugo, making her think, "They know me now, don't they?"

As she left the stage and walked toward her wheelchair-bound mother, who was sitting in the first row, she sprinted down the stairs to hug her tightly.

"Mom, you are the greatest role model in the world. Thank you for always being there for me. Your butterfly has come home."

"You received what every child on Earth deserves, a mother's love. Fly high, my darling Maria. Fly high."

Chapter 12

The Discussion

Mount Kisco, New York
Wednesday, August 26, 2020
11:22 P.M.

Professor Joseph and Dominique had been watching every moment of the convention. Upon discussion of the president's broken kneecap each thought that the accident had occurred at an inconvenient time.

"The man was about to accept his party's nomination for the White House," said Tyson. "That's pretty bad timing."

"That didn't sound too genuine on your part," replied Dominique.

With a clear look of bewilderment on his face Tyson said, "I find it very strange that a man who was an accomplished skier, one who, at one time, had Olympic aspirations, couldn't step out of his own bathtub without falling."

"What are you getting at?" asked Dominique.

"I'm not sure, but I think that the accident's sort of odd. That's all."

"But accidents happen. Other presidents have had accidents. Didn't it seem like President Ford was falling down some flight of steps once a month or so?"

"Perhaps."

"Do you think that he'll miss the convention and not speak tomorrow night?"

"I think that he'll be there. Either way, he's following a tough act. Martinez was great tonight. One of the most invigorating speeches I have ever heard."

"I agree. Compare her speech with the one given by Bishop, the Democratic candidate for vice president, and there is no comparison. She's going to make a difference in the election for sure. I thought that

Elgin got a raw deal, but she's convinced me that she's the real deal."

"I'm sure that a lot of people forgot about Elgin Hathaway tonight."

"Maybe. Meanwhile, let's see what happens tomorrow."

"Have you seen his polling numbers lately? At last week's convention, Governor Ryan and the Democrats got a big boost in their numbers. People like this guy. I'm telling you that he's going to be tough to beat and the president needs every advantage that he can get."

"And a broken knee gives him that advantage?"

"Certainly. The knee took Ryan off the front page and placed the focus back on Faulkner. Even when Ryan was being nominated, the questions were being asked about Faulkner's knee. Now everyone is asking will he speak tomorrow. Despite what has been, until tonight, a lackluster Republican convention, no one is talking about the governor right now are they? All the talk has changed from being about the up-and-coming governor back to the president and the mystery surrounding whether he will speak or not."

Chapter 13

The Drawn Curtains

Madison Square Garden
Thursday, August 27, 2020
10:16 P.M.

The mood at Madison Square Garden was subdued, remarkably, even more subdued than it had been during the years in which Isiah Thomas had haplessly coached the Knicks. After three nights of speeches the crowd had anticipated that tonight would be the night that President James Augustus Faulkner would have been giving his acceptance speech. Almost every person in the arena had wanted to hear their party's leader give some inspiring remarks.

The crowd was not happy, yet still they were respectable, as host Danny McAvoy stepped to the microphone. In his high-pitched voice he said, "Ladies and gentlemen! Ladies and gentlemen! Ladies and gentlemen, we are all saddened by the recent accident that took place at Camp David several days ago. We are happy to announce that the surgery was successful and that President Faulkner is feeling much better. The accident damaged his body, but not his spirit. He is grateful for your support and promises you that he will serve his next four years with vigor and with enthusiasm unmatched in our nation's history.

"Tonight was scheduled to be the president's acceptance speech. His unfortunate accident caused us to plan a video conference with the president, but he has chosen not to go in that direction, canceling the conference."

With those words, the crowd became uneasy, with sporadic boos being heard. One man yelled out, "What's happening? Is he okay?" Another shouted, "No video? He couldn't even make a stinking video for us?"

At first disappointed that they would not see the president live, they were now led to believe that they would not even see a video of their beloved President. Then McAvoy continued, "No, your President has chosen not to speak to you via video. Instead, your President has chosen to be here in person. Yes, he's here! Yes, the next President of the United States, James Augustus Faulkner is here."

The last time that the Garden had been this alive was in 1993 when John Starks dunked over Michael Jordan and Horace Grant. The crowd rose, cheering in unison, "Faulk-ner! Faulk-ner." Suddenly the house lights dimmed, and the cheering quickly subsided to the point that a proverbial dropped pin could be heard. A spotlight shone on a pair of bright red curtains that slowly parted, revealing a darkened stage.

McAvoy then shouted into the microphone, "Heeerre he is, the next President of the United States, James Augustus Faulkner!" A small spotlight, about four inches across, appeared on the back curtain, slowly doubling in size to about eight inches and then finally to about three feet. The back curtain opened, revealing a ten-foot square box wrapped with silver paper and adorned with a huge red bow. The crowd sensed something great was about to happen and they were right. All were fixated upon the box when suddenly the front of the box dropped to the floor.

At first it was difficult for the crowd to realize that there was a man sitting in a wheelchair. As the image was shown upon the giant screens, the crowd burst into their familiar, unanimous cheer, "Faulk-ner! Faulk-ner!" At that point the president raised his arms and then motioned to the crowd for silence. More than ten times he frantically waved his arms until finally the crowd reluctantly silenced themselves. However, the quiet remained in place only momentarily, as Faulkner, using a suspended triangular-shaped bar, slowly pulled himself from the chair and stood before the again loudly vocal audience.

On cue, two young men ran from each side of the stage and handed the president a pair of crutches. Holding the crutches above his head, he slowly lowered them to their more customary position. While putting his weight upon the stainless steel instruments, he painstakingly walked to the podium. Twelve, thirteen, and then, finally, after fourteen tedious steps, he reached his destination, the crowd cheering louder with each step. With a huge smile on his face, the president shouted into the microphone, "So, America, how the hell are you?" Laughing, he acknowledged the crowd's cheers. "Well I hope you're okay, because I'm feeling fine! That's right, I'm feeling fine, America. And although you saw me slowly walk here to the microphone, let me tell you, I'm ready to run! That's right, run. I say, I'm ready to run for another term."

A thunderous round of applause followed, and the president, as if he were an Olympic sprinter, reacted as if he was running the 100-meter dash, making a fast motion of pumping his arms.

"I've been in the news the last couple of days, for reasons that were not planned. My back foot caught the top of a bathtub, and I fell hard to the floor. Perhaps you heard the noise in your homes. The only noise I heard that night was a solid crack of my kneecap. Painful, yes! Debilitating, no!

"Like this great nation of ours, we can take a hit, and we can keep moving on. I'm ready to move on. And I hope America's ready to move on with me."

Faulkner was interrupted by cheers of "Yes, we are! Yes, we are!"

"But I must start slowly, as those are the doctor's orders. I was told to convalesce at the White House, but nothing was going to keep me from being here with you. During the next few months I must take it slow. They feel it is in my best interest to stay put in the White House. However, I promise you that I will take care of all of my presidential business from there. It saddens me that I have to be under house arrest, not traveling around this great nation, sharing stories with you.

"Would you forgive me, America, if I don't travel around the nation and campaign? Well, would you?"

The crowd gave him the response he had sought. The audience was telling the president that he could stay in the White House to do his campaigning. His broad smile, though apparently a sign of their approval, actually had had a more sinister origin. He realized that his master plan was working.

He spoke for another thirty-six minutes, making comparisons between himself and the recently nominated Governor Ryan. The speech that night was one for the ages, regarded by many pundits to be among the greatest acceptance speeches in presidential election history. His highly demonstrative gestures perfectly accompanied his skillfully crafted words, which featured several hilarious ad-libs centering mostly on the topics of falling, bathtubs, and broken bones.

Much of the speech spoke of the improving economy. He emphasized standing on one's own, not waiting for government bailouts. Several other issues were compared to one's ability to walk without help. Each topic was greeted with overwhelming applause, which made the president feel pleased with himself. Faulkner had the Garden audience, and millions of television viewers, in the palm of his hand. As he finished his speech, he refused a wheelchair and waved goodbye to the now frenzied gathering of supporters. As he left the stage, using his crutches for support, he stopped, turned back toward the audience and waved once more. Then, drawing the loudest response of the night, while balancing himself on one leg, he held his crutches above his head; then he threw them to the floor and hopped through the side curtains.

Chapter 14

The Knee

Gramercy Park Hotel
New York, New York
Friday, August 28, 2020
5:30 A.M.

The president and Caroline congratulated and comforted each other until the wee hours of the early morning. The couple sat in bed having had only a few hours of sleep. It was there in bed that they talked about their upcoming schedule. However, each was exhausted, especially the president, who, in addition to having a lack of sleep, was also feeling ill.

"Are you in much pain?" asked the First Lady.

"Honey, I'm not going to lie, my knee is aching, a great deal, but the abdominal pain seems to have subsided," responded the president. "But, it's manageable. I'm glad we will be heading back to the White House."

"I am, too. Honey, you know that I would never hurt you intentionally?"

"Hey, we do what we have to do, now let's just hope that it worked."

"It will. I am certain that it will. I just feel horrible about whacking you on the knee. The sound keeps echoing in my head."

The president smiled, "Please stop worrying about it, like I said, you did what you had to do. And now people are going to understand why I can't travel too often. The campaign will be so much easier to run from the White House."

"We could have our first debate there," Caroline said. Faulkner was scheduled to meet the Democratic candidate, Governor Robert Ryan of Indiana.

"Can't do it," Faulkner said. "I don't want to look like a chump who can't travel at all. Besides, the last thing that I want is to give voters a chance to picture that clown at 1600 Pennsylvania Avenue."

"How about Georgetown or American? The college kids would eat it up. It would freshen up your image. Let's run it by Mike." She punched in the cell number of the campaign director Michael "King Maker" O'Sullivan.

"No good," Mike told them. "Ryan's team will never go for it; they'll think that it gives you a home court advantage. Let's try something in Virginia or Maryland. I'll get Bob Gittings on the phone and we'll figure it out." Caroline hung up so O'Sullivan could call his Democratic counterpart and fix the place and date for the all-important first debate.

Chapter 15

The Debate

Baltimore, Maryland
Wednesday, October 7, 2020
9:00 P.M.

President Faulkner wanted to stay as visible to the public as possible. This thought had been shaped by the plight of a recently semi-demolished shopping mall in Maryland. As he traveled to and from Andrews Air Force Base, he noticed that the demolition process seemed to progress according to the frequency by which the president passed the site. If he made frequent trips to and from the airport, there seemed to be little work done. If, however, his trips were less frequent, he seemed to notice, while passing the site, a great deal of change.

It was this "Mall Theory" that made the president want to be in the public eye, as if the public were to see him several times a week, they might not be as quick to notice what were to be the certain changes that he and his body would be making. His thinking was that if the public were to see him only once in a while, his changes would be much more easily seen. It was his plan to be in the public eye several times a week. That was, as long as his health held up.

The night of the debate had been the first of five times in seven days that the president would be seen by the public, always making sure that the events were covered by the national media. Up to this point, he had successfully hidden his illness, and his constant media exposure had raised few public outcries about his slight weight loss. Besides, if there was any clamor about it, he could fall back upon the excuse of his broken knee and his desire to diet to keep the weight off.

But his opponent, Robert Ryan, had raised several other questions about Faulkner, questions that were going to make it tough for the president to get re-elected. Constantly Ryan had commented upon the Faulkner administration's failures in the areas of unemployment, foreign policy, and what was perceived as a lack of a substantial energy policy. But foremost in the Democratic challenger's arsenal were his attacks on Faulkner's inability to stop the terrorism that had invaded our shores during the president's administration, killing dozens of innocent Americans from coast to coast.

"The last time that the shores of the United States were repeatedly attacked in this manner was during the War of 1812. In your minds have you asked, 'Mr. President, when will it all end? Have you figured out that the American people have had enough? Do you feel safer than you were four years ago?'

"I promise to find out the answers for you in the upcoming presidential debate. He won't be able to stay in the White House. He'll be there, America, and so will I—representing all of you."

The public had anxiously awaited this first debate, one that many felt would put the president back on his heels, in a defensive position. It had been agreed upon that both Faulkner and Ryan would be seated, a compromise made to the president's knee injury. Ryan had made a public decree that the president's health would be, as far as his campaign would be concerned, a non-issue.

For more than an hour, McManus Theatre, on the beautiful grounds of Loyola University, had been filling to capacity. This site, in Baltimore, had been a compromise spot agreed upon by each candidate's team. The president favored it because of its close proximity to the White House, whereas Ryan and his camp liked the fact that it was situated within a state that for years had voted Democratic.

The stage of McManus had been adorned with red, white, and blue bunting. At mid-stage was a table equipped with four microphones, one for each contestant and two in the middle for the mediator, WBFF news anchor Jessica Gilmartin, and her guest, Leah Manders. The overcapacity audience of 355 was comprised of many students from campus, the majority being political science and history majors. All of them were eager to take part in their first presidential debate.

The audience roundly applauded Ms. Gilmartin as she was called to the stage, where the drawn curtain concealed the table and chairs behind it. The veteran newscaster said, "Tonight's presidential debate features two outstanding speakers and a famed journalist." An introduction of Leah was followed by a reading of the debate's rules. After several interruptions for applause, she introduced the two men by saying, "And so, with no further delay, let me introduce the two men who are here tonight to speak to each other and to America. For the Democratic Party we have the governor of the great state of Indiana, Robert Ryan."

As she said his name the sound of heavy applause filled the theatre. Gilmartin continued, "And here from Oregon, by way of Washington, D.C., is the President of the United States, James Augustus Faulkner."

As her last words were spoken, the curtain slowly opened, revealing each man standing in front of the table, the president using crutches. Ryan was dressed in a dark grey pinstriped suit, which was accented by his light grey shirt and blue tie. Meanwhile President Faulkner wore a solid navy blue suit, white shirt, and bright red tie, making him dressed as patriotically as anyone could possibly be.

Each man waved to the crowd and then took several steps toward each other, the president using visible caution. It was at mid-stage that they shook hands and then took their respective seats, the president to the right side facing the audience, Ryan to the left.

Gilbert began with "Mr. President, in a few months, the American people will be going to the polls, with the choice of either re-electing you or electing Governor Ryan. In your opinion, Mr. President, with terrorism ravaging the American spirit, why should the electorate trust you to protect them and think that you are the person that will bring an end to these blatant attacks?"

The president smiled and said, "Jessica, let me first thank you and Loyola University for housing this wonderful event. I hope the audience here at McManus Theatre will take a second to applaud your efforts and those of this beautiful university."

A modest round of applause followed, and then he continued. "Well, Jessica, the American public should trust me because we have addressed the problems that face our nation, and my administration is working hard to further the cause of all Americans. Do we still have work to do? Certainly. But, with the help of all of our fine citizens, we will be able to finish the job that we started. Specifically, I am in charge of a network of individuals and agencies who are working diligently to bring those cowardly attacks under control and to prosecute those individuals who are responsible.

"It takes time to track down our leads and to substantiate the tips that come in. But we are closer today to arrests than we were a day ago."

After rather quiet applause, Gilmartin turned to his opponent. "Governor Ryan, I will ask you the same question. Why should the electorate trust you to protect them and think that you are the person that will bring an end to these blatant attacks?"

Inching closer to the microphone, the JFK look-alike, two-term governor replied, "Jessica, the president and his administration are going nowhere with their investigations. 'Closer today'? How many yesterdays have we experienced since the first attack? How about the one in this fair city's harbor? No answers yet, for the citizens of Baltimore, Mr. President? That was almost a year ago! Scarier, how many tomorrows will we have to wait in fear of what will be the eventual next attack? When describing the efforts of the Faulkner administration, 'trust' is not a word that comes to mind. It's time for our nation to go in another direction, one that will end these attacks once and for all. We have lost our way, and we need someone to take the helm of the ship and get us out of the rough waters and back to a more tranquil way of life. The numbers that are reported for unemployment in this nation are such that the president should be embarrassed. The economy is as bad as it was when President George W. Bush was in office. The American people need an alternate path, one that will lead us back to prosperity. As for terrorism, I certainly will do a better job than my opponent. The president's time in the White House seems to have caused a loss of vision for him in terms of what is troubling our citizens. There has been little response to the attacks, other than using Elgin Hathaway as a sacrificial lamb.

"These facts coupled with the apparent lack of effectiveness shown by the president and his administration against the vicious attacks strongly suggest that it is time for a change. He has failed to find those responsible and, in essence, has failed the American people."

Gilbert asked, "Is Governor Ryan correct, Mr. President? Have you failed the American people?"

"Certainly not, Jessica. My challenger, based in Indiana, is a long way away from the inner workings of Washington and my administration, as we earnestly put forth efforts to bring these malicious attacks under control."

"Governor Ryan, your reply?"

"Not close to the inner workings of Washington? Mr. President, how close to those inner workings does one need to be to fear what is going on? How close were the children who died in the Inner Harbor of Baltimore? Were the people of Utica, New York, close enough? How about the dead citizens of Chicago, Cleveland, Milwaukee and the other cities? Just how close does one have to be not to have to worry about whether or not the next train or bus that they get on will be blown up by a group of terrorists that your administration has allowed to run amok among us? Inner workings, indeed. Perhaps we should label them inner 'non-workings.'"

The applause made Faulkner uneasy and aware that Governor Ryan was going to live up to the term "challenger."

"Governor, it's easy for one to be critical when one is relegated to the sidelines."

"Sidelines, Mr. President? The terrorists have put everyone into the game! The playing field now stretches from Hawaii and Alaska in the west to the entire East Coast. There are no sidelines, and the people in the state of Indiana are as worried as people are anywhere in this great nation. Tell the families of the hundreds who have died that they are on the sidelines and see what they have to say. We're all fair game, Mr. President—there are no more sidelines thanks to you."

Like every presidential debate since the famed 1960 Kennedy-Nixon debate, the contestants sparred with one another over various topics. Jessica Gilmartin was able to keep the two men focused and often served in a capacity similar to that of a teacher who had to discipline two novice members of a high school debate squad.

Most of the debate followed a predictable script, with each man making salient points. However, there was one major exception. All throughout the debate the governor pressed the issue of unemployment. However, at one point, Ryan quoted the wrong numbers, giving figures that many people in the audience knew were incorrect. When the chance for rebuttal came about, President Faulkner vigorously corrected him.

Pouncing like a hungry mountain lion on some defenseless prey, Faulkner attacked. "Ladies and gentlemen, when I was in high school, back in Oregon, my science teacher, Gertrude Higgins, taught my class that light travels faster than sound. Governor Ryan has proven that Mrs. Higgins was right, because at least on this point, he appears bright until you hear his words."

Upon hearing those words the audience exploded with laughter. Jessica Gilmartin struggled to regain order, possibly because she had been chuckling, too. After a couple of moments President Faulkner continued. "The governor just stated that the national unemployment rate is at 6.8 percent. Perhaps he, too, should be unemployed, as the rate in his state is, indeed, 6.8 percent, while the national percentage is 5.7. I agree that even the correct number is too high, and my administration is working to bring that number down. But for the good governor to misrepresent the facts is unacceptable to me and should be unacceptable to the American people."

Gilmartin asked, "Governor, do you care to comment?"

Ryan smiled, shook his head and said, "I may have made a mistake, but I hope that the American public will forgive me for the mistake of one night. On the other hand, Mr. President, you have to be held accountable for the mistakes of the last four years! Quoting incorrect numbers is forgettable by most people—but the policies that have created those numbers are not acceptable at all. Your administration has been a failure in terms of employment—the only ones seemingly employed are the terrorists who are wreaking havoc upon our citizens and cities. I'll apologize for my mistake tonight. Can you apologize for the last four years?"

"I have nothing to apologize for. The nation will rebound."

"'Rebound?' In basketball a rebound follows an attempt that has missed the mark, one that has been a failure to connect. Mr. President, you've been putting up a great many air balls lately."

"Thank you, Governor Ryan" injected Gilmartin. "On that note, we come to our next topic."

"Jessica, can I respond to that comment?"

"Mr. President, we have to move ahead."

"Please. Governor, you have been on the junior varsity all of your life. It's tougher to make shots stick here on varsity."

After the crowd became much louder, with their response to Faulkner's statement, Manders asked for quiet and then asked, "Mr. President, what can you say to the people in the audience and to the viewers at home to make them feel more secure?"

"Leah, with the exception of those people who have been directly in harm's way, no one in this nation has been affected more by those callous, cowardly attacks than me. And although my opponent seems to feel as if a switch can be pulled, ending these attacks, it is something upon which my administration has been working diligently. It may not appear so, but we have made stellar progress."

"Stellar progress, Mr. President?" interrupted Ryan. "You can't be serious. Tell that to the people of the cities that are yet to be attacked! Or to the friends and relatives of those who have already died under your watch."

As the suddenly enthused crowd cheered wildly, Gilmartin called for quiet. After several attempts to regain order, she asked the governor to wait until the president had finished.

Regaining his composure, Faulkner continued, "Governor Ryan, you are doing a fine job in Indianapolis. However, you are not privy to the information that I have. So, you must admit, you have no idea what I'm talking about when I use the term 'stellar progress.'"

"My fear, Mr. President, is that *you* have no idea about what you're talking about when *you* use the term!"

Again the crowd erupted, signaling their support for the challenger. Once again Gilmartin called for order, finally receiving it after her fourth request.

The debate continued for more than an hour, with most in attendance feeling that President Faulkner was clearly behind. Of more importance, Governor Ryan had raised several questions for which the president had had to do damage control. Yet, the most harmful portion of the evening was not generated by the governor, but rather, toward the end of the debate, by Leah Manders, when she asked, "Mr. President, there are unsubstantiated reports that you are not in good health. These reports have nothing to do with your knee injury. Rather, they express concern about what is being reported as a tremendous amount of weight loss and an appearance that has some inside the Beltway commenting that you look, to use their term, 'sickly.' In fact, to further these concerns, some suggest that you and your medical staff are hiding a serious condition and have been referring to you as President 'Fake-ner.' In addition, it is reported that on the night of your bathtub incident, you refused to allow the hospital staff to administer blood tests, perhaps fearing the discovery of some illness. Mr. President, would you please comment on these allegations and can you, in light of these claims, assure the American public that come this November, those people who choose to vote for you will, indeed, be voting for a healthy candidate?"

The capacity audience drew silent; the only noise that could be heard within McManus was the sound of cameras taking pictures of the president's angry expressions. He was not pleased to hear this question and of course was even more unhappy that allegations had been brought to light within the confines of the debate. Although he was seething inside, he smiled and said, "Ms. Manders, and to everyone watching or listening to this debate, let me say the following. Over my many years in Washington

I have put on weight, weight that has been a result of the fine cuisine that is served at the White House, at state functions, and on the road. These pounds have been a burden, and so late in the spring, I chose to go on a strict diet and a vigorous workout regimen, both of which were working well. When I had my mishap in the bathtub, I was told that I would be wheelchair-bound for some time and would certainly not be able to continue my rigorous training sessions. So, I chose to enhance the diet to compensate for the inactivity that I would be facing.

"What you are witnessing are the results of the extreme diet upon which I and my medical staff have placed myself. As for the night of the accident, I was experiencing a tremendous amount of pain. With knowledge of a potential attack by terrorists, which we feared might transpire during that night; I was concerned about a lengthy hospital stay, wanting to leave as soon as I could. My chief physician, Brook Rider, overrode the decision of the emergency room team and told them to operate at once. I did not see then, and I continue not to see now, anything controversial about that decision. Any discussion that might infer any negativity is frivolous and at best, inaccurate."

Gilmartin sensed the irritation from the president and quickly turned the attention toward his opponent, asking, "Governor Ryan, your thoughts about the president's health?"

Ryan, speaking clearly and deliberately said, "The American people have to take the president for his word. I believe that the president is an honest man and that there would be nothing to gain by keeping information away from the public. I promise that no one on my team, to my knowledge, has been responsible for the rumors to which you have alluded. In fact, my campaign would not seek political gains based upon the condition of the president's health."

Looking first at Ms. Gilmartin, and then into the camera, Ryan cleverly concluded, "I promise you that if my health becomes an issue, there will be no need for rumors to be generated, as I will be forthright with the public and the media. And I add, if I may, I am sure that the president will be honest and transparent too. There is no place in this campaign for either of us to be disingenuous with anyone. And I am sure that if there were any truth to the questions about the president's health, or lack thereof, he would be at the forefront of the conversation."

The president wanted the debate to end immediately. Although he didn't do a "George Herbert Walker Bush" and check his watch to acknowledge the time, his body language did suggest to many observers that he was done for the evening. However, the debate lasted two more questions and what seemed to be a never-ending twenty minutes. Moments later, no one on Earth was more pleased than the president when he heard Jessica Gilmartin say, "And with that, ladies and gentlemen, we conclude the first presidential debate of 2020. Our thanks go to the fine people here at Loyola University and to the people of Maryland. And of course we thank the governor of the state of Indiana, Robert Ryan, and the President of the United States, James Augustus Faulkner."

After shaking hands with almost everyone on stage, the president and Governor Ryan shook hands and then, for several moments, spoke cordially.

"Great job, Mr. President. How's the knee holding up?"

"I'm fine—although it made it hard for me to get around those jabs you were throwing in my direction."

"You did fine. I'll see you down the road. Travel safely."

"You too, Robert."

After that brief exchange, Faulkner was helped back stage to his dressing room. It was there that the exhausted president was able to relax for a couple of minutes, taking two pain pills and an anti-inflammation pill.

His schedule called for him to go back to the White House, but he was allowed the luxury of a few minutes' rest. He reflected upon the events of the last two hours and thought that he had performed well. In fact, he thought that he had been the superior candidate on stage. However, he was dogged by one question: "Did the question from Leah Manders damage his chances of fooling the nation?"

Chapter 16

The VP

Mt. Kisco, New York
Sunday, October 11, 2020
10:34 P.M.

As he pushed the seven button, the last of the eleven digits needed to connect to the vice president, the professor thought about what he would say to his former teammate.

"How may I direct your call?" asked the soft voice on the other end of the phone.

"May I speak to Dudley?"

"Give me a minute sir."

An inquisitive Dominique asked, "Dudley?"

"Oh, when we were kids Elgin always did everything right. We called him 'Dudley Do-right' after the character. So, he told me to use it as my password."

After a short wait, a familiar voice was heard on the phone's other end. "Hello, this is Vice President Hathaway. To whom do I have the pleasure of speaking?"

A pleased professor looked at Dominique and mouthed the words, "It's him."

"Mr. Vice President, this is Tyson Joseph."

An awkward pause occurred, making the professor rather uncomfortable. Then, the voice on the other end of the phone erupted in perceived joy and exclaimed, "I told you to never call me . . . Vice President. To you, I'm always Elgin. How are you?"

The relieved professor answered, "I'm okay. Well, in fact. But I heard that things aren't good for you. Faulkner's heading in a different direction."

"Yeah, but, I'll talk to you about that some other time—maybe when

I'm in New York. But right now, I'm on a very tight schedule, and I don't have much time to talk."

"Yes, Mr. Vice.. . . . , I mean, Elgin. I won't keep you too long."

"I am sorry," said the vice president, "but so many things are happening around here that need to be addressed. With the president being hobbled, I have to get out in the public more often."

"Yes, I understand. Listen, what I need to speak to you about isn't for the phone. I would need to come into your office to speak with you."

"Yes, first, thank you for the information that you dropped off to me in July. Like I told you last month, I've been researching it, as often as I could. The topic is an interesting one. However, to be honest, I haven't been able to study it too much. I've seen that the names that I've come across do fit the historical records of the White House. So, indeed, there could be authenticity there.

"The other thing that I will say is that if all of the information is factual, then we have a mess on our hands."

"It could be overpowering in scope. Releasing the information could harm many people."

"True, Tyson, but it could also benefit many others."

"Elgin, just like me, you're in the legal business. Really the people who will benefit will be the lawyers."

"Yeah, somehow no matter what the circumstances are, the lawyers always are on the winning side of things."

"I don't envy you—you're in the potential position to be the hero to many and the villain to others."

"Yeah, I'm damned if I do and damned if I don't. Meanwhile who do you know that knows about this?"

"Just me and my friend Dominique. Oh, and Woodman, the guy who turned me onto the papers."

"Can he be trusted?"

"He's worried about his pension. He doesn't want any part of it— and told me so. However, I was thinking about talking to someone else about it."

"Someone like who?"

"Manders."

"Leah Manders? It would be on the news by six o'clock. I'm not sure about her involvement."

"She can be trusted. I'll tell her that everything is off the record. She'll be fine with that."

"Okay, if you think so. But keep one thing in mind."

"What's that?"

"The final decision is mine and mine alone."

"Certainly. By the way," asked Tyson, "Just one more thing. You never got back to me about the track team reunion. Are you going?"

"Tyson, it's hard for me to take part in those types of get-togethers. I'd love to see all of the guys, but . . . Man, did we have a squad. I think that coaches Panaroy and Singletary were so proud when we won the state championship in the four by four."

"You were a tough leadoff man, Elgin."

"And you a great anchor leg."

"Well, it's set for the night of May eighth, right after the Loucks Games."

"Man, let me tell you, by next May I'll have no idea where I'll be or what I'll be doing. But, if I can make it—I'll be there."

"Okay, get working on that other item if you get a chance."

"I will—but I gotta go."

Chapter 17

The Unveiling

Blue Duck Tavern
Washington, D.C.
Tuesday, October 13, 2020
11:45 A.M.

The lunch crowd was too busy eating to notice Leah Manders's entrance. The professor had asked for a private room and the out-of-breath Leah needed an extra minute to find him.

"The president is on the move; traffic is backed up everywhere. Sorry I'm late. Did you order?"

"I took the liberty of ordering for you. After all, I've eaten enough meals with you to know what you like."

Just as Leah was about to ask about a drink, Paola, the waitress, brought her a White Russian, a drink that the journalist was famous for requesting at important gatherings.

"Thanks, I needed that. How are you, Tyson? It's been a while."

"I'm doing well. Listen, can we get down to business?"

"Certainly. What's up?"

"I have some important information for you that, for now, has to be kept off the record."

"It must be something pretty special to get you to travel down here. What'cha got?"

"Let me hear the words first."

"Okay, until further notice, whatever we discuss here today is off the record. What gives?"

"I have some papers that prove that there's been a presidential cover-up that has lasted over one hundred fifty years."

"Excuse me. Did you say one hundred fifty years?"

"You heard me. Since 1865 and the Johnson Administration."

"So every president from Johnson to Faulkner has known about this thing?"

"The only ones that I can confirm are up to Wilson. After that, there's no trace of the cover-up."

"So, I'm here to find out about something that possibly ended one hundred years ago? It's old news, Tyson. You need a history teacher like yourself, not someone in the news business."

"Leah, that's cute. You know me better than that. Despite its age, the information remains pertinent today. Does the idea of a secret law created by Congress during the Lincoln Administration interest you?"

"Honestly, maybe a little."

"And that the Congress probably planned the law in such a way that it would lead to Lincoln's assassination. Also, the law has discriminated against millions of our unsuspecting citizens and is still on the books."

"Okay, that sounds much more interesting."

"Finally, I have the proof right here in my briefcase that ties in every president—here is a sample."

Leah quietly read, "March 4, 1893: After returning to the White House, President Cleveland sat and sipped some beer. When the president was handed an envelope marked 'Harrison to Cleveland' he said, 'I'll read it later. It's the same information that Chester gave to me in my first term and that I turned around and gave to Benjamin when he defeated me. Now he's feeding it back to me.'"

"Okay, so what does this mean?"

"Those are the writings of one of my ancestors who took those notes. In fact, my family noted the presidential conversations that they were privy to for more than half a century. As for the materials that you read, this system of envelopes was handed down from one White House occupant to another from Grant to Wilson, being passed from one president to his successor. The exceptions were T.R. and Chester Arthur, who received the information after assassinations in envelopes marked 'In case of my sudden death, give to the next president.'"

"Now you have me. But why?"

"This is all about this secret law that I was telling you about, letting each know of its existence. They kept the cover-up going."

"It's a little late to arrest the bunch don't you think? They've all been dead for more than one hundred years."

"Cute. Here's the law. You tell me what you think. Remember, it is still on the books."

Reading for about a minute, Leah's eyes lit up. "Holy crap! It's unbelievable. What are you gonna do with this stuff? You can't sit on it, you know."

"I've contacted Elgin about it to see what we should do."

"We?"

"You're not French. We includes you. Remember, not a word of this to anyone, you promised. It's all off the record."

"Okay, if I have to."

"You have to, at least until I say it's okay."

Chapter 18

The Dalles

The Dalles, Oregon
Tuesday, November 3, 2020—Election Day
3:30 A.M.

Few people in the small town of The Dalles, Oregon, remembered a colder day in November. Certainly the zero-degree day of 1985 had been discussed—rightfully so, it was among the coldest November days in The Dalles[i]. But that had been beyond the memory of many of the town's younger residents.

Among those residents who did remember the 1985 cold spell were its two most famous residents, James and Caroline Faulkner, who were in town to cast their votes in the presidential election. James Augustus Faulkner was among the fifth generation of his family to call The Dalles home and the fourth generation to live on the Flying Faulkner Farm, the name a reference to the farm's founder Jeremiah Faulkner who, a few years after the flight of the Wright Brothers, had built and flown the first airplane in the state of Oregon. The farm, the largest cherry farm in Wasco County (and the second largest in the state), had made the Faulkners rich and powerful players in state politics, and James had served two terms as governor before being elected senator.

Like millions of Americans across the nation, the president woke up knowing that Election Day had arrived. He gently elbowed Caroline in the ribs, making her jump up and exclaim, "I'm awake, dammit! I'm awake."

The president responded, "It's 3:30. We're due for a photo-op at 5:00."

Vigorously rubbing her eyes, the First Lady said, "Did you say 3:30?"

"Yep, I did, but think of it as 6:30 back home," said the president with a smile. "By the way, who are you voting for this morning?"

Laughing, and giving her husband a big hug, the First Lady responded,

"Why you, of course. I want to be able to keep telling people that I am sleeping with the President of the United States!"

After each had had a quick cup of coffee and a bagel, the couple was escorted to the waiting Presidential State Car, which was to take them to the Wasco County Clerk's Office. Each was bundled up with several layers, the cold temperatures reminding each of them of a cold D.C. winter. As they were about to enter the car, Caroline squeezed James's right hand, pulling it toward her. As he turned to see what she wanted to say, he opened his mouth to speak. The First Lady placed her index finger to her mouth, indicating that she wanted silence. Even though no words had been exchanged, he understood what she was saying. They took a moment to look back at their farm, knowing that the events of the day would determine whether in a few months they would be back there to visit or to live out the last days of their lives.

The car drove them to the County Clerk's Office, their assigned location to hand in the ballots. As the car drove to Washington Street, despite the darkness of the hour, the president could make out hundreds of people waiting for their arrival, many straining their necks to gain a better glimpse of the power couple. As the doors were opened and the couple stepped out of the car, the crowd applauded loudly. The First Lady waved feverishly with both hands, while the president only used one— his other was steadying the cane that he was using to help him walk.

The mostly partisan crowd continued to cheer, almost certainly waking up anyone in the neighborhood who wasn't on the street.

As James walked by the adoring crowd, he couldn't help but think about the five-month deception that he had pulled off. Part of him felt sad that he had done it, but the crowd's exuberant cheers seemed to make any feelings of guilt subside. Yet he realized that the vote that he was soon to cast was going to be a hollow one, the internal pains a constant reminder of his certain fate.

As he slowly made his way to the Clerk's Office, he thanked the workers for opening early to accommodate his schedule. He shook so many hands and received so many well wishes that he couldn't count them all.

He wasn't certain which pain was worse, the one within his abdomen caused by the cancer or the one in his head caused by the deceit. Despite these inner storms, he slowly moved forward.

Now, with paper ballot in hand, he was within three feet of the desk. Without warning, he was hit with the most severe pain that he had ever felt in his life, pain so overwhelming that the president felt overcome with an agonizing throbbing that made beads of sweat trickle from his forehead and his hands to start to wobble.

In a scene reminiscent of Howard Cosell's immortal call of "Down goes Frazier. Down goes Frazier. Down goes Frazier," from the 1973 heavyweight bout between Joe Frazier and George Foreman[ii], the president doubled over and fell face-first onto the wood floor, dozens shouting, "Look, the president has fallen." A loud gasp was heard from the crowd, and a desperate Caroline, who was only inches away from being within arm's length of her spouse, was unable to reach him prior to his fall. Onlookers, too, were unable to reach out, ironically, victims of the security rope that had been placed to keep the public away from the president. In what seemed like an eternity, but in actuality was only a few breathtaking seconds, Faulkner hit the floor and for a moment lay there, motionless.

As a bevy of Secret Service men and his loving wife rushed to his aid, the president, despite his internal pains, motioned them to stay away with a wave of his hand. When they continued in his direction he sternly shouted, "Do not help me! I will get up on my own."

With those words, his would-be rescuers stopped in their tracks, not wanting to be the one to defy a presidential order or spousal request. With dozens of horrified onlookers, the president took a deep breath then, skillfully using his cane, was able to push himself up to one knee. As Caroline stood with her arms open in a gesture of help, the defiant president shook his head, indicating that he was going to do this alone. As he successfully navigated his ascent, the crowd applauded. Only upon reaching a full standing position did Faulkner allow his wife and his security team to approach.

Waving to those in attendance, he proceeded to vote, handing his ballot to the County Clerk, Emma Powell. The pain level had subsided to the point of being tolerable, so he was able to wave to his audience and shout out, "Oops"—which received a loud laugh. After Caroline had voted, the couple walked slowly to the waiting limo.

After a final wave to his well-wishers, the couple, sitting in the back of the quickly departing car, was able to quite literally catch their collective breath. As the limo turned from East Second Street onto Route 197, the car, headed for the airport, thousands of his followers waved to him and Caroline, all hopeful that he would win.

The president, who by this point had seemed to fully recover, turned to his wife and smugly said, "I should have done a freaking absentee ballot, just mailing it from the White House. This crap never would have happened. I'm embarrassed. Hell, demoralized. Here I am the most powerful man on the planet, flopping around like a fish out of water!"

"Honey," said the First Lady with a smile, "you got off the floor, voted, and walked out of the place with dignity. You'll be fine."

"You think so?" asked the president.

"I sure do," said a disingenuous First Lady. "I sure do."

---

i. http://weather-warehouse.com/WeatherHistory/PastWeatherData_TheDalles_TheD-alles_OR_November.html December 26, 2012

ii. Wikipedia Article, "Howard Cosell" December 16, 2012

CHAPTER 19

The Long Ride Home

The Dalles, Oregon
Tuesday, November 3, 2020
5:48 A.M.

The trip to The Dalles Municipal Airport was short but filled with soul-searching thoughts for the president, who was still upset about his mishap. Once at the airport, the First Couple and their entourage boarded Marine One, which, along with four decoy helicopters, took off bound for Portland International Airport, where Air Force One awaited. The president could not wait to get back to Washington, D.C.; election results awaited.

After being welcomed by the crew, the First Couple chose to settle into the private sleeping area of the airplane. Both were tired, but the president was also in pain, more than he had grown accustomed to handling. The president loosened his tie, took off his shoes, and reclined on the bed, with the First Lady being only moments behind him.

Caroline was very concerned about the health of her husband, who had fallen asleep just prior to her sitting on the bed. After twenty minutes of rest, there was a sharp but polite knock on the door. Faulkner was far too deep into his sleep to be aware of the knock, but it awakened the First Lady, who jumped out of bed to quickly answer the door before a possible second knock could accidentally awaken her husband. With a quiet voice she answered, "Yes, who is it?"

"Excuse me, Mrs. Faulkner. I am sorry to disturb you, but we have a problem up here," said the president's Chief of Staff, William Coughlin.

"It's not a problem with the airplane is it?" asked a concerned Caroline.

"I'm sorry. I didn't mean to startle you. It's nothing like that. I just have something that the two of you need to see as soon as possible."

"The president's sound asleep, and I don't want to wake him. Can

I be of help?"

"Yes, please come into the office area. I will meet you there," answered Coughlin.

A few minutes later a slightly annoyed First Lady joined Coughlin in the office.

"What's up?" asked Caroline.

"If you could take a seat, I want to show you something related to this morning's fall."

"He's not injured badly," voiced a protective Caroline.

After explaining that it had nothing to do with any possible physical injuries, and seeing that the First Lady was more at ease, Coughlin told her, "For lack of a better word, there has been some 'fallout' associated with his tumble."

"What do you mean?"

"I'll show you on the tape. Here let me hit play. It's all over the Internet and the TV."

"Bill, I was there, remember?" said the unimpressed First Lady. "This is what you called me in here for, Bill? So! Everyone is seeing the fall! We knew that that was going to happen. We knew that the freaking video would be swarming all over the place. What do you expect? The president falling is big news! How many times did the media get mileage out of Gerald Ford and his falls?"

"Just calm down and watch it again."

"Again? And who the hell do you think that you're telling to calm down? This is calm, buddy. But in a minute—"

"Please, just watch this."

"I've replayed it in my head a thousand times already. What could I possibly learn from watching it one more time?"

Getting an affirmative nod of approval, Coughlin continued. "Caroline, you haven't seen it like this, I promise you. Please watch carefully. It will answer your questions—all of them—and then make you think of a thousand new ones!"

With that, he showed the video one more time, but this time in slow motion. At the decreased speed the video seemed to show nothing new, and the First Lady was quick to point out that fact. As the video approached what would be the moment at which the president fell, Coughlin told her, "Now, look carefully at the slow motion."

As that moment approached, the First Lady looked intently at the screen. Suddenly, and with a gasp, Caroline jumped out of her seat and screamed, "Oh my God! It can't be! Show me that again!"

Coughlin was not eased by the fact that he was able to shut up the First Lady, making her finally stop talking and have to listen for a change. "You see what I was talking about? This is real serious. How are we going to handle this? What the hell have you been hiding from me? What is wrong with him? Why couldn't you trust me with the truth?"

Showing the video again, the First Lady could not believe her eyes, as she saw her husband walking with the cane and then suddenly doubling over while holding his mid-section, appearing to be in excruciating pain. It was clear that he didn't fall because of his knee; the video clearly showed that he was in pain prior to his fall, grabbing as if someone had hit him in the gut with a bowling ball. As he doubled over, he dropped the cane, and for a moment he seemed to perilously cling in mid-air, cane-less and holding onto himself—in clear view, he was having abdominal pain.

"I'm telling you, Caroline, this film will be watched by more people than any other film clip, including the Zapruder film of the Kennedy assassination."

Caroline kept thinking, "We're screwed, dammit, we're screwed." Then looking straight at Coughlin she said, "Bill, I have so much to tell you. But let me start by saying that what I tell you must stop here. Do you understand? It stops here and is never to be repeated to anyone! Is that clear?"

"Of course," he said in a reassuring manner. Coughlin started to listen to the amazing string of events that had led to their present conversation. His anger intensified as he heard the First Lady speak about items of which he had been left out of the loop. The plot cooked up by the First Couple sickened him to the point that he finally had to say, "How the hell did you think you were going to get this by the American public? You broke his knee? And why did you keep the entire thing from me?"

The First Lady had no response, only a blank look on her face. Then it hit Coughlin. "Wait a minute. Wait a minute. The reason why you didn't tell me was because you knew that I would do what I am about to do—blow the whistle on the entire thing. That's it, isn't it?"

Caroline became incredulous, saying to him with anger, "And just who the hell do you think you're speaking to? I am the First Lady of the United States. And don't get all righteous on me! My husband has told me some of the little secrets that you have shared with him. You're no choirboy, buddy. He's told me about your women friends, some being the same as his! One call to your wife and you're toast, Bill. So let's get something straight. If we are going down in flames, I will make sure we all burn. Do you read me? After he dies my book will come out and Bill Coughlin will stink like rotten fish. You won't be able to get a job as an underarm sniffer at a deodorant factory when I get finished with you. So back the hell off and sit down in your damned seat and tell me what the world outside of this office is talking about."

Realizing that she held the upper hand, Coughlin sat back in his chair and followed her directions.

"I have already received 1,128 tweets about this, and it only aired fifteen to twenty minutes ago. By the time we land in a few hours that number will be over 10,000 and still climbing. What the, ah, what do you think we should say?"

Looking at the clock on the wall the First Lady thought for a second and then said, "He told me to wake him in about fifteen minutes. I will do that and talk it over with him. Then he'll tell us what to do."

"This is something that we'll have to deal with."

"Hey, I know. I've been in the spin business a lot longer than you have."

Quickly the First Lady pushed her chair away from the desk, stood on her feet and told the Chief of Staff that upon her return, along with the president, a decision would have been made and that he should wait here until then. Again reminding Coughlin to remain silent, she left the room to return to the sleeping president.

Standing above the still-sleeping President, she had so many things on her mind. How would he want to handle this new crisis? What were the people on the ground saying about him? Would he be able to survive the controversy? How would they be able to explain away this mess?

The president looked so peaceful resting before her. Little did he know what was swirling around him. Caroline didn't want to disturb him, perhaps letting him stay above the fray a little longer.

But after a few minutes of safeguarding him, she realized that it was time to face the realities of the situation. She thought about what the video had revealed, showing that the president was now in more pain than ever. Never had he exhibited such signs of agony. Never had his pain been in the public theater. How could she handle seeing him slowly fade before her?

As she reached to wake him, she drew back her hand. She wasn't ready to subject him to the fact that almost everyone on the planet had access to the video showing him in despair. She concentrated upon some of the finer days of their lives, like the day they met in high school—she a city girl from The Dalles, and he a farm boy. There was the day in April of their junior year when he first kissed her. A tear slowly fell from her eye as her thoughts concentrated upon the prom, their wedding and their deceased son, James Jr. Yes, their relationship was a complicated one, mostly due to his infidelities, but Caroline realized that deep inside of her burned a love for him that endured. Questions, however, were still popping off in her head.

The cancer, yes, the cancer, which was at the heart of all of this, how advanced had it become? What lay ahead for him? For her? For the nation? Was this the beginning of the end?

As her hand shook him, the president looked up at her and instantly knew that something was wrong. "What is it, Caroline? I can see it in your eyes! Tell me."

Tearfully, the First Lady lowered herself to the bed, every downward inch seeming like a mile. She struggled, at first, to begin, but somehow found the inner strength to say, "James, there is something that you need to see."

"Not another attack? Where did those bastards hit now?"

"No, nothing like that. I'll show you."

Reaching for the phone next to the bed, Caroline called for the video feed to be shown in the bedroom. A few grueling minutes later, after watching the slow-motion action, a depressed president looked sadly at his wife and said, "The jig's up. It's time to come clean with the American people."

During a long, satisfying hug, Caroline suddenly broke away, prompting the curious president to ask what was wrong. "I just had a thought. Hold it. Let me think this thing out for a minute." After a brief delay, the First Lady said, "No offense, Honey, but you are not guaranteed a victory. The race is pretty darn close."

The president replied, "And what does that have to do with the price of Nikes in Oregon?"

"Well, a great deal. If you lose the election, why would we have to say anything at all? You would just hold onto the secret until January twentieth and then let Ryan take over. We could explain the incident as the result of a bad meal or something."

"I hate to be a downer, but there is a good chance that I will win the darn election, you know. Then, Miss Smarty-pants, what do we do then? Besides, do you think the clamor this is going to cause can wait until January?"

"It would be your choice. You can continue the cover-up, hopeful that there are no more incidents like this one and hang in there as long as you can. Just remember the public isn't going to buy this knee thing forever. Your other option would simply be to tell the truth or as much of it as you would like to share with the public. But those are your three choices; say nothing, say everything, or say part of everything."

The president thought about it for a moment and after a brief discussion with Caroline made his decision, calling Coughlin into the bedroom.

As Bill walked in, he saw the couple, each sitting up on the side of the bed. First the president and then Caroline apologized for not including him in their plans. After Coughlin revealed the extent of his hurt feelings, the couple rose from the bed and walked over to where he was standing, Faulkner leaning upon his wife's arm. Caroline's hug was followed by a more substantial one from the president.

"Okay, let's get back to work," said a beaming Coughlin. "What the hell do we do now?"

A short explanation of the president's plan was presented by the First Lady, one that Coughlin thought might actually work. After several minutes he excused himself and went back to what he called "The Office at 40,000 Feet." Then after monitoring the tweets, emails, and Facebook pages, he saw that his original estimates had been a tad low, as there had been 27,328 inquiries about the president's fall. Following the presidential orders that he had received, Coughlin put out the following press release:

"As covered by various news agencies across the nation, many Americans and people around the world have become aware of the fall that President James Augustus Faulkner took at the Wasco County Clerk's Office. As most of you are aware, he was able to quickly gather himself and walk to the desk to hand in his vote, just as millions of Americans were able to do across our great nation.

"Although there appeared to be something drastically wrong with the president, be assured that he dropped his cane and clutched his abdomen because of one problem—a severe reaction to flu-like symptoms, brought about from his very busy schedule. It was nothing more, nor anything less.

"The president hopes the prolonged coverage of the incident has not deterred anyone from making the trip to their polling places. He is urging all eligible Americans to use their right to vote. He will address the issue in his after-the-election-results speech tonight."

Chapter 20

The Popular Vote

Andrews Air Force Base
Tuesday, November 3, 2020
4:16 P.M.

The president was disappointed to learn that the weather in Washington, D.C., was worse than what he had left in Oregon. Although the temperature was warmer on the East Coast, the freakish winter storm reminded many of the October storm of 2011. When told that eight inches of snow had already fallen and that another four or five were due to hit the ground by morning, all that Faulkner could think about was the effect that it might have on the election. With Maryland, northern Virginia, and D.C. all in the storm's bull's-eye, he was concerned about voter turnout.

"Jim, don't worry. Those are Democratic areas being hit."

"Hell, then let it snow, let it snow, let it snow," he musically replied.

Arriving at Andrews Air Force Base, the decision had been made that the presidential party would drive back to the White House rather than risk the helicopter ride. Inside the car there was a quiet atmosphere as the couple monitored television coverage of the election turnout around the nation. Except for the areas that were being hit by the storm, the turnout was reported to have been fairly heavy throughout the rest of the Northeast and in the Midwest.

As the car made a sharp turn, the president saw the familiar mall along the roadside had had all of its exterior walls removed, exposing the insides. He wondered if the incident at the polling place had done the same thing for him. "In a few hours I'll have the answer," he thought.

After arriving at the White House, the couple went directly to the ballroom that had been set up for them and several hundred others to watch the evening results. It was in an adjoining room that arrangements had been made to contact field agents who were present at several of the key districts in the highly competitive states of Virginia, Florida, Ohio, and New Jersey. Others were spread throughout the rest of the nation.

As the Faulkners entered the room, they were greeted by dozens of anxiously waiting people, all of whom were concerned about the health of the president. Assuring them that he felt fine, he chose to address the entire gathering at once, and with the assistance of several White House aides, he slowly climbed the ramp to the stage where he carefully positioned himself to step in front of the microphone.

"Thank you for the warm ovation. We've had a long trip today, and we're hopeful that it'll be a short night. Thank you for coming out in this weather, but it'll be worth it as you'll be on hand as the American people re-elect me. We'll offer overnight accommodations as the combination of snow and victory champagne usually are not conducive to good driving."

After waiting for the laughter to subside he continued, "I'm fine, despite what you saw in Oregon. Nothing's going to stop us now. I feel it in my bones that we're going to win tonight. It might end up as a close victory, but we're going to win it. Now excuse me while I freshen up."

The crowd erupted with applause, cheering the familiar "Faulk-ner, Faulk-ner, Faulk-ner!" the president responding with a vibrant wave of his hand.

By 7:00 the first states were about to close their polls and that meant that the networks would all start making their projections. Dozens of the partygoers sat in the carefully arranged rows of seats.

As the volume on the set was turned up, the crowd quieted down, anticipating the night's excitement. By 7:00, only seven states would have their polls closed; Florida, Georgia, Indiana, Kentucky, South Carolina, Vermont, and Virginia. In particular, the crowd in the ballroom was anxious to hear the results from Florida and Virginia, as pre-election polls had indicated the likely winners of the others. With the expectation of a very close electoral college battle, the president and the Republicans had hoped to duplicate the victory plan of then-candidate George W.

Bush, who in 2000 eventually and controversially defeated Al Gore by winning the middle of the nation and Florida.

At 7:10, as television anchor Leah Manders announced, "As expected, Georgia and South Carolina were being projected to go to President Faulkner," the crowd erupted with excitement. Faulkner was said to have a big lead in each. Several minutes later the crowd had little reaction to the news that Vermont had been projected to fall to Governor Ryan, as after all, Vermont was a state that usually went Democratic[i].

As he had done during the successful 2016 election, the president, with the help of two aides, took out a two foot by four-foot white magnetic board, upon which there were two columns, labeled "US" and "THEM."

Next to the board was a pile of magnetic strips, each with the name of one of the states or "The District" upon it, and written in parentheses was the number of Electoral College votes for the respective state or district. These strips were lined up in alphabetical order, making their selection easy for the president. There was also a pile of strips that had upon them numbers, these to be used to mark the total of votes that had been projected for each candidate.

Leah Manders made her announcement, and with a broad smile, Faulkner moved the Georgia and South Carolina strips into the "US" column. "Here are the first two states." The crowd cheered loudly as he displayed the results. A smattering of boos could be heard as he moved the Vermont strip onto the board. He vigorously waved off the negativity and shouted out with a laugh, "Hey, he had to win *one* state, didn't he?"

Moments later it was announced that Kentucky had voted in favor of the president and soon following that news, Manders announced, to no one's surprise, that Governor Ryan had won his home state of Indiana. Despite that expected setback, the president, at that moment, had an Electoral College lead of 33–14.

After several short conversations, mostly centered on his health, the president and the First Lady took a short stroll to the buffet table, where awaiting them was a feast fit for a king, or at least, one fit for an incumbent president. He ate sparingly, his still upset abdomen curtailing his appetite. Meanwhile, the First Lady, who was hungry, dined like a queen.

Rather than sitting at their reserved seats, the couple chose to sit in two chairs that they found in the hall, far away from the hustle and bustle in the ballroom. As they sat with their plates on their laps, they looked at each other, smiling. Holding her hand, he quietly said, "Well, Honey, we made it."

Caroline smiled, "I still feel bad about a couple of things—the knee and the fall. Both stayed on my mind during the entire flight. I'm so sorry for the pain that you must be feeling."

"So am I, but not as sorry as I am for all of the pain that I have caused you over the years. I've always loved you and none of those other women ever meant anything to me. If I could take it back, I would. I've lived a life of many lies, including all of the ones that I told you. Part of me wants all of this over; maybe a loss tonight will allow me some private time with you before the inevitable happens. You deserve that much."

"What I deserve is a win tonight. If indeed you're not getting any better, let's go out of here as the president and First Lady. As for the other stuff, yes, you have had a very strange way of showing your love for me. The truth be told, Jim, I've forgiven you for your, let's call them, indiscretions. I just knew that that was your way. I've forgiven you, but I'll never forget the tears, the embarrassment or the years of mistrust. You put a hurt on me that still lingers. But we can talk about this after you're re-elected. Tonight is a night for happy tears and champagne, not tears of pain and drinks to drown one's sorrows.

"Look, it's close to 7:30. The second round of states is about to be announced. We can talk about this later."

Before the president could reply, one of the invited guests, Nathaniel Vine of Los Angeles, known to everyone as "*Hollywood* N. Vine," ran over to the couple and shouted, "Leah Manders is about to make her announcement."

"Thanks, Hollywood. The president and I will be there in a minute."

Slowly climbing out of their seats, with the help of Hollywood, the First Couple was able to take their regular reserved seats just as Manders, doing the national network feed, was about to say, "It is 7:35 here on the East Coast and WGDC is projecting that President James Augustus Faulkner will be victorious in the Mountain State of West Virginia. It was expected that he would take West Virginia, as he had had a landslide victory there four years ago. This year, the victory may not be as large, perhaps an indication of his lack of campaigning. Nonetheless, we are projecting a victory for the president in West Virginia.

"We are also projecting that Governor Ryan will take the fifteen electoral college votes from the Tar Heel State of North Carolina. Our projections indicate that he will win there, the first Democratic victory there since Barack Obama's 2008 win. Recently, North Carolina has bucked the trend set by the other former seceding states. Starting in the 1860s most of those states voted Democratic in reaction to and in opposition to Lincoln's Republican Party. That was the standard for one hundred years, until the 1960s when the Democratic Party, the party previously supported by the Southern states, pushed for civil rights, causing the allegiance of the Southern states to switch to the Republican Party. But in 2008 Virginia and North Carolina voted for the Democrat Barak Obama. This year the Democrats have once again won the Tar Heel State.

"The evening has just started, and the president has been victorious in much of the Southeast, which is not a surprise to many. He had always been a favorite of these typically Republican-voting states. It was also reported that the state of Ohio has closed its polls, but because the battle for the state was expected to be a very close one, we are not, at this time, projecting a victory for either candidate."

With fourteen states closing their polls at 8:00, all in attendance were anticipating a chance to get more Republican victories. The crowd was excited when Faulkner placed West Virginia in the "US" column, hopeful that several others would be following soon.

As he had his third glass of cranberry juice—the only plans for alcohol that evening involved victory champagne—an intense pain, radiating from the same area that had earlier dropped him to his knees, hit him harder than a Mike Tyson uppercut. Fortunately, he had been sitting in the hallway, so the only person that witnessed his demonstrative reaction to the pain was Caroline, who held his hand and told him that when he was ready, he should accompany her into the private living area of the White House, away from the crowd. After several moments, Faulkner gingerly rose to his feet, the pain still severe. He slowly walked with her, leaving behind several bewildered partygoers.

By 8:15, Leah Manders was projecting several losses for the president, as Connecticut, Delaware, Maine, Maryland, Massachusetts, New Hampshire, and the District of Columbia all favored Governor Ryan, providing him with forty-two additional votes. Those who had thought that the president was going to run away with the election were starting to come to the realization that there was going to be a fight for the 270 Electoral College votes that were needed for victory.

But, despite these defeats, Faulkner had received his own good news. According to Leah Manders, the president was able to pull off projected victories in Alabama, Mississippi, Missouri, Tennessee, and Oklahoma, as each provided an easy victory for the president. Those states totaled forty-three electoral votes, more than neutralizing the gains of the governor.

But the 8:00 news, although mostly good for the president, did leave his followers with some concerns. Manders announced that four large electoral states with 8:00 closing times, Florida, Illinois, Michigan, and, New Jersey were all too close to call. Even more concern developed as an important state from the 7:00 group, Virginia, was announced to be still too close to call.

Faulkner missed these reports, as he was in the bathroom vomiting. But his wife, standing outside the bathroom door, kept abreast of the developments by watching the bedroom television. In her mind, no matter how the election turned out, she felt that she was going to have to prepare for some type of defeat.

By 8:45 Manders announced, "Arkansas has joined the Faulkner group, giving the president control of seven of the eleven states of the Old Confederacy, with only the still-not-reporting Texas and Louisiana and the still-too-close-to-call Virginia and Florida not within his grasp."

Several hundred miles away in Bar Harbor, Maine, Professor Joseph had concerns of his own. Sensing that the election would be a tight one, he saw a pattern developing similar to the one in 2000. His concerns centered on the middle of the nation, as well as the states of Arizona and Washington. He knew that if the Democratic candidate was to have any chance of winning, Governor Ryan needed victories in at least three of the states from the Midwest and Great Plains. Arizona would be a key state, but for years Ryan had been critical of the state's immigration policies, perhaps pushing the voters toward the direction of the president. Washington, felt the professor, would be a toss-up state, but Faulkner, in a great political move, had pushed for federal funds for instate projects that helped the region, which had had a tremendous impact on the state named for our first president.

But of much more concern for the professor was the poor health of his son Robert, which was the reason for his trip to Maine. The previous night, Tyson had been contacted by the medical facility with news that Robert was suffering from a very high fever, the origin of which was unknown to the doctors. His condition was labeled as "critical," and the entire staff was scrambling to find out what had led to his sudden turn for the worst. Tyson had chartered a flight and arrived at Bar Harbor late into the night. Although he had missed his opportunity to vote, he was more concerned with tracking the condition of his son than he was with tracking the voting habits of the American public.

At about the same moment that the president had learned about the results of the 8:00 states, the professor had learned what had caused Robert's temperature to rise—the flu that had overtaken the area. Hearing that his son's health was slipping away, the professor broke down in tears. After taking several minutes to console himself, he gathered the strength to call Dominique.

"Hi, Honey," said Dominique, upon receiving the 8:46 call. "How is Robert doing?"

"Not good. His condition is listed as 'extremely dangerous.'"

"What? Oh my God, Tyson. I am so sorry. What's going on with him?"

"The flu. It's killing him, Dominique. I think we're going to lose him. I'm so worried. I'm devastated."

Trying to remain strong, she sensed the despair within the professor and was worried about his ability to withstand the stress of the night. She tried to comfort him as well as she could, but being hundreds of miles away, she felt helpless.

"Honey, he's in good hands there. The doctors all know him and have cared for him in the past—for a long time, too. It'll be fine."

"He's losing the battle, honey. He's losing it fast. Listen, the nurse just stopped in and waved for me to follow her. I'll talk with you later."

The click as he hung up reverberated within her head, causing her to become despondent, losing herself in tears.

At 9:15, Faulkner, too, was feeling despondent. He said to Caroline, "You should go back out there so our guests see at least one of us there."

"And leave you—the way you're throwing up? No way!"

"I'm okay; at least I will be in a few minutes. Go out there and tell 'em that I'm just resting—the knee's acting up."

"Yeah, maybe you're right. But if I don't see you in a few minutes—"

"I'll be there—one way or another."

Caroline put on her game face and proceeded to the ballroom, where she explained to numerous people that in preparation of a late night of celebrating, the president was resting.

Just as she sat down with a glass of her best friend, Johnnie Walker Blue, in her hand, the news of the 9:00 states was being announced. The room became eerily quiet as Leah Manders began to say, "Several states have seen their polls close at 9:00, and we are ready to make several projections. It appears at this hour, that our fourth largest state, New York, has chosen to side with the challenger, Governor Robert Ryan of Indiana. As expected, it is safe to put the twenty-nine electoral votes into the Democratic column.

"Meanwhile, in a state that at first appeared to be a toss-up, the ten votes of Wisconsin seem headed to the governor. too. This was a pivotal state, and many had thought that the president might be able to carry it. But it appears that the governor has been carrying a few areas that were thought to have been Republican strongholds. Add those to his substantial leads in Milwaukee, Madison, and some other urban areas, and we now feel confident that we can report that Governor Ryan will win the state handily."

After a short conversation with Wisconsin correspondent Sue Bruno, Manders continued, "Back east, Rhode Island is also to be placed in the Democratic column; that coming as no surprise, as the governor was favored there. And in what might be considered to be a small surprise, in what looks like it will be a squeaker, the governor will also take the state of Minnesota and its ten votes."

After a short discussion with several of the reporters from each of those states, Manders continued. "Well, the followers of the president can rejoice in that he claimed the second biggest prize in the nation, the state of Texas and its thirty-eight votes. This was as close to a guaranteed win for the president as he was going to have this year, so it is no surprise at all that he is the winner in the Lone Star State.

"Also, our projections for three of the Mountain States of Colorado, New Mexico, and Wyoming are in. It appears that, in what appeared to have been a toss-up, Colorado will end up in the column of the president. Governor Ryan had made four trips to the Centennial State, but it appears that the president has won Colorado. Meanwhile as predicted by many, Wyoming and New Mexico will head toward Faulkner. The two latter states are not surprises, while Colorado going to the president is… Wait a minute. It appears that we will have to backtrack and say that our reports are now saying that Colorado is headed for the camp of the governor. I must apologize as it appears that we reversed the numbers that we were reporting and so that caused us to miscalculate our projection. Repeating, Colorado is being projected for Governor Robert Ryan. I guess those trips really paid off for him."

After a momentary pause, perhaps allowing time for the person or persons who made the mistake time to receive a verbal lashing, Manders continued. "So far we still don't have a projection for Ohio, whose polls closed more than ninety minutes ago. As always that state seems to come down to a battle between the Republicans of the southern part of the state and the Democrats of the north. Meanwhile, regarding two key states, Virginia and Florida, both of which had their polls close at 7:00 Eastern, we have to announce that the voting is still too close to call."

Manders spoke for several minutes with Ohio correspondents Nikki Awutey and Miranda Sweeny to discuss aspects of the Buckeye State voting.

Then she continued. "In other 9:00 states, it appears that the president will be victorious in Louisiana, which appears to be a landslide victory for him. Also going red will be Nebraska, and the Dakotas, North and South. The results are in from Kansas, and there too, the president has appeared to use his strength in the western part of the state to defeat the forces of Governor Ryan, most of whom were centered in the city of Kansas City. So, at 9:38 Eastern Time, with all of our projections some-what up-to-date, it appears that the president has extended his lead to twenty-five points, now ahead 158 to 133."

A short station break ensued, after which Manders reported, "We are presently projecting President Faulkner with a twenty-five-point lead in the electoral college vote. But let me get back to Florida and Virginia. In each of these key states—remember Virginia has thirteen votes, while Florida has a whopping twenty-nine—there is little variation in the estab-lished voting patterns. These patterns had indicated prior to the election that the two states in question would be toss-up states, and nothing has happened to change that opinion, although the weather is a factor in northern Virginia, cutting into areas that normally vote Democratic. It appears that we are in for a long night in each of those important states."

Leah was starting to tire, but a message in her ear quickly revitalized her. "This just in! We are reporting that the Wolverine State, Michigan, is going to be won by Governor Robert Ryan of Indiana. This state was originally considered to be a toss-up, but it appears that the several trips that the governor made to Michigan have paid off for him. Again, WGDC is projecting a victory in Michigan for the governor."

By 9:45 the president had not rejoined the party, which caused concern for the First Lady. She quietly left the ballroom to check on her husband, asking Dr. Rider to accompany her. Arriving in the bedroom, her mouth opened with a gasp, as stretched before her on the floor was her husband, lying in a pool of his own vomit. She could not believe the amount of sweat that had accumulated upon his forehead and face.

"He's in bad shape," said Rider. "Listen, I think he may have had enough of the bright lights for one day. Let me check out his vitals."

Performing a fast examination, Rider assured the First Lady that her husband would soon be fine, but cautioned her, "He's on the downside now."

"Oh, my God, Jim," she said to the semi-conscious President. "What the hell is going on with you? Let's get you in the shower and clean you up a little. People are waiting to see you."

Pulling the president's head up slowly, Rider and Caroline used a wet hand towel to clean the accumulated mess off of his face. From there they maneuvered his prone body so that his head and back were resting upon the side of the bed. Talking to him all of the time, she started to undress him, preparing him for the shower that was already running. Using all of their combined strength, Caroline and Rider dragged him toward the waiting cascade of water.

"Jim, help us out a little, dammit. Pull yourself up. Come on, dammit. The water's gonna feel great."

They dragged his now-naked body over the cold shower tiles and sat him in the shower. Angling the showerhead to pour upon him, Caroline jumped out of the way so that she would not get wet. His first reaction was to swiftly move his arms and legs and he screamed, "Get that freaking water out of my face. Get it off!" Although upset at first, after several moments, he seemed to enjoy the feeling that the shower was giving him. Slowly but steadily he regained his strength and stood up on his own. And after repositioning the showerhead, he was able to capture the full value of the pulsating water. Wow, what a difference did it make!

After stepping out of the shower, the president was handed a white towel, and while wiping himself off thanked the First Lady for the help and kissed her. Acknowledging her for the much-needed support, he said, "Honey, I don't know what I'd do without you. Thank you for everything tonight and for all of the years we have been together."

Caroline smiled and said, "I couldn't imagine life without you," although the events of the day had placed those very thoughts in the back of her head. Pointing to the bed she said, "I've laid out some clothes for you," not mentioning that these clothes looked similar to the ones that he had worn previously—a deception she hoped would fool those waiting in the ballroom. Looking around the bedroom the president wondered where Rider had gone.

"He went back to the ballroom—he didn't want people to see all of us coming out of here at the same time, afraid of the speculation that that might cause."

As he was getting dressed Faulkner asked the First Lady, "How's it going so far tonight?"

"I'd say just about as expected. No real surprises. Ryan is holding his own, and there are a few states that are too close to call. But don't worry, when it is all said and done, you will win."

"Do you guarantee it?"

"Just like my guarantee when we first met, that you had never been around anyone like me before."

"Well, I have to admit, that that one worked out very well," he said with a soft laugh.

She told him that it was close to 10:00 and that a few more states would soon be closing their polls. She suggested that she would return to the ballroom and tell the others that the president would be back as soon as he was through on the telephone. "So, I'll see you in a few minutes?" she asked.

After a confirming answer from the president, Caroline checked her makeup and left the room. Before he started to get dressed, the president laid back down on the bed, his tired body begging him for a few more minutes of rest.

At 10:12 Caroline looked up and saw her husband walking into the room, greeted by guests with each step. He was able to join her, and requested a cranberry juice from one of the attendants. Although he looked to be at full strength, the internal pains were still prevalent, but at a somewhat-diminished level, allowing him to be able to move around and speak freely to others.

As the president spoke with Senator Charlie Vandenberg of Ohio, Caroline approached her husband and whispered in his ear. He thanked her and told her that he would be right with her. Vandenberg finished his statement, assuring Faulkner that victory would be his in Ohio. "I guarantee it, Mr. President," he was overheard saying to the president. Faulkner shook his hand, thanked him, then walked toward Caroline, hopeful that the Senator's guarantee worked as well as the one that he had received from his wife.

Walking about fifteen feet, he sat with Caroline who had positioned herself just in front of the large television. "Manders is about to announce the 10:00 states. This should go a long way to finishing off the governor. Wait, I think she is about to talk about it."

With that, she directed that the sound be turned up even higher than it had already been set, and then all in the room could hear Leah Manders say, "It is now, let's see, 10:18 here in our Washington, D.C., studio. We are ready to project the results of a few more states. Right now, the president, James Augustus Faulkner, holds a lead of nine Electoral College votes, 158 to 149. With their respective point totals, both men are more than half way to the magic number of 270.

"Let's see if the 10:00 states help the president or Governor Ryan achieve that number. First up is the Midwestern state of Iowa. And we are projecting that Iowa has gone to the challenger, Robert Ryan, whose presidential bid was launched in Iowa many months ago. Iowa's six votes go to the governor."

A brief conversation with correspondent Keith Smithson revealed that the people of Iowa had fully endorsed the governor, with exit polls suggesting that the governor might win by as many as twelve points or more.

After another short break Manders reported, "WGDC is now projecting that the great state of Montana, and its three electoral votes, is going into the win column for President Faulkner. That was a state that appeared to have been his for the taking. Likewise, Utah and its six votes are going for the president. Again, Utah, which has a history of voting Republican, has chosen the incumbent president. Meanwhile, Nevada appears to be, right now, too close to call just yet."

Once again the president took out his trusted magnetic board and noticed that, during his absence, someone had filled in several states. He was applauded as he placed Utah and Montana in the "US" column. After acknowledging the cheers, Faulkner looked at the board and after reading the names of the states that were there, he realized that there was really only one major round of states to be contested, those in the Far West. Between the results from those states and the results from those that had closed but had yet to be announced, the president realized that his future, at least the political part of it, would be determined during the next few hours.

Anxiously he was waiting for 11:00 and the report from the states that would be closing their polls then, as much of the final story would be told by then. Meanwhile, he entertained everyone who approached him, many offering clever sayings, memories and even songs, although the president refused to join in a chorus of "California Here We Come," knowing that, in most likelihood, the Golden State would end up siding with Governor Ryan.

Meanwhile, his threshold of pain was starting to wither away, as each minute he felt more and more uncomfortable. He told Caroline that he would have to go back to the bedroom to relax, but she insisted that he should try to maintain a presence in the room. He agreed that her suggestion made sense, but he insisted that he would only stay until the pain reached a certain point, and that upon reaching that point, he was heading to the bedroom for relief.

Just as he and Caroline had completed their conversation, "Hollywood" walked toward the couple and reminded them that the results from the next group of states were about to be announced.

Leah Manders was now at center stage, not only here at the White House, but on televisions all across the nation. "It is now 11:15 here in the East, and it appears that the race has gotten a little closer. President Faulkner has won his home state of Oregon with its seven electoral votes, but the state of California, as expected, has gone to the Democrat, Robert Ryan. That is a whopping total of fifty-five more votes for the challenger, making this race very close. The state of Washington is at this moment said to be too close to call, and, in no surprise, the state of Idaho has voted for the president. The last time that Idaho voted in favor of a Democrat was in 1964, when the state backed Lyndon Johnson over Barry Goldwater.

"And this just in, we have just heard from two of the major states from the East. With almost all of the districts reporting, Virginia is reported to be headed to the column of the Republicans. Yes, President James Augustus Faulkner has won the Commonwealth of Virginia and its thirteen votes. The weather may have played a factor in this win, although there are reports that in the heart of the Democratic areas there were many carpools that tried to get people to the polling places. Nonetheless, the state is now projected to be in favor of the president."

Leah spoke with Virginia correspondent Carmen Claussen, who was in Alexandria. "Leah, the weather has certainly paid a part in the election results here in the counties of northern Virginia. It has been snowing steadily here in the area, and I have been told that the percentage of those actually voting is down between eleven to thirteen percent compared to the number of voters who participated in the 2016 election."

"That certainly wasn't good news for Governor Ryan was it?"

"No, Leah. To counteract the Republican counties of the western part of the commonwealth, the governor needed to hit a home run here in the D.C. suburbs. I'm afraid, for his sake, that that did not happen."

"Thank you, Carmen.

"Further north and away from the storm, the Commonwealth of Pennsylvania has chosen Governor Ryan. That's right, in what was considered to be one of the key contests of the night, the Keystone State is going into the Democratic column, and Governor Ryan has received its twenty important votes. That was a close race, but it appears that the governor has won it."

Several minutes passed, and a great deal of conversation took place in the ballroom, most of it centered upon figuring out the final results of the election. There was much debate, but most of those involved thought that the president would still be able to win what was turning into one of the closest elections in history. Then Manders's next announcement caused a wave of silence in the ballroom.

"We are now projecting that the Garden State of New Jersey will be won by Governor Robert Ryan. Many thought that President Faulkner would win that state, but with stunning ease it will go to the Democrat.

"So not counting Ohio and several other states that are yet to be decided, Governor Ryan has taken the lead—244 to 191. How about that? We certainly have a race on our hands, and with several states from the East still undecided and a few states in the West yet to close their polling places, it could be one of the closest races in history.

"This is going to be some finish. But 244 votes are not 270, there are still some 103 votes out there, and those latter votes will determine the eventual winner."

Leah took a break as Pat Leon spoke for several minutes about the races in the House and the Senate. Pat was a popular person at WGDC, and his reports were always favorites with viewers. After another commercial break, Leah reappeared.

"It has been a good hour for Governor Ryan, but remember, the key number is 270, as the first person to get there limits his opponent to a possible high total of 268. We have a long way to go, and we are yet to hear from Alaska and Hawaii who close at midnight Eastern Time. We still have to see what happens in the states of Arizona, Ohio, Florida, Illinois, Nevada, and Washington. This could be an historic finish, ladies and gentlemen.

"It is still anyone's race, and it could go either way, but there is one thing that will be easy to predict, that WGDC will be ready with all of the evening's results. We will be there, no matter how late into the night the election goes. We will be right back." With those words the network broke for local news.

By 11:45 President Faulkner had once again dismissed himself from the group, walking back to the private living area to get some more rest. He missed the latest news, having told a disappointed Caroline that he would be back a few minutes after midnight, and if he hadn't returned by then, that she should come wake him up. The level of noise in the ballroom rose tremendously, most of it centering upon conversations about the closeness of the election. Absent from the room was the swagger that had appeared earlier in the night, as reality had set in—Ryan wasn't going to go away without a fight.

A dejected president asked his wife where the last bit of news left him. Once she reported the score, he asked, "How the hell can we win this thing?"

"Honey, if things fall into line, you'll win."

"You think that'll happen?"

"Remember my guarantee!"

The explanation that Caroline provided seemed plausible, so the president felt a bit more relieved.

A few minutes later, at 12:17 on Wednesday morning, Leah Manders announced, "Just like he did in 2016, the president has lost the state of Hawaii and its four votes. Most people expected that victory for the governor. Again, Robert Ryan has taken Hawaii."

The president took the defeat in stride and soon heard Manders announce, "It is now projected that President Faulkner will win the state of Alaska and its three votes. Like Idaho, Alaska has not voted for a Democrat since 1964[ii]. Many Alaskans were pleased that the president was so visible in their state after the Great Earthquake of June 2017, traveling to that faraway state twice.

"We are still awaiting word from some of the larger states in the country, as they will determine the final results of this year's election. We will have to sit back and see what these states bring to the table."

Fifteen minutes later, according to Leah Manders, the state of Illinois, an 8:00 state, was ready. Anticipation rose to the highest level of the evening, as the twenty electoral votes were seen as a game-changer, one that could put the governor on the precipice of victory. No one in the ballroom uttered a word as the volume was turned up. "It looks as if the state of Illinois, the Land of Lincoln, will be disappointing the Republican Party. We are now declaring that Illinois, with its twenty Electoral College votes, has been won by Governor Ryan and the Democrats. Ladies and gentlemen, that puts the challenger at 268 votes, one away from a tie and two away from certain victory. Think about it, Florida and Ohio are still not reporting a winner. This could be a tremendous night for the governor. We are still waiting for those two states, plus the states of Arizona and Washington to be declared one way or another."

Manders spent the next few minutes explaining the voting history of each of the aforementioned states, explaining that according to the numbers that were being projected, the president had to win each of the remaining states to gain the 270 that were necessary to win.

Hearing this, and already being aware of it, the people in the room saw their cell phones light up, both inbound and outbound, as worried partygoers were now thinking that, for lack of a better term, the party *was* over. Some relief was on hand when, at 12:33 it was announced that Arizona and its eleven votes had been won by the president, but, in most circles, that had been expected.

Although it was important, the crowd didn't focus on Manders as she spent the next fifteen minutes reviewing congressional and Senate results from around the nation. It appeared that the Republicans would continue to have the majority in the House and that the Democrats would have superior numbers, although barely, in the Senate. These numbers, however, mattered little to many of the partygoers, fixated as they were upon the presidential returns.

A few minutes later Manders shifted her attention back to the race for the White House. "We can confirm that the state of Nevada has placed its six votes behind . . ." she paused for dramatic effect. "The incumbent,

James Augustus Faulkner. Repeating, the president has won the state of Nevada.

"So with only three states yet to report, Washington, Ohio, and Florida, the president has closed to within fifty-seven votes, 268–211. The good news for the Ryan camp is that a victory in any one of the three states guarantees him a victory. The bad news for the camp is that polls had indicated that in two of the states, Washington and Florida, the projections favored the president. Ohio had always been seen as a pick 'em state. So there is still much of the story to be told. Stick with us and we will figure out who will be the next president of the United States."

With that, the station broke for a commercial break, planned to last five minutes. However, after three minutes and twenty-one seconds, the scheduled Cadillac ad was interrupted by Manders.

"It is 1:08 here in the East, and one of the three remaining states has just projected a winning candidate. And it continues to be good news for President James Augustus Faulkner. The rays of the Sunshine State have shown their light upon him, giving him twenty-nine additional votes. It appears that a huge turnout in the panhandle counties and a lack of a Democratic turnout in Miami may be responsible for his victory. Add in the fact that his running mate, popular governor Maria Martinez of Fort Lauderdale, may have been a key. She has been a respected leader of the state, backed by all ethnic groups there. The once-questioned move of dumping Elgin Hathaway from the ticket may actually prove to have been beneficial for the president. However, without victories in the states of Washington and Ohio, it might not mean a thing."

By 1:35 Wednesday morning, Leah Manders was so tired that she had trouble seeing. A rundown of the closest electoral votes in American history was able to fill some of the waiting time. Indeed, she was able to spend one minute on the controversial election of 1876, the one in which Ohio governor Rutherford B. Hayes was able to defeat New York governor Samuel Tilden by a single vote, 185 to 184[iii]. The 2000 election in which George Bush defeated Al Gore consumed another three minutes.

"If the president pulls this thing off, he will win by two votes, the closest margin since Hayes, one hundred forty-four years ago. We are not sure when the results from the two states on polar opposite sides of the nation will be in, but we will be here when they do."

By this time the president had been back in his bedroom, waiting for Caroline to walk in with news that was either good or bad. He was not feeling well and was worried that no matter which way the news came out, he wouldn't be able to provide much of an after-the-election speech.

By 1:55, the news got better for one of the candidates, as Leah Manders reported, "It is pretty late here in the East, but the last of the Eastern states has spoken. We here at WGDC are reporting that, with ninety-eight percent of the precincts reporting, the eighteen electoral votes for Ohio will go to . . . ," again, waiting for the purpose of dramatic effect, "President James A. Faulkner. We will have a report from the Buckeye State in a minute, but, first, let me say that it is all coming down to the state of Washington, as the president has won Ohio. By the narrowest of margins, President James Augustus Faulkner is projected to win the state of Ohio, which is often referred to as The Mother of Presidents, giving birth to new hope for the president.

"So, in the end, it is established that the western Washington will determine who will serve for the next four years in the eastern Washington. We have had some dramatic endings in these elections, but I cannot recall one that has been so riveting. So right now, the vote totals are as follows: Ryan 268, Faulkner 258. If Governor Ryan wins the Evergreen State's twelve votes, he'll finish with 280 votes. However, if the president pulls it out, he will have the minimum amount of votes that it takes to win, 270, guaranteeing him a second term."

Manders then turned to field reporter Milton Earl who was reporting from Spokane. "Leah, the state is often split between the Democrats of the western part of the state and the Republicans here in the east. One thing to look for is the amount of an effect that Faulkner's popularity in bordering Oregon has had upon the eastern part of Washington. He is very popular here, and if he can get a large turnout of voters, it could counteract the Democratic votes for Ryan in places like Seattle and Olympia."

"Thank you, Milton. Now we'll turn to Eleanor Elizabeths in Seattle. How is the turnout Ellie?"

"Not as heavy as in previous years, Leah. Exit polls indicate that the voters here in the state's largest city are split fairly even, although trending toward Ryan. However, I'd say that the president would be happy to be trailing by the slim margin that he is in this part of the state."

As the minutes passed Caroline wondered how long it would take to count the votes. She thought, "The state doesn't have *that* many people." She walked to the residential area, and while peaking in saw her husband kneeling at the side of the bed, in prayer. Not wanting to disturb him, she turned to go back to the ballroom, when she was greeted by a thunderous cheer.

Vine ran down the hall, gave her a bear hug and shouted in her ear. A huge fan of the New York Mets, he paraphrased the famous line of longtime announcer Bob Murphy by saying "The game is over. We won it. We win the damn thing[iv] by a score of 270 to 268!" They just announced that Washington has sided with us. It is o-v-e-r! Get Jim, get him out here now. He did it."

Overwhelmed with joy, Caroline didn't know whether to laugh or cry, so she did both. Following Vine's suggestion, she managed to pry herself from his bear-hug embrace and hurried to the room in which the president had risen from his knees, his prayers being over. He had just started to exit the room when a hurried Caroline ran right into him, almost knocking him down. Staggered but stable, he was able to gain his composure and ask her what all the excitement was all about.

"Jim, you did it. Washington State is ours and so is Washington, D.C. You've been re-elected!"

The president heard her, but asked her to repeat the message.

"You did it, baby! You won."

Looking at his leg, he then looked up at his tearful wife and softly said, "It was worth it. All of the pain, it was worth it. There were times that I thought that we had made a mistake, and that God was punishing me. But I see it was through *His* will that we won. Are you ready?

Let's go to the party."

The couple wasted no time in getting back to the ballroom. In fact, the limp that had been noticeable for the last few months seemed to disappear. Once entering the room, the couple was greeted by the band's rendition of "Hail to the Chief."

Acknowledging all of the attention, the newly re-elected Faulkner took Caroline's hand, motioned to the band leader and walked his wife to the middle of the dance floor. As they reached their destination, the crowd applauded as they heard the band play the president's favorite song, "The Lady in Red" by Chris de Burgh, the song that they had first danced to in 1986. Still too tired and ill to be his usual self, the president danced with Caroline for about ninety seconds before he asked her if he could stop and sit down.

Looking very sharp in her Republican red dress, Caroline whispered in his ear, "I love you so much, Mr. President. Jim, you did it. I love you."

The president whispered back, "I love you too. Now, can we get all of these people to go home so that we can get some freaking sleep? I'm as tired as hell."

Several minutes later he received a phone call from Governor Ryan who said, "The American people have spoken and you have received the majority of their votes. Congratulations my old friend. Congratulations."

"Thanks, Bob. It was a great contest, a real slug fest. You and your team should be proud. We can work together to bring the splintered nation together."

"I'd be honored, Mr. President."

Soon after hanging up the phone, the First Couple were back in their hallway seats, resting, until they heard the band play "Celebrate" by Kool and the Gang, which made them stand up and rejoin the party. Faulkner told Caroline that he wanted to observe, choosing, rather, to sit down before he collapsed in a chair. However, rest was out of the question, as a line of well-wishers formed, each eager to congratulate him. After several minutes of sitting and shaking hands, the procession was halted as there was a call for the president to speak.

"This is going to be brief. I want to thank all of you for your great support and for all of your efforts. This was a team victory tonight. Team Faulkner has done it! I want to give a special thank you to my wife, Caroline, who is my strength and the love of my life. And I also want to thank Governor Ryan, who just called to congratulate me. Of course, I want to thank God for giving us all the strength that we needed to win. It was a great victory for our nation."

As he finished his last words, he broke into laughter as two aides walked up to his side carrying his "Us/Them" board, which now had the completed score of 270 for Faulkner and 268 for Ryan. Smiling, the president concluded his remarks by saying, "Well, I guess *this* means that it's official."

At 3:15 a fatigued president and Caroline waved goodnight to the few people who were still there and went to the bedroom, where they kissed repeatedly, giddy as they could be. After several minutes a violent pain erupted inside of the president, causing him to double over. It took several minutes for him to recover from the latest reminder of his cancer. Helped by Caroline, he got undressed and went to sleep, unaware, as was the nation, of what lay ahead.

---

i. http://www.270towin.com/states/Vermont December 26, 2012

ii. http://www.270towin.com/states/Alaska December 26, 2012

iii. http://en.wikipedia.org/wiki/Rutherford_B._Hayes December 26, 2012

iv. Wikipedia Article, "Bob Murphy" December 26, 2012

Chapter 21

The Sad Goodbye

Bar Harbor, Maine
Wednesday, November 4, 2020
9:05 A.M.

The text was simple and to the point, "I have landed. Be there soon." Its briefness made the professor smile and think, "That is so Dominique." Despite the brevity, he was warmed by it, as he knew that he would see her soon.

As the nation had spent the night choosing its president, Professor Tyson Joseph had spent the night by the bedside of his dying son, Robert, Dominique's message the only break from his sad vigil. He looked at her words several times, hopeful that they would help him escape the reality that confronted him. But sadly, each time his eyes would leave the glow of his Smartphone, they were drawn back to the dank, darkness of the hospital room and the motionless body who lay in front of him.

All night he had spoken to Robert, trying to encourage him to keep fighting for his life. The previous night, as the roll call of states and their decisions were being announced, Tyson sat in his uncomfortable chair searching for answers, wondering why it had been his son whose fate had been determined by the car accident. Was there some earthly explanation to all of this?

He had started so many sentences with "Robert, it's Dad," or "Robert, it's your father," hopeful that his words would make some kind of difference. The occasional sounds of his son's monitors had indicated that perhaps there was still some life left within Robert. But soon after the people of Ohio and the state of Washington had finished speaking their collective voices, Tyson had silenced his, falling asleep in a position that would later that morning cause him to awaken with a stiff neck.

But now it was 9:20, and the professor was hopeful for one more miracle, perhaps one like the one that had aided the president, who was able to grasp victory from the jaws of defeat. As he quickly looked at his iPhone's edition of the *New York Times* to be able to receive the full story of the election, his attention was suddenly directed to the monitors that were attached to his son and the loud, steady beeping that they were making. His first thought was, "Crap, this isn't good."

Two nurses burst into the room, one calling the front desk asking for Dr. Rosenstein to come immediately. The professor, forgetting the stiffness in his neck, leaped out of his seat and moved toward the bed, only to be pushed away by Nurse Patti Jo. "We will have to ask you to step into the hallway, sir."

"I'm not going anywhere. I will move to the other side of the room, but I'm staying here."

"Sir, you—"

In a stern and assertive voice the professor interrupted, "I said that I was staying. Now put all of your attention on him."

Despite her strength and toughness, Nurse Patti Jo did not want to create an altercation; perhaps Dr. Rosenstein would be more successful. As the doctor entered the room, he acknowledged the concerned father and told him to stay out of the way. After several anxious moments the lack of sound from his stethoscope supported his earlier thoughts, and he announced that Robert was dead.

A distraught Tyson asked permission to be left alone with his son, and Rosenstein escorted the nurses out of the room. Turning, the doctor told Tyson, "Take as much time as you need." Thanking them, he closed the door behind them and sat once again in the chair. "As much time as I need?" he repeatedly asked himself. "When will I know?"

He started to speak, but the contrasting dryness of his mouth and wetness from his tears slowed him down.

"Robert, the divorce wasn't my fault. I was in a loveless marriage with your mother. It's tough when you love someone who doesn't want to love you back! She had no interest in me, other than my money, which she spent like water going over Niagara Falls. I was patient with her, for the first few years, but it got to be so very bad. I couldn't take it anymore. So I asked for a divorce and she refused. I wanted to leave, but it was my house. Why would I leave it to her?

"Finally the arguing was too much, and she chose to leave with you. I am so sorry that things didn't work out, but I tried. I really tried. Needless to say, the split cost me valuable time with you. I will regret that the rest of my life."

With a steady flow of tears he continued, "You deserved so much better. I was so busy with every other aspect of my life, law, the college, philanthropy; it must have seemed like everything but you. It certainly wasn't intentional. I was just trying to provide for you and your future. And look where that got you. Robert, I am so, so sorry. Please forgive me."

By this time the professor was sobbing out of control, bending over and hugging his lifeless son with a hug that lasted several minutes. A soft knock on the door interrupted him; it was Dominique, who ran across the room, bent over and kissed her boyfriend on the back of his neck. Her embrace made Tyson feel so good, yet he turned and openly wept in her arms.

"It's all right," she said in an attempt to comfort him. "I'm here. It will be all right."

"Thank you for coming, Honey. You are the best. I can't believe that he's gone. It seems like he just got here. It's so unfair; it should be me there, not him!"

"Tyson, no. God took him for a reason."

"What possible reason could—"

"Because He didn't want him to suffer anymore. There will be no more suffering for him, Tyson."

The couple stayed in the room for more than an hour, then Tyson suggested that they allow the staff to take care of the body. He also suggested that he had to make arrangements for the funeral.

Dominique had taken a cab from the Hancock County-Bar Harbor Airport, so she and the professor loaded her luggage in the back of his rental car and drove to Tyson's house, which was about forty-five minutes away. Upon arrival she was amazed at the beautiful A-frame log cabin, which had been built on the shores of his private lake. She had never smelled that strong a scent of pine in her life, instantly falling in love with the place.

Commending him upon his selection of the property and house, she followed him into the interior of the house, a move that took away her breath.

"Tyson, this place is absolutely gorgeous, and the land around it is unbelievable. How long did you say that you've owned it?"

The professor was unresponsive, mired in his grief. Dominique wasn't concerned with the answer, instead reaching for his hand and saying, "Honey, why don't you just lie down for a few minutes. Just go into the bedroom and take a quick nap. It'll make you feel better."

"Maybe I will."

"Don't worry about me. I have that symposium next week, and I have to make a few calls."

"In the cabinet near the fridge is a list of food places that deliver. I have an account with each; there's no need to pay."

"You get some rest, and I'll take care of it."

Tyson walked to the bedroom, and Dominique called her former colleague, "Mary Frances, it's me, Dominique."

"How are you? You are really missed around here. The new person is—"

"Fill me in next time I'm in town. I'm in Maine. I just need to know how many more reservations have been made over the last few days."

"Fifteen more! That brings the total to, let's see, four hundred twenty-six. The hotel is going to be happy."

"Do me a favor and call Katarina at the hotel and give her the new numbers."

"She'll be excited."

"Okay, let me get going—I have a few things to do up here in preparation for the funeral. My friend's son died the other day."

"Oh, I'm so sorry to hear that. He's been sick for a while hasn't he?"

"Yes, but it's still very sad."

"I'm sure that it is. Good luck with everything. If you need anything, please contact me."

"Thank you. See you soon."

Dominique left Tyson a note telling him that she had called for food deliveries and that she was taking a walk around the property. After thirty minutes, the professor woke, read the note, and took a moment to look out the window to observe Dominique walking through the snow toward the other side of the frozen lake. He had told her that even though it had been very cold, the ice might not be safe to walk upon. He smiled as he saw her heeding his advice to walk several yards away from the edge of the frozen water.

Checking his voicemail, the professor heard that he had received a message from Doctor Rosenstein, who had called to provide his condolences. Returning the call led the professor into a lengthy, but informative conversation about the flu pandemic that, a month ago, had arrived in Boston and had now, some two weeks later, spread throughout New England and into the Middle Atlantic states. Robert was now among the latest of the more than two thousand victims claimed by the disease. The professor thanked Doctor Rosenstein for his long work with Robert, reminding him that at some point they would play the golf match that they had talked about for years. Walking back to the kitchen, the professor picked up the phone and called the Lorenzo Jamison Funeral Home and was able to speak directly with Mrs. Eileen Jamison.

"Yes, Mr. Joseph, thank you for calling. Of course I remember our discussion last year. I am so sorry to hear about the loss of your son Robert. These events are never pleasant, even if they are well-planned like yours. I appreciate your remembering us. We happen to still have the services that you and I spoke about last year. Is that still your interest?"

"Yes, certainly, whatever you suggest."

"When would you like the service?"

"In two days if it is possible. Would that be enough time for you?"

"Of course, sir. We'll make the arrangements with the hospital."

The sad call finished, Tyson put on his coat and boots and walked toward Dominique, who at that moment had found the swing set that was located in the recreational area that the professor had built for Robert. Sadly, she was the first person to use it. Sitting next to her on an adjacent swing, he began to pump his legs to provide some lift.

"You're the first person to use this. Robert never got to play on it."

"I'm sure that he'll appreciate that we're using it. Look, there's someone coming up the road!"

"That's a truck from Maguire's Deli. Let's go inside."

Two days later the couple found themselves at the Lorenzo Jamison Funeral Home in downtown Bar Harbor, where they were greeted: "Hello, Mr. Joseph. I'm Eileen Jamison. I'm so sorry for your loss."

"Thank you. Please call me Tyson. This is my good friend Dominique Dalton."

"Welcome to you, too and, again, I am so sorry for your loss. Let me take you into the receiving room where I can introduce you to Reverend Darwin Stogel. You'll see why we call him the 'Voice from Heaven'."

As the reverend walked over to them and with a booming voice said, "Mr. Joseph, I want to express my deepest concerns for you and your family. We here in Bar Harbor all loved Robert, and we are so very sorry for your loss."

Dominique, after being introduced, asked why there were so many chairs arranged in the room.

"Most of the staff from the hospital will be on hand, ranging from the Chief Administrator all the way to single-day volunteers. The ninety chairs will easily be filled."

Within the hour dozens of people were in attendance, and Stogel began, "I want to thank the good people of Bar Harbor and the surrounding area for being in attendance on this day of remembrance for Robert Garrison Joseph, one of God's children.

"I have heard so many people comment that it was a shame that Robert died at such a young age, that he had so much time ahead of him. And although it is true we all would have loved to have seen Robert live into his seventies or eighties, let us not forget, God had a plan for Robert, just as He has a plan for all of His children.

"Who are we to want more from Robert or, for that matter, from anyone else, than what God wants from that person? Do we have the gall to suggest that we know better than He? Stand up if you feel that you know better than the Almighty."

The reverend waited a moment and upon seeing that he had no takers, continued, "Robert has done all that God wanted him to do. It was meant for others to build skyscrapers. Still others were meant to fly to the Moon. Still others were made to write the love songs. These were not assigned to Robert. He did what God wanted him to do. Don't raise questions about what Robert didn't do. Please don't speculate about what Robert could have done if given more time. He did what the Lord wanted him to do. Nothing more! Nothing less! He did what he was supposed to do, and might I add, he did it well, in the eyes of God. Can I get an amen?"

"Amen," was the unison response.

"I am told that young Robert was brought to our state by his father many years ago, from the wonderful state of New York. As a youngster, he tried to say, "Bar Harbor!" His pronunciation sounded more like this, "Ba Ha Ba." Let me tell you this. I too was from New York; Plattsburgh to be precise. Like Robert, I too came to this area at a young age. And let me say this, listening to the accents of the people who were natives of this area, to me, it sounded as if they were saying the same thing that Robert was saying, Ba Ha Ba."

As a pleasant laugh was shared by all in the room, the smiling reverend continued. "Yes, that was young Robert's favorite phrase, one that he would repeat no matter where he was! So, fittingly, after the near-fatal accident that almost claimed his life, his father chose to have him reside here, in a place that he loved and that could provide him the care that he needed.

"Many of you might consider the short life of Robert to be less than a success. But I know the Lord better than most, and he got from Robert everything that was planned. Again, nothing more, nothing less. Can I get an amen?"

"Amen," was the response.

"So what was it that the Lord had planned for Robert? The plan was to have his father, Tyson come to love this area of our nation. Of more importance, the plan called for Tyson to depend upon this part of the nation, Ba Ha Ba in particular. It brought together Maine and Tyson.

"Without that meeting the new children's wing on the hospital wouldn't have been built. For years, that wing has helped hundreds of young men and women to recover so that they could live what most of us would call a normal life. After recovering at the hospital, several of its former patients went forward and, with God's help, had children—children who would have never been born if it were not for Robert's stay in Ba Ha Ba. Perhaps one of them will build the skyscrapers, or fly to the moon, or write the love songs. Robert's job, according to God, was to get the new wing of the hospital built so that others could be helped. And that job he did very well. Can I get an amen?"

"Amen."

"In the end, Tyson was thankful for the dedication that the hospital staff gave to his son, and the staff is thankful for his dedication of the new wing that the professor has given to us. I am sure that I am not speaking out of turn here; we all know that his donation was for many millions of dollars, fifty-three to be precise. Tyson then raised another forty-seven million dollars."

Applause could be heard throughout the small room, with Tyson nodding his head to acknowledge it. Dominique was amazed by the gesture, something that Tyson had never mentioned, and as she held her man even closer, the pride became more evident.

"So, the Lord had a plan," continued the reverend. "One that Robert followed to a T."

Stogel spoke for another ten minutes, making the audience more aware that the little things that each person does, each and every day, may not seem to have a purpose or an impact but indeed are part of what

God had planned for each of them.

"So, my people, do not question the time that any of us has here on Earth. That is determined by God. Of more importance, question what you will do with your allotted time. Along the way, help as many people as you can, just like Robert and Tyson have done. This concludes our ceremony. Please allow Tyson and Dominique to walk ahead of the rest of you, as they will be carrying Robert's ashes. Amen."

Leaving the funeral house, and after a ten-minute ride, the couple found themselves at the Crestwood Yacht Club, where waiting for them was Captain Mario Scranton who, along with his crew, would take the couple ten miles out to sea. As the boat approached its destination, it slowed, eventually coming to a complete stop. Reverend Stogel stood and proclaimed, "All tears eventually end up in the ocean, so if some of you feel as if you have to cry, let the tears flow freely.

"I choose to rejoice as Robert Garrison Joseph has returned to his Lord. Ashes to ashes, dust to dust, God, please allow Robert an easy passage to see you. Thank you for sending him to us. Amen."

Upon hearing those words, Tyson stood up and asked Dominique to join him. He then loosened the top of the urn, spreading its contents into the ocean, and said, "Robert, you and your beloved Ba Ha Ba are now, and forever will be, one. Amen."

Chapter 22

The Better Thing

The White House
Sunday, November 8, 2020
9:06 A.M.

A very concerned Brook Rider was greeted by Caroline Faulkner. "I got here as fast as I could," he said.

"I'm sorry about your loss, Brook. How was Texas?" asked the First Lady.

"As good as could be expected. My brother-in-law had been ill for a very long time. His passing was a blessing of sorts."

"How's the family doing?"

"We all took the hit and have pretty much moved on. But forget about me, it's been a week since the election and during that time, while I was in El Paso, I heard that Jim's been hiding from the press and that his health's really slipped. What's happening around here?"

"Brook, we didn't want to bother you—you had family business to take care of. But ever since the election he has been losing weight, has had no energy, and has had trouble keeping things down. His weight, well you'll be shocked when you see him. It happened overnight. He has no appetite and has been talking about the end of his life. Brook, I really think this is the beginning of the end. I'm scared. Really sacred! I think that I'm going to lose him!"

"Caroline, we knew that things weren't going to get any better and that this day would be upon us sooner than later. I hate to be the bearer of the news, but he's probably on the downward slope."

Caroline, pulling herself together, said, "Can you speak with Dr. Perlman, to review the most recent findings? He's been trying to help as much as he could while you were away, but Jim's been unresponsive and not cooperating."

"Jim not cooperating?" he replied with a smile, provoking a similar response from Caroline.

After giving Caroline a hug, Rider walked down to his office and saw Perlman sitting in his chair.

After a twenty-minute discussion, the doctors agreed that all they could do would be to provide the president with the best quality of life that they could. "Thanks, Perls. I guess I better get up there and see him."

A few moments later he saw an emotional First Lady. "Caroline, it's not good at all. Much has happened since I saw you last week. He's not going to have any miraculous recoveries. There's nothing more to do."

Caroline could hardly speak. "I know. I know."

"Save your strength; let's go see him."

Entering the room, the befuddled doctor was shocked by what he saw. "Has it only been a week since I last saw you?"

"No, I'd say it was more like a week," said the frail president, clearly indicating his severe loss of hearing and comprehension.

The doctor looked at his friend, trying to be as kind as he could be, yet trying to be truthful at the same time. Sighing, he looked at the president and said, "Look, there's no easy way for me to say this but to say that there's very little time left, my friend. Not much time at all. You've kept out of the public eye, and many have believed that you have the flu that is killing so many Americans. But I don't know just how long you'll be able to get away with that story, as the epidemic has greatly decreased, and is almost a non-story now. The press is getting hungry for more facts and parading your press secretary out there a couple of times a day to tell them about the flu isn't going to cut it anymore.

"Jim, they've seen hundreds of people dying from the flu around us, and you're claiming that you have the same illness. They've seen others passing away, and disingenuously, you're claiming to have the same ailment. Time is of the essence, man. Come clean with the public."

"I've been clean with them. I'm sick dammit! They all know that."

"They don't know that you're *this* sick!"

"You've been gone for a while. Don't come in here and start laying guilt trips on me."

"Will you come to your senses, man?"

The pair sparred for several minutes, with the defiant president several times using all of his remaining strength to emphasize, "I'll keep this illness a secret all the way to my grave." But upon the arrival of a still sobbing Caroline, the president started to soften.

Caroline quietly said, "Jim, think of your legacy and the effect this secret will have on it. The real word will get out. Do you want people in the future calling you a liar? I don't know about you, but I don't want that for you. I'll be the one stuck trying to defend you—do you want that for me? After all of the freaking crap that you put me through while you were alive, don't stick me with this crap after you're dead!"

"Damn, if you put it that way, do I have a freaking choice?"

Caroline hugged her weak husband, "Jim, everything will be alright, and leaving would be the best thing for everyone."

"Caroline, I—"

"You can leave, Jim. Brook get everyone else in here."

A few minutes later the somber meeting took place on time, with all in attendance. The visibly weakened president tried to shape and dominate the agenda, but he had to get help remembering many of the details surrounding the issue. After two or so minutes of bystander status, Dr. Rider took control of things. "Jim, Dr. Perlman and I agree that you have about a week to live, maybe a little more, but probably less. You have to go public with this and stop hiding out here in the White House. People think that the flu epidemic is behind us, but if they think that it killed the president, too, we'll have more of a panic on our hands."

Although reluctant, the president agreed that he would hold the conference. However, it was the next suggestion of Brook Rider with which the president totally disagreed. "Jim, I feel that during your conference you should resign, living your last days with Caroline, perhaps on your farm in Oregon."

Faulkner wanted no part of that. "I want to die as the President of the United States, not someone who will be linked with Nixon as the only ones to resign the office. I won't have it, you hear. I won't quit on the people."

His defiance was more than an attempt to be strong. He knew that if he turned over the presidency to Elgin Hathaway, that the vice president might, in time, learn of the secret papers that Mrs. Wilson had buried. After all, they were still in his office. It was a secret that he feared that Hathaway would share with others. But despite his pain, despite his suffering, he realized that he was leaving the White House one way or the other, so why not return to his beloved Oregon. Caroline tearfully said, "Honey, give it up. Let's go home. It's time."

"Look, I'm too weak to fight all of you. Perhaps I should just go home. I was born on the ranch, why not die there too. I'll announce it at 2:00 tomorrow. The networks will love the extra time to get ready for the evening news. Set up a meeting with Hathaway for about an hour from now to bring him up to speed on all of this. Now, each of you get out of here, and let me talk with my wife."

One by one, each person gave the president a firm handshake and then exited the room. Alone, Caroline embraced her sickened husband, tears flowing down both of their faces. Suddenly the First Lady pulled away from her husband, exclaiming, "Elgin should hear this from you, Jim. You need to get him here and explain things."

"Yeah, I guess you're right. I hate turning things over to him."

"Jim, let it go. I'll call him in here."

"Get him."

Picking up the phone, the First Lady said, "Elgin, it's Caroline. Jim needs you in the residential area now."

"Okay, I'll be there in a little while. I'm working on a report for him."

"Drop it. Come up now."

"But—"

"No buts, now."

After she finished the call the president said, "You know that I don't like that bastard. Not from day one did I like him. He was forced upon the ticket by the damned liberal faction of the party."

An indifferent First Lady snapped back, "Hey, buddy, just drop it. I think you have bigger fish to fry, don't you? He's a good man, and you're lucky that you have him. Hell, we'll all be lucky that we have him."

As he quickly walked toward the presidential bedroom, Elgin kept thinking about some of the heated moments that he had shared with the president.

A few minutes later, there was a knock on the door and Hathaway walked in saying, "I was informed that I should be here." Hathaway for years had felt that he was out of the loop. Although he had greeted them with a smile, inside he was looking at a man that he loathed; Faulkner was the man who had stifled Hathaway's political career.

In front of him was the man who had sent him on meaningless trips to Panama, Costa Rica, and Detroit. Even after the president's infamous bathtub accident, he only trusted Hathaway to travel to local events in the Capitol's immediate vicinity, never allowing him to do anything that might bolster his own career.

Hathaway was now standing only a few feet away from the man who had derailed his aspirations for a 2024 run at the presidency. But when he looked at the frail man in front of him, he found no anger, only curiosity and compassion. "You wanted to see me, Jim?"

"Just come on in, sit down, and be quiet," Faulkner said. The order took both Caroline and the vice president by surprise. "I have a great deal to say to you and very little time to say it. But, the biggest thing's that at 2:00 tomorrow afternoon I'm holding a press conference to announce that I'm resigning as the president and moving back to Oregon."

A staggered Hathaway couldn't believe what he had just heard, causing him to jump out of his chair. "Jim, what? You're thinking about stepping down?"

"I'm not thinking about it; I'm doing it, man. Don't you freaking listen?"

Hathaway ignored the jibe. "But why?"

"Let's just say that I want to be like Dickens's character Sydney Carton and say, 'It is a far, far better thing that I do, than I have ever done; it is a far, far better rest that I go to than I have ever known.'[i] I'm dying and I don't have much time left. I want to die at home—on my farm.

"The bottom line is that you will finish out what's left of my term. That's about a month and a half. You'll hold that position until January 20th when the vice president-elect will be sworn in as president. You won't hold the office long, but I'm giving you the shot at what you've always wanted. If you don't screw it up, you'll be eligible to run for the office again in 2024.

"With Caroline as my witness, I want to apologize to you for the way that I've treated you; no man should be shown the disrespect that I've shown you. You're a good man, one who will rebound from this and will be able to move forward. I've set up a briefing for you; you'll have to cover a lot of ground very quickly. I'm sure you'll handle it." Faulkner closed his eyes briefly. "As I said, you're a good man. One that I hope will be able to keep the contents of this conversation quiet. I hope I can trust you to do that. Please keep silent on the topic of my resignation until I've delivered my speech."

A stunned Hathaway stood in front of Faulkner, not knowing what to do or say. But even though the president had not fully explained the actual reasoning behind his decision, Hathaway knew. Just looking at the man, he knew.

"Mr. President, may I say that it has been an honor serving under you."

"You don't have to say a word. Just be ready for your briefing. I believe it will start in about thirty minutes or so. There are a great many things for you to learn, many of which were kept from you. But, once you're president, you may be approached about one particular item, one that if handled the wrong way might bring this nation to its knees. Be careful; don't let your ethnic loyalties get in the way of what's best for the country." Faulkner paused as a wince of pain creased his face. "Now, if you will excuse me, I have to write the last speech of my life."

"Don't let your ethnic loyalties get in the way. Hmmm. That could only mean one thing," repeated Hathaway slowly walking toward the exhausted

president. Extending his right hand, he said to the president, "Go out of here with dignity, just the way you came in. Perhaps you might want to address with the American people the item to which you just alluded— one of which I have gained knowledge. You owe it to the public. It has been a pleasure, make that an honor, to have been your vice president."

With those words, Elgin turned and quickly walked toward the door.

"Wait, Elgin," Faulkner yelled. "Let me talk with you for a minute. Caroline, would you mind giving us a couple of minutes?"

After the First Lady had closed the door behind her Elgin asked, "You needed to speak to me?"

"You're damned right I do. What item is it that you've gained knowledge of?"

"I think we both know what I'm talking about . . . . President Johnson's administration. The secret law."

"But . . . but, how could you be aware of it? I only found out about it through a document left behind from Wilson. How did you—"

"Was that in the private letter in the time capsule?" Hathaway asked.

"Yes, Wilson's wife left the information behind. I was the first president to know about it since he found out more than a hundred years ago."

Hathaway nodded. "Okay, that explains a lot. I wondered why there was no link to the more recent presidents."

"So, that explains how I knew . . . how the hell did you find out about it?" Faulkner asked.

"Jim, a historian approached me with documents that he uncovered. It was a diary one of the White House servants had written. That servant knew about the secret act. There were many interesting ideas attached to them."

"I'm sure that there were. But of course those ideas will remain in the White House, right?"

"Perhaps. They might be found to be interesting to millions of people."

"You're kidding, right?"

"No, not at all. The ideas brought out are of such magnitude that they could help a lot of people who don't know that they're the beneficiaries of what's available."

"You stupid bastard! The people haven't known anything about this crap for more than one hundred fifty years. Why the hell do you think that they need to know about it now?"

"For a million years people didn't know that germs caused diseases," said Hathaway, exasperated. "Clearly that was knowledge that was good for them to learn. Same goes for this."

"Like hell it does!" Faulkner raised his voice as much as he was able. "I don't want it released! I'm telling you not to release it."

"You're not in a position to be telling me anything. Tomorrow afternoon you'll be on a plane heading back to Oregon and I'll be the one in charge."

Faulkner labored to bring himself up to sitting. "Screw you, you bastard! You're only doing this to get back at me for not putting you on the ticket. Admit it, that's what this is all about.

"As I told you before, I think that you're a freaking liability. I thought that the Democrats were going to nominate Ryan from Indiana because he's so liberal. I needed to bulk up my conservative base, and I didn't think that I could do it with someone like you."

"Yeah, I remember you telling me that crap about being forced to have a minority on the ticket like you were in 2016, and that you wanted a Latino, because, in your words, they are the up-and-coming minority in this nation, not like my people whose heyday was in the 1960s.

"You are so out of order with that, Jim. Your bigotry's showing, and it isn't pleasant to look at. Keep it the hell away from me. But, you've got no clue. It's got nothing to do with you—I'd go public because some people could possibly get what is rightfully theirs. They're entitled to it."

"Entitled? Entitled! Those bastards aren't entitled to a freaking thing. They don't even know that—"

"Well, someone has to tell them what's theirs. That's where I come in."

"Those people—"

"*Those* people are my people, and they deserve the opportunity—"

"Crap, because they're related to a bunch of ignorant slaves?"

"If you remember, we almost came to blows once before. You're lucky you're in that bed."

'Why, because you and some of your black people friends would beat me up? Yeah, I wish I wasn't in this bed either. I'd kick your ass back to the plantation."

"Not only are you sick, but you're a sick bastard. I see you'll take your racism to the grave with you. I'm out of here, and the next time I'll see you is when you're waving like Nixon after they load your sorry ass onto the helicopter. Now, excuse me, something stinks in here."

"Before you go, why? It's going to cause chaos."

"Because, unlike you, I plan to follow the laws—all of them, even those from one hundred fifty years ago. See you tomorrow."

Leaving the room, Elgin hurried back to his office where he picked up the phone, "Tyson, it's me. I just left Faulkner. It's all true. He learned about it from the time capsule. We'll have to meet soon to talk about how to proceed with the information."

"Certainly, I can be down there tomorrow."

"No good. Tomorrow's a big day around here—one like no other."

"What's up?"

"Just watch the news, my man. I'll contact you soon, when I get a chance."

---

i. Dickens, Charles. "A Tale of Two Cities". Chapman and Hall 1859

Chapter 23

The Decision

Washington, D.C.
Monday, November 9, 2020
10:00 A.M.

Monday, November 9th, was the first sunny day that the residents of the nation's capital had seen in a week. The clouds had cleared, revealing a bright blue, sun-bathed sky. Although only a few people knew it that morning, the weather was fitting for an important day in American history, as political clouds were likewise being replaced by clarity.

By 10:15 A.M., President Faulkner had finished writing his speech, a speech for which he felt he would forever be remembered. The historical significance alone guaranteed him to be placed in the textbooks; he saw his speech listed alongside FDR's "Day of Infamy," MLK, Jr.'s "I Had a Dream," and JFK's "Ask Not" inauguration speech.

Twenty minutes later he met with Caroline, who a few hours earlier had picked out the attire to be worn by the president. Of course, that was picked after she had chosen her own. The First Couple studied every line, every word, and every syllable of the speech and after a few alterations, Caroline agreed with her husband that it was ready. They also agreed that it was time to show it to the next set of eyes, those of William Coughlin.

Coughlin was called into the Oval Office and asked to read what the couple had thought would be the final version of the speech. Mindful of their pride, he chose to cautiously make suggestions before all agreed that it was ready to go. The president offered his hand to his Chief of Staff, "Will, from the very beginning, you've been the Rock of Gibraltar around this place. Thank you and please keep an eye on Elgin."

"Thank you, Mr. President. It's been my pleasure. And, yes, I will keep an eye on him."

Coughlin left the room with a smile, although inside he was as sad as he had ever been in his life, knowing that after today, in all probability, he would never see the president again.

When the First Lady asked to be excused to talk to some of her staff, the president was alone. Re-reading the text again, he was confident that he had captured the full intent of his thoughts. Putting the speech down, Faulkner paused to think about some of the major events of his administration. Most of his thoughts were positive, giving himself high grades in most areas. The major negative was his failure to get terrorism under control, mindful that a possible attack had become an everyday fear for Americans, although thankful that there seemed to have been a temporary lull in the attacks. "Dammed terrorists! I'll go to my freaking grave not knowing who they are."

At 1:30 he was set to make the final preparations for the televised announcement. Faulkner looked at the furniture, out the window at the snow-covered lawn, which glistened in the sun, and then turned the light switch off. Caroline joined him, looking pretty in another one of her famed red Republican dresses. Her hair had been cut short, just the way the president liked it. As she walked into the room, the president slowly tried to rise from his chair and greet her with a kiss, but chose, instead, to go back to a seated position.

"Are you ready?" she asked her husband.

He answered, "Baby, I was born ready, and I will go out ready too."

Several sound checks were made, and the cameras were set and ready. The president, as he had done so many times before, sat behind the Resolute desk. He thought of the many times that he had addressed the nation from that chair, cognizant that this would be the last time he would have that privilege. He cleared his throat as he nervously awaited his cue.

"Mr. President," said Guy Mathewson, the producer, "It's 1:55. We are ready to go. The networks will start their coverage at 2:00 and have a five-minute lead time. After that, I will point to you, and it'll be show time."

Faulkner looked at the teleprompters one last time, turned to Caroline and gave her a wink. The passing of the seconds seemed like an eternity, his heart's pounding becoming a distraction. Then, before he knew it, Mathewson started his countdown, "5, 4, 3, 2, 1," and then his finger pointed in the direction of the president.

"My fellow Americans, I have scheduled this hastily arranged broadcast to share with you several important items.

"First, and foremost, I want to thank you for your support in the recent election, re-electing me to the highest office our great democracy has to offer. I know the election was close, but our system has allowed me to once again be your leader. Vice President-elect Maria Martinez is also very thankful for your wonderful support.

"For these last four years it has been an honor serving you. In the recent election, I ran against a man for whom I have the utmost respect. Governor Robert Ryan ran a fine campaign, and the closeness of the results suggest that although the majority of you supported my candidacy, a percentage of you wanted change. In a sense, which I will spell out in a moment, all of you will achieve your goal.

"Looking back, does it seem that long ago that the campaign for this month's election began? I am sure that you remember my bathtub accident, one that resulted in a limitation of movement being placed upon me. My inability to travel among the world's greatest people saddened me tremendously. I chuckle when some people suggest that I won the election because I didn't get out among you. I missed campaigning. I missed interacting with all of you.

"The night prior to the election I felt very ill, and the ride to Oregon on Air Force One was, for lack of a better word, a nightmare. I developed a high fever, and it now appears that a severe sinus infection had a bad effect upon my sense of equilibrium. Every newspaper and television news channel covered the results of that difficulty—my fall from grace on Election Day."

Faulkner paused to take a deep breath and then continued. "It was the result from a medical test at the time that suggested the true nature of my health. Subsequent tests and procedures diagnosed my disorder.

Alas, it was one that was much more serious than originally thought. Although I didn't believe it at first, I soon realized that I was a very sick man. It turns out that I have inoperative stage four pancreatic cancer, which has metastasized into several other key organs of my body. The best doctors in the world have agreed that the chances of survival are slim and that I quickly need to get my affairs in order."

As he became more emotional, he continued. "Having had many discussions with my wife, Caroline, and with members of my staff, both medical and presidential, I have chosen to take their advice, which is the only sensible thing to do. I fought the good fight, but you deserve a president who can concentrate upon your needs, not one who needs you to concentrate upon his."

As his emotions were starting to get the best of him, the president took a deep swallow before continuing. "During the history of our great Republic we have had nine men leave this prestigious office before their tenure was complete. William Henry Harrison, Zachary Taylor, Warren G. Harding, and Franklin D. Roosevelt all, due to medical reasons, died in office, while Abraham Lincoln, James Garfield, William McKinley, and John F. Kennedy died by the hands of others. A ninth, Richard M. Nixon, resigned his position. Whether it was by the hands of a deranged assassin, or by a disease-carrying assassin from within, these men did not complete the time that the voters had provided them.

"For the best interests of our great nation, I have chosen to add my name to the list. And so, I will be returning to my beloved Oregon ranch to wait for the soon-to-be-gathering darkest of storm clouds. Effective at noon tomorrow, I will resign as your president, turning over the presidency to Vice President Elgin Hathaway, who will be in office until January 20th, when, according to the Twentieth Amendment, Vice President-Elect Martinez will assume the office."

Faulkner slowed down, took a deep breath and continued. "According to the previously addressed Amendment to the United States Constitution, in a scenario in which the president-elect dies prior to his or her inauguration, the vice president-elect will be sworn in on Inauguration Day.

Thus, tomorrow Mr. Hathaway will become the forty-sixth president of the United States, while on January 20th Ms. Martinez will become the forty-seventh.

"Our nation will be in good hands. Presently we are fighting a war against terrorism, both abroad and upon our shores. Despite my absence, the struggle against these groups will continue. I am confident that under the leadership of these future presidents, these individuals will be successfully eradicated from the world.

"Presently there has been a cessation of the attacks that have paralyzed our nation. Although we are pleased with this situation, we are constantly vigilant—aware that at any moment they may again begin to attack us.

"Our nation, during the struggles of World War II, survived the death of Franklin Roosevelt, as President Harry S Truman led our great nation and the rest of the free world to victory. I have the utmost confidence that Elgin Hathaway and Maria Martinez will be the Harry Trumans of this generation. With their leadership and with the grace of God, we will be triumphant."

Faulkner tried not to tear up, but found it difficult to hold back the tears. Another deep breath helped. Then he continued, "Tomorrow, at 11:00 A.M., one hour prior to leaving office, I will sign papers authorizing the creation of the James Faulkner Cancer Foundation—whose goal it will be to eradicate this dread disease. My wonderful wife, Caroline, has agreed to donate five million dollars as the inaugural gift to the charity. Just as Franklin D. Roosevelt called for scientists of his generation to create the Manhattan Project and John F. Kennedy asked the scientists of his generation to get us to, and back from, the Moon safely, I call upon our top medical scientists to rid our planet of this scourge. Just like these two great leaders who were not alive to see the successful fruits of their convictions, I too expect cancer to be eliminated by this assault by our scientists, but unfortunately for me, I will not be witness to its end. We have eradicated polio and smallpox from the planet, so let America lead the way in ending this dread disease. The Manhattan Project took six years to reach a successful conclusion, while Neil Armstrong took his famous small step some eight years after President Kennedy called for it to happen. I propose that our scientists, the best in the world, rid us of cancer within ten years. With God's help, these scientists will make sure that I am the first and only president to be driven from office by cancer. Of more importance, the millions of people who have died from this disease will not be followed into cemeteries around the world by descendants who fall to a similar fate. When asked, please donate generously to this new foundation.

"I leave here tomorrow, not as a defeated man, but rather as a hopeful man. It has been my pleasure serving all of you. May God bless each and every one of you, and may God bless the United States of America."

The president stared into the camera until the red light turned off. The pain was worse than ever and he had trouble rising to his feet, causing Caroline to rush over to aid him. However, she was a step too slow and the president collapsed into her arms.

As she started to lay him gently on the floor, she was aided by Brook Rider and several others.

"Jim! Jim," agonized Caroline.

Rider shouted, "We need to get him to a hospital. Now!"

Sadly, this was the last time that James Augustus Faulkner would be seen in the White House.

Chapter 24

The Long Trip

Indianapolis, Indiana
Monday, November 9, 2020
3:07 P.M.

"Of course I watched it. My wife and I were having a late lunch at Binkley's and we watched the whole thing at the bar. I'm in a Yellow Cab on North College Avenue. Governor, I will be at your office in about—" The cab driver, Rahim, interrupted with his Pakistani accent, "Ten minutes, sir."

Thanking the driver with a nod of his head, Bob Gittings continued, "About ten minutes. I let my wife take the car home, so that's why I'm in a cab. I've some ideas for you."

Rahim, looking back in the rear view mirror said, "Sir, if you don't mind, there is construction on Massachusetts. I will take St. Clair over to Capital Ave. It might save some time."

Gittings, who was in a favorable mood replied, "Whatever you think is best. I'm in a hurry, but if you think that that will save us some time, go for it."

Rahim continued the conversation, "Sir, if you don't mind. I don't think that it is fair."

"What's that?" asked Gittings.

"It's not fair. The governor should be the one going to the White House in January, not that woman. No one voted for her. The person who people voted for is about to die and his substitute is taking over. No one voted for her. That stinks. I recognize you from the news, Mr. Gittings. When you see him, please tell the governor that everyone who comes into Rahim's cab thinks that he should be the president. Everyone—no exception! Everyone!"

"Well, thank you for that message," said an amused Gittings. "I'll certainly let the governor know that the people are behind him. We'll see what can be done."

As Rahim pulled in front of the State Capitol Building, Gittings reached into his pocket and handed him three ten-dollar bills. "Keep the change," he told the enthused driver. "You made this trip very interesting. I hope to see you again."

"You will, sir. You will. Here's my card and please give the governor my regards."

"Will do, Rahim."

Stepping out of the cab and into the sixteen-degree weather made Gittings button his top coat button and pull his hat over his ears. Having grown up in San Diego and being educated at UCLA, despite his six years of living in the Hoosier State, he had not fully acclimated to the winters. Rushing into the building like Olympic sprinter Usain Bolt, he saw an elevator door closing in front of him and jumped in.

Arriving at the governor's office, and seeing the door open to Ryan's massive office, Gittings walked right in. "How are you today?" he asked the governor.

With a stern look on his face Ryan replied, "Well to be honest, I can't believe that I lost this election to a freaking dead guy. And now a woman who wasn't even running for president will be taking office in a little more than a month. Does that suck or what?"

"Hold your horses, governor. Hold them tight," said Gittings with a smile. "To paraphrase the great Yogi Berra, 'It ain't over till it's over.'[i]

"Meaning what?"

"Okay, first of all, everything that the president said about the Constitution was correct. The Twentieth Amendment does state that if the president-elect dies prior to taking office that the vice president-elect would, on January 20th, become president. My point is this, what if Faulkner isn't the president-elect?"

"What are you talking about," asked the perplexed governor.

"My point is fairly obvious. Faulkner won the November election.

But the real election doesn't take place until December 14th, the day that the Electoral College votes. Remember what your civics teacher taught you, 'The people elect electors, the electors, in turn, elect presidents.' Technically, he is not the president-elect, because *that* person will not be chosen until next month, by the electors. No votes have been cast yet!"

The governor seemed a bit confused by these words, and Gittings could read the bewilderment on his face. So he continued, "Faulkner's supposedly received 270 votes, and you've supposedly received 268. But neither of you has received those votes yet. The voting doesn't take place until December, when the electors gather in their respective state capitals. We have between now and that election to convince hopefully two, but if need be, only one of the electors who voted for him, to change their mind and vote for you. If we get two of them, you win. If we get one of them, it's a tie."

"Then what?"

"Sir, let's go back to that civics class. According to the Constitution, if no candidate wins the majority of the Electoral College, then the House of Representatives votes, one state at a time. Each state gets one vote, so the representatives from the state vote among themselves. The state gives its one and only vote to the candidate who wins its election. In a state like North Dakota, it's easy—there's only one representative, so whomever he or she wants to vote for, gets the vote. But in California there are 53 representatives. Imagine that vote! Democrats and Republicans together, slugging it out. But in the end, the Golden State will have just one vote. Then, there is a tally of the state votes with the first candidate to receive the votes from at least 26 of the states to be declared the winner."

The governor smiled and said, "Okay Mr. Civics Teacher, what happens if some of the electors chose to vote for Martinez instead of for Faulkner?"

Smiling, Gittings replied, "That is what I'm banking upon to happen. If I can't convince some of the electors to switch to you, then I hope that they'll switch to her."

"But, then she'll have the 270, and she'll win."

"No, not at all. Let's say that 100 stay with Faulkner and 170 go with Martinez. You will still have your 268. No one will have the majority. It will be left to the House of Representatives. The magic number will be 26, a majority of the states. I believe we won 21 states outright, while they won 29."

"So Martinez would win?"

"No, not necessarily. What if some of them vote for her, while others vote for Faulkner?"

"What a mess."

"Let's hope so, sir. Let's hope so. Okay, set aside the uniqueness of this election for a second. Never in our nation's history, has the perceived—and I'm only saying perceived—winner died previous to taking over the presidency. The fundamental question is 'How will the electors handle the idea of voting for a dead man?' I am sure that there will be loyalists who want to give him his due and vote for him because the people in their respective states had voted for him. Likewise, I'm sure that there will be those electors who want no part of voting for a dead man, as they feel as if they are wasting a vote. I know that if I were to be in that position, I wouldn't want to waste a vote."

The governor smiled and said, "You know, that's all well and good, but the fact remains that Faulkner isn't dead."

"True, but he will be soon. He wouldn't have made that speech if there was any chance of him being around for the inauguration on January 20th. He would have just waited and resigned after the ceremony. Then his new vice president would have had a clear path to the presidency.

"He made the speech to remove any uncertainty from the minds of the public. How many people, besides history teachers, know the details of the Twentieth Amendment? Rest assured, only a few people know anything about it. That's why he told everyone. But I think he's missing the point about the president-elect. Hey, wait, I get it. He's banking on staying alive until December 14th, while the electors vote. If he can do that, it is over for us because she will officially become the vice president-elect. We have to hope that he dies prior to that date—keeping our hopes alive."

"Wow, what a way to win an election."

"Yeah, but the operative term there is 'win an election!'"

The two men sat discussing the likelihood of electors voting for whomever they wanted in the 2020 election, to which Gittings said, "One good thing—we don't have to research all 538 electors. We need to concentrate on the 270 who voted for Faulkner."

"Why not all of them?"

"We don't have to worry about the states that we won; those electors will still vote for you. We're trying to convince the ones who didn't vote for you. So we are going to concentrate upon the states that went Republican and their 270 votes.

"The only item that could make some trouble for us is that the fact that there are some states with laws that require the electors to vote for the candidate to which they are pledged. That could keep some of the electors from changing their votes.

"I think we have to get started on this immediately. If we hesitate, we're dead."

The governor started to chuckle and then said to the confused Gittings, "Bob, under the circumstances, don't you think that the use of the word 'dead' is a bit inappropriate?"

The pair started to laugh, then after composing themselves, Gittings added, "Nothing should originate out of this office or building. I will do the work from my home office or from my wife's computer.

"I was going to say that the one big piece of information that I had for you was that I have learned of five electors who would probably vote for Faulkner. I think for the right price we could get a couple of them to change their allegiance."

"Interesting," said Ryan with a wry smile. "Who are they and what do they want?"

"Well, the first place I wanted to look was in the three states that have the worst reputations for politicians: Illinois, New Jersey, and New York. But that was useless; they were already on our side," he said with a laugh. "So, I looked into several of the Faulkner states, and I checked with some of the people in those states who owe me favors. After a few hours I came up with this list."

Reaching into his shirt pocket, he pulled out a tightly folded piece of paper. Slowly unfolding the paper, he handed it to Ryan, who snatched it from his hand. Ryan studied the paper, reading each name two or three times. He looked at the state in which each of the people resided, their respective political positions, and the notes that Gittings wrote about each.

'When did you have time to make up this list?"

Gittings replied, "It's been a week since the election. I've had plenty of time to look into this possibility."

"But why?"

"I had someone close to me die of cancer, and the few times that I saw Faulkner's picture I saw a similarity."

After a few moments of studying the list, Ryan put it down and asked, "Do you think we can get two of them?"

"Hell, if you want to be president, we have to!"

The men began to prioritize the names, when Gittings mentioned their finances.

"You looked into all of their financial records? Wow. No wonder we keep you on the payroll! This is very impressive. You know, if this pans out, you can have any job in the administration that you want."

"I'm going to hold you to that. Remember that you said it.

"I will start with the people in the West and then hit those farther east. Before I leave, let me suggest a few things to say to the press. I noticed this pile of telephone calls that you have to return. I am sure that they are looking for you to comment about what the president had to say today."

Leaving the governor, Gittings went to his office, where he used his cell phone to call each of his targeted electors, hopeful that he could set up a meeting with each. After receiving a positive response from almost every one of them, he sat down with his traveling secretary, Megan McDonald, to plan the flights, hotels, and land transportation in each of the cities that he would visit.

The next day, Gittings was on US Air Flight 24[ii], bound for Phoenix, to meet with Arizona state senator Stacey Dapice, an elector who Gittings felt might be willing to switch her vote from Faulkner to Ryan.

Landing on time, he was greeted by the limousine service that McDonald had suggested, the driver, Lamont Cameron, holding a sign welcoming him to Arizona. "How was your flight?" asked the tall, lean, well-attired driver.

"It was your typical flight," answered an enthusiastic Gittings. "Thanks for asking. We're heading for the Arizona Biltmore on East Missouri Ave."

"I will get you there in a few minutes, sir. Please sit back and relax," suggested Cameron and closed the door behind his client.

After getting to the hotel, checking into his room, and after a good night's sleep, the ringing telephone signaled the arrival of Stacey Dapice. Gittings answered the phone, "Good morning, Senator. Yes, I'll meet you in the lobby in five minutes."

After a brief introduction and after being welcomed to Phoenix, Gittings said, "Senator Dapice, thank you for meeting me."

"Oh, it's my pleasure. I hope you find this part of the country to your liking."

"I'm originally from California, so it's nice to get back into the warmth."

"Well, we're happy to have you. What is it that I can help you with?"

"I came out here to see if you'd be willing to help Governor Ryan next month."

"Just how could I do that?"

"Are you aware of the possibilities regarding President Faulkner?"

"I am aware that a unique situation exists. So, yes, I think that I know why you are here."

"Senator Dapice, I need your support. We have, as you mentioned, 'a unique situation,' one that might be unprecedented in our history. We all know that the president is not doing well. If he passes away, his electors will have to make a decision; will they vote for him or will they vote for someone else? I am interested in knowing what it would take to have your vote go to our candidate, Governor Ryan."

The senator didn't seem surprised by the comment and certainly didn't appear to be offended by it. Her body language reflected that of interest. "You would be asking me to betray the will of the people. I would also betray the political party that has been loyal to me and to which I have been loyal for more than forty years. I would be ostracized by the state and would be criticized until the day that I died. It would take a great deal for me to consider changing my vote, let alone to a candidate of the opposing party. I'm not sure if you are reading me correctly; it would take a great deal to get me to change."

Taking a small yellow writing pad out of his jacket pocket, Gittings wrote the number 100,000 on the first page of the pad. Emphatically folding the paper and handing it to Dapice, he asked her if this figure would help her handle any problems that might arise in the future.

Smiling, Senator Dapice said, "That's not even in the neighborhood. We're talking ten times that amount, plus I'm going to have to relocate out of the state, perhaps to Hawaii. You know it's expensive out there. Nothing short of that could get me to change my mind."

"You're asking for how much?" asked a stunned Gittings. Shaking his head demonstratively, he told her, "That's much more than I was authorized to provide."

"Authorized to provide?" asked Dapice with an attitude. "Are you kidding me? This man wants to be president and all that he is willing to offer is $100,000? Mr. Gittings, it is year 2020, please don't come to my state and offer me the kind of money that was handed out for votes way back in 1960.

"If this man wants the big time, it'll take big bucks. You have my number; call me when you are serious."

With those words, Dapice demonstratively pushed back her chair, rose to her feet, and stormed out of the room, leaving Gittings in stunned disbelief. Getting up from the table, he took out his cell phone and called the governor, and sounding like Roy Scheider in the movie Jaws said, "We're gonna need a bigger budget."

"Look, just make your rounds. We only need one of them to say yes."

By the time he ended the conversation, Gittings was back in his room, where he called Lamont Cameron, telling him to be ready shortly afterward.

At approximately 11:00 Cameron sped off toward Sky Harbor International Airport, where Gittings thanked him for the service and wished him a Happy Thanksgiving.

Inside the terminal, Gittings made a call to the next person with whom he was to meet. Once he was told that the meeting was still a go, he checked in for his next destination, Las Vegas, Nevada.

Upon his arrival Gittings grabbed a cab from McCarran Airport and took it to The Palms Casino, where, at 6:00 P.M. he was to meet the Nevada lieutenant governor, Bryant Christopher. Arriving at the hotel at 4:15, Gittings settled into his room and then went downstairs to the crap table, quickly losing $1,000 before he could blink.

At 6:00 Gittings arrived in the lobby, the location requested by Christopher. There he was met by one of the lieutenant governor's assistants who said, "Look, he's a little nervous about this. He'll meet you in his car in the parking lot."

Gittings walked with the assistant and then stepped into the car.

"Mr. Gittings, I'll assume that you are in town looking to gamble—on the tables and on the idea that my electoral vote is for sale."

"I flew all the way out here for this? That could be correct on both counts."

"I'm sorry to have misled you. I have had a change of heart, and I'm not in a position to help you."

"That's a bunch of crap. Why not?"

"I'm the youngest lieutenant governor in state history. The governor has lost favor with the party, and just after speaking with you earlier today, I've been assured to have a shot at the top spot in the next election. Talk is that he won't get the chance to run again. So I have to back off—I'm sorry. I'd be foolish to risk that opportunity."

"I traveled a long way to see you and earlier everything seemed okay, as if you were willing to talk. Now this!"

"Things developed while you were in the air. I've changed my mind."

"Great—excuse me, I'm getting out of here."

An hour after his second disappointing meeting of the day, Gittings was at a blackjack table, winning more than $5,000 in a little more than an hour. After leaving the table, he took a cab to one of his favorite places in the world, the Top of the World Restaurant, to just sit and relax.

After several drinks he left the restaurant a refreshed man, traveling back to the Palms where, at the roulette table, he lost a large portion of his earlier gains. Still ahead for the day, he went to his room determined to have a better day tomorrow.

The next morning at 6:45, Gittings left Las Vegas bound for Denver, where he would switch to another flight bound for Cheyenne, Wyoming, a location where he hoped to get his first positive response. Arriving at 11:05, he took a cab to Mitchell's BBQ, one of the best restaurants in town. An hour later State Representative Gabby Cook of District 1, from, of all places, Crook County, walked over to his table, the one in the corner that she had requested.

She presented a tenseness that neither of his subjects from the previous day had shown. Her uneasiness was with good reason. A year earlier she had been investigated by her colleagues for unethical behavior. Having beaten those charges, she was always apprehensive when meeting people about whom she didn't know much, and Gittings fit firmly into that category.

After Gittings made his usual offer, she countered, "How about $250,000, and by the way, how will the payments be distributed?"

Gittings replied, "Within an hour I could provide $50,000 and then another $200,000 after your vote is recorded."

"No, try this: $150,000 ahead of time and $100,000 later."

After a slight delay he agreed, but asked, "What assurance do I have that you'll vote for Ryan?"

"I guess there is no assurance."

When she said that Gittings stood to leave and said, "Thank you for your time."

She forcefully grabbed his arm, preventing him from moving forward and said, "Okay, here's the deal." Handing him an index card with several numbers upon it, she said, "In December I'll be the only one voting from this state; check my vote when they're announced in January. If it goes for Ryan, wire $300,000 to this Swiss account. You've nothing to lose. You leave here having spent nothing and if I agree to change my vote, I get more money than I was originally seeking."

"And what assurance do you want that we'll pay?"

"Honor among thieves? Besides, I requested this table because it's the one that I use to videotape my private meetings. I have our entire conversation recorded. The three hundred thousand assures you that it will all go away—I don't want to be implicated in anything illegal."

Smiling, Gittings shook her hand in agreement and then watched Gabby get into her car and leave. He called a cab and headed back to Cheyenne Airport, asking the driver to hurry, "I have to catch a 4:00 to Denver."

Rushing through the terminal, he arrived in time to board the plane to the Mile High City, where he would make connections to New Orleans. Sitting and catching his breath, he put on his earphones, plugging them into his iPhone. The short flight lasting thirty-five minutes was in stark contrast to the three-hour layover that he had for the second plane. He spent most of his waiting time on the phone with his wife and with Governor Ryan. It was with the latter that he had his longer conversation, explaining his progress and/or lack of progress up to that moment.

By 7:30 his next flight was in the air; he always loved going to New Orleans, as he felt that the food and clubs were the best in the country. Arriving on time, he took a cab to the Hotel St. Marie. His driver, Paul Roget, got him there in what might be considered record time, two near accidents notwithstanding. A breathless Gittings entered the hotel and took his room on the second floor. Moments later he was on the move again, entering his favorite restaurant in the city, Mulate's on Julia Street.

At 11:00 A.M., thirty minutes late, the mayor of Shreveport, Donnie Lamb sat down across the table from him. Lamb, tall and with a thick

Cajun accent, asked Gittings for some information about Governor Ryan, information that Gittings was extremely happy to supply. Lamb looked at him and said, "I hope you enjoyed your meal, because I am doubtful that you will like what I have to say. I'm thinking about running for the US Senate and I can't take any chances that could derail my goal. I'm not a big fan of Faulkner, but I have to remain loyal to my people. Thus, I can't help you."

"I understand. I considered it a real reach to get you to come on board. But if you reconsider, here's my card. Good luck with everything. Have another drink on me anyway."

The two had several drinks together, Gittings having one, or two, or, perhaps, three too many. After Lamb helped him to a waiting cab, Gittings staggered into the back seat, arriving back at the hotel, somehow finding the correct room, where, within two minutes, he fell asleep on the bed with his clothes on.

Four thirty A.M. never seemed to come as early for Bob Gittings as it did that next morning. His phone's alarm and the wakeup call from the front desk collaborated to get him to move a little, enough for him to peek at the clock. He realized that he couldn't stay in bed any longer, slowly finding his way into a fine-feeling shower. Afterward, Gittings dressed quickly, calling the front desk to arrange a ride for him to the airport. Running out of the lobby, the taxi awaiting, Gittings was on his way to Louis Armstrong Airport, asking the driver to "Step on it."

To the still-not-completely sober Gittings, the ride to the airport seemed like a ride through a video game, his driver Raoul passing through every yellow, and sometimes red light, that he encountered. The ride to the airport was very quick, arriving in what Gittings called "Fifteen minutes before we left." He thanked his driver with a thirty-five-dollar tip.

Landing on time in Atlanta, by 10:30 his arranged driver, Romeo, took him to McCormick & Schmick's, another of his favorite restaurants, for a meeting with the mayor of Macon, Noah Pryor. The mayor, who was eighty-one years old and in poor health, seemed to be the person most likely to be swayed by Gittings. Always considered a political rebel, after this present term he was going to leave politics for his favorite fishing spots across the nation. Having recently been re-elected in 2019, he had no desire to run for another term; in fact, he had indicated that he had, at times, considered leaving his present term.

"Mr. Mayor, thank you for meeting me. I'm Bob Gittings from Indiana and I appreciate you giving me a few minutes of your valuable time."

"Son," said the mayor in a voice that reminded the Hoosier of cartoon character Foghorn Leghorn, "It's my pleasure to meet with you. Hell, I'm eighty-one years old, overworked, and in poor health. I'm closer to my tomb than I am to my mother's womb, so I reckon I'm glad to be meeting with just about anyone at this time."

"That's a good one, sir. I'm here to discuss an important issue with you."

"Son, I might be old, but I'm not stupid. You're here from Indiana for one reason, and I'm sure it's not the shrimp and grits—although, let me tell you, it's worth the trip. Look, they are deee-licious. Anyway, I have an electoral vote that you want. Need we beat around the bush anymore?"

"No, sir, we shouldn't and please, by all means, please call me 'Bob.'"

"Okay, Bob. What'd ja say your last name was, 'Forapples?' Get it, son, Bob Forapples?"

"No," Gittings said acknowledging the joke, "I said it was Gittings, Mr. Mayor."

"Okay, Gittings, let me lay it out for you, son. You tell me if I stray in the wrong direction with this. You're in a pickle with a 270–268 defeat looking you smack in the face. You're hopeful that you can convince me to change my vote, knowing that Faulkner is about to buy the proverbial farm. Is that putting the horse in the right corral?"

"Well, Mr. Mayor, I think you hit the nail on the head."

"Good, cause, carpentry's always been a specialty of mine, built my own barn with these two hands. My other specialty's being an elected official. I was just re-elected last year, and I've no intention of ever running again. In fact, I'm thinking about leaving my term early—I want to spend more time exploring some the fishing holes in upstate New York."

"How early are you thinking about leaving?"

"Hell, if the fish are biting the right way, I might be out of here tomorrow morning! Seriously, I don't know when I'm out of here—it's a thought I've be rassling with. Maybe the Good Lord will decide for me?"

"So, Mr. Mayor, what would it take for me to get you to switch your vote from Faulkner to Ryan? Is there a dollar sum that might convince you to join our side?"

"You want me to do what?" a seemingly annoyed mayor asked.

"Switch your vote to Faulkner, sir."

"Son, do I need to lecture you about the concept of party loyalty?"

"No you don't, sir. I came down here with the hope that I could get you to switch your vote to Ryan, sir. I thought that you understood."

"Sir, I understand plenty," he said, pointing his finger at Gittings. "There is no way that you can pay me to vote against James Augustus Faulkner. Do you hear me? There is no amount of money that I would accept to vote against James Faulkner."

A dejected Gittings said, "Thank you, Mr. Mayor. I appreciate the meeting and, yes, I understand your position. Listen, no hard feelings— enjoy those fishing holes."

Suddenly, Pryor rose up from his chair and said, "Sir, I think you misunderstand me. There is no way that you could pay me to vote against him. I'll do it for free."

A stunned Gittings asked the mayor to sit down and explain what he meant. He listened as Pryor spoke for several moments about crawfish, extramarital affairs, and the economy, before finally saying, "Sir, I'm out of here soon; I'm leaving the political arena. Why not go out with a real bang? Besides, I hate that bastard. It will be a pleasure to vote against him."

"So, you'll vote for the governor?"

"You at a hearing loss, son? You can put it in the bank."

Gittings hesitated for a moment, afraid to upset the mayor. Then he said, "If you don't mind me asking you a question, what is your hatred for the president based upon?"

As he began to sit back down, Pryor reached into his pocket and brought out a thick, worn-out brown wallet, much of the leather cracked from age. Opening it up, he searched through a group of pictures, finally selecting one that he handed to the perplexed Gittings. "See this beautiful girl? That's my baby doll, my daughter Priscilla Anne."

Gittings looked at the picture of a beautiful buxom woman, one that he considered to be a knockout. He listened as Pryor explained, "So, three years ago, I am invited to the White House, along with dozens of other mayors from across the country. The invitation was for two, but since '02, when my beloved wife Claire passed away, I have taken Priscilla Anne along with me on these special trips. Son, you would have loved Claire, she was smarter than the day is long. She knew everything. I called her 'Claire Voyence'. You get it, son? Like in clairvoyance—she knew everything, I say! Anyway, we get to the White House, and there is the president to greet us. He looked at Priscilla Anne like a rooster looks at a hen, giving her that, 'Let's go somewhere and make a dozen eggs' look. You know what I mean?"

Smiling, Gittings acknowledged the thought, laughing respectfully.

Continuing, Pryor said, "So we have the luncheon, and let me say, the food was good, real good, best Maryland crabs that I've ever had. Afterward, Priscilla Anne goes to the washroom, where she is met by three female Secret Servicemen. Would they be called 'servicemen' or 'servicewomen'? Sometimes I fall victim to this language of ours. I've been speaking it nearly all of my life, but, anyway, they tell her that the president wants to meet with her in the Oval Office.

"Oval Office, my behind! He had designs on her oval office, if you know what I mean, son. He put his hands on my Priscilla Anne and starts working his hands like he's reading Braille or something. Well, my Priscilla Anne whacks him right in the side of his head and tells him, now get this one, 'Acting like that, you should be the vice president, in charge of vice.' Get it, son, in charge of vice. Girl inherited her mother's looks and my sense of humor. I'm glad it was in that order, would've been a nightmare otherwise.

"So she smacks him one more time and tells him, you'll like this one,

'If you want to get a look at some mountains, then you better travel to Colorado.' Oh, that girl is so funny."

"That's a good one, Mr. Mayor."

"Please call me Noah, son. Like the man who had to clean up after all of dem animals on the boat.

"My Priscilla Anne told me about the whole thang a few months later, and let me tell you I am glad that she waited. There would have been an incident like no one in the White House had ever witnessed before. Anyway, son, that is why I would be glad to vote for your Governor Ryan."

After several more minutes of being entertained by Pryor, a hearty handshake ended their meeting, and by 1:00, Gittings was in the back of a taxi, on his way to Hartsfield-Jackson Airport, this time for a 4:14 flight to Memphis.

His Delta flight arrived in the River City at 5:00 and he was picked up by a limo service, the driver getting him to the Hampton Inn on Beale Street so far ahead of his 8:00 meeting that he was able to go to the Rum Boogie Café and eat a fast Beale Street BBQ Special, the hickory smoked ribs highlighting the meal, describing it as his favorite meal—ever.

Returning to the hotel, he met with State Senator Olivia Waite. Knowing that he had made at least one positive connection, he was cautious with the senator, asking her what her thoughts were concerning faithless voters. Once she said that she could consider a Faulkner vote, for $500,000, Gittings promptly ended the meeting so that he could see the late show at the Jaguar Jazz & Blues Club; the Joe Moss Band was performing and he loved the sound that they produced. Later the music had Gittings tapping his toes all night and once again, he had to be helped into a cab so that he could get to his hotel bed, where after a good night's sleep he'd awaken knowing he was heading home.

Gittings was bothered by the morning alarms, each of which seemed louder than the other. But as he showered, he was smiling, knowing that he was going home. After a regular, uneventful flight, by 11:30 A.M. Gittings was walking out the airport door and into Rahim's taxi. "You look tired, sir. Rahim is happy to see you. Thank you for calling me. Did you get done what you wanted?"

"It was a long trip, but all in all, a good one. I'm glad to be home."

"Knowing you, sir, I am sure that it was a success. Rahim knows these things. Believe me. It's the one thing that I do even better than driving—that's knowing people.

"Home or the office, sir?"

"It's time to go back to work, Rahim. Take me to the governor's mansion."

"Very good, sir. I will have you at the office momentarily."

Gittings hardly heard a word that Rahim said, as he fell asleep within two minutes of the departure from the airport. Arriving at the Statehouse, Gittings made Rahim promise that they would stay in touch with each other, a suggestion that was embraced by the happy cabbie.

"Thank you for calling me. Do you need another card, Mr. Gittings? I have a private limo for hire—call me anytime."

"I'll see you the next time I'm heading out of town."

"Rahim will be ready, sir. Just call."

Heading into the governor's office, Gittings was excited to tell Ryan that the mission had gone well.

"You look like death warmed over," said a smiling Ryan. "Welcome home. Thank you for making the trip. So tell me about it."

For the next two hours Gittings told the governor about every detail, at least those that he could remember. He explained that after all of his travels, "Boss, I think we have one of the votes that we were seeking, maybe two. Now, just don't piss off any of the electors that are supposed to vote for you and we'll win this thing!"

---

i. http://www.baseball-almanac.com/quotes/quoberra.shtml December 28, 2012

ii. http://shopping.usairways.com/Flights/BuildItinerary.aspx December 29, 2012

Chapter 25

The Inevitable Happens

Washington, D.C.
Friday, November 13, 2020
6:22 P.M.

Jeannie Hospie was one of America's favorite meteorologists. Her forecasts were accurate, her sense of humor was well-appreciated and her appearance was flawless—her attire almost always caused viewers to take a second look.

". . . So once again, big snows are expected for Arkansas, Oklahoma, and the panhandle of Texas. Also, heavy rains are expected for the western part of Washington State. All other parts of the nation should have normal or near-normal temperatures."

Just as she was about to provide accumulation totals for cities like Amarillo, Tulsa, and Fayetteville, she was interrupted by Leah Manders. "We interrupt the weather broadcast to make this special announcement. This is just in to our news desk; Former President James Augustus Faulkner has died at his Oregon farm. Repeating, President James Augustus Faulkner has died on his beloved Flying Faulkner ranch in Oregon.

"Although reports are still coming in, it is being reported that the president, after leaving Washington, D.C. three days ago, became ill on Air Force Two and upon landing in Portland, chose to be driven to his ranch. Accompanying him was his medical team, which was led by famed Dr. Brook Rider.

"At this moment we do not have any of the medical details, but, again, former President James Augustus Faulkner has died.

"Please stay tuned to us as we will receive more details."

As the news broke, Bob Gittings was on the phone with Governor Robert Ryan.

"Governor, I just heard the news."

"Yeah, it was just announced."

"Well, I feel bad for his wife, but for us, it's very good news. He didn't make it to the electors' vote, so there's a new race for the White House."

"Did you say 'race'? Man, I'm ready to run!"

"Good one, sir. Good one. I'll see you later."

CHAPTER 26

The Panel

Washington, D.C.
Sunday, November 15, 2020
8:00 P.M.

Millions of viewers across the nation tuned in to WGDC's news special entitled "The Election Crisis: Where Do We Go from Here?" which tried to help citizens understand the issues that laid ahead concerning the presidency.

Host Leah Manders introduced herself and said, "Unless you have been hiding under a rock, you have to be aware of the constitutional crisis that confronts our nation, the first one our nation has seen since the Clinton impeachment trial or, further back, the Nixon years in which the 37th president was pitted against Congress concerning his secret tapes.

"Tonight our network's correspondents and our panel will analyze the situation that, hopefully, by January 20th will have resolved itself. That is the date that the new president is to be sworn in. Usually the process presents no problems. This year, it appears to present nothing but problems. We are aware that, last night, millions of people watched our tribute to the late president—one that featured James Faulkner's rise to power, his resignation from office, and then his much-too-sudden death."

Manders turned to the left, as directed, to look directly into Camera Two. "By now we think that you know the facts; incumbent James Augustus Faulkner was re-elected by the American public but died prior to next month's voting of the Electoral College. However, he is the first candidate who apparently won the election who then met his demise prior to the Electoral College's vote.

"So what happens now? Here are some questions to consider:

"When exactly does the electoral college meet? Are the votes that are pledged to the president his and his alone? If not, how many of the 270 pledged votes that he received will he actually get? Will the votes that were supposed to be his be given, instead, to the Vice President-elect Maria Martinez? Or will she have to earn them somehow? What about the many states that require the members to vote for the pledged candidate? Suppose one or two of them don't want to vote for the president; considering the extraordinary circumstances, will they still be forced to? And finally, will the United States Supreme Court be called into action to make a last second determination of the facts?

"To address all of these questions and many others, we have assembled a very impressive group who, we hope, will be able to provide some answers. Included in this group is Washington insider and columnist for the *Washington Post*, Grover Ellington Benson."

As the camera put Mr. Benson's close-up into focus, Manders introduced the next members of the panel, Anne Marie Fishkis, a constitutional expert from Georgetown University and Columbia University Professor of American History, Tyson Joseph.

Manders began, "Is there anyone in America, including the three of you, who has ever seen anything like this before?"

Fishkis answered, "Leah, no person that is alive has seen anything like this. This is an historic first. I can assure you that there is no one in America who has witnessed anything like this."

Manders asked, "Grover, what are your thoughts about this? Is this a once in a lifetime experience?"

"Leah, it certainly is. But, on the other hand, it has to be an exciting time for educators all across the nation. I can see new lesson plans being developed according to what happens from here on out. No one saw this one coming. The timing of the president's resignation and subsequent death may compromise the Twentieth Amendment."

"I agree," emphatically said Professor Joseph. "We are in new territory here; an unprecedented series of events has led us to what might be a major constitutional crisis! If the late Marvin Gaye were to look at this he'd say, 'Mercy, Mercy, Me'".

"Constitutional crisis?" asked Manders. "Although my opening lines mentioned it, could you, Professor Tyson, explain it further?"

"The question at hand deals with the Twentieth Amendment. It states that in case of death, the president-elect will be replaced by the vice president-elect. Leah, we have no president-elect. The people didn't elect Faulkner; they elected his electors. The electors are yet to vote, not doing so until December 14th—a month from now! We have no president-elect. That is a constitutional crisis because there is nothing in the Constitution that explains how to handle this situation. Nothing!"

"I am not sure if I agree with you on that point," said Fishkis. "It would only become a crisis if the electors stick to, or are forced to stick to, their votes. If all 270 of Faulkner's voters change to Martinez, we have no problem!"

Professor Joseph loudly replied, "Are you kidding me? The odds of all of the electors for Faulkner voting for Martinez are so remote that I can't see any way that that would happen. Besides, there are laws in some of those states that require some of those Faulkner voters to vote for him. What would happen if the states require their members to vote for Faulkner? Does the name 'Supreme Court' mean anything to you?"

Manders continued, "Perhaps. But what if those who aren't *required* to vote for Faulkner decide to vote for Martinez, while those who *are* required to vote for him, do vote for him? Then what?"

Joseph replied, "I don't know if my colleagues agree, but constitutionally, that would be the best option, as the Constitution has outlined that scenario for us—since no one would have a majority, the House of Representatives picks the winner from the top three candidates. In this case, that would be Ryan with an assumed still-standing 268, and a combination of 270 voters for Martinez and Faulkner. Take note of this, no one would have the majority. If I might add, the last time that the House was called into action was in 1824, when there were four candidates vying for the majority of electoral votes. No one received the necessary 131 Electoral College votes—the amount needed for a majority at the time—so the House came into play. Although Andrew Jackson had been leading the Electoral College vote with 99, he didn't win.

"In what famously went on to be called 'The Corrupt Bargain,' Henry Clay threw his support behind eventual winner John Quincy Adams and Clay's supporters followed suit. Adams won the presidency and Henry Clay became his Secretary of State."[i]

Benson interrupted, "If it were left to me, I would do away with those requirements, as I think they are unconstitutional. They appear to, at least in my mind, go against the right of freedom of speech. Even if a person is an elector, doesn't he or she still have fundamental rights? Well, don't they?"

Fishkis asked, "But Grover, when one goes to work for, let's say, Pepsi, one is subject to their confidentiality agreement—I'm assuming that Pepsi has some type of confidentiality agreement. If one doesn't like the agreement, one would leave the company or perhaps not become an employee in the first place. My point is that an elector shouldn't be allowed to put him or herself in the position of becoming an elector if he or she isn't willing to follow the rules of the job. And according to the 1952 United States Supreme Court Case of *Ray v Blair*, the Court ruled that the electors work for their respective states, and thus, are required to follow the guidelines presented by their state. That case, I might add, was almost seventy years ago, and no one has challenged it successfully. Using that as a point of fact, in my opinion, the electors who are required by their states to vote for Faulkner will have to vote for Faulkner."

Manders asked, "Even though he is dead?"

To which Fishkis sighed and replied, "Yes, Leah, even though he is dead."

Benson quickly interrupted, "With all due respect, how the heck can that be the best scenario? The way I see that vote going is like this, the Democratic electors will continue to vote for Governor Ryan, while those who are Republicans will be split between Faulkner and Martinez. How many rounds of voting in the House will we have to have to determine a winner? There will be no one with a majority, and the procedure will become a stalemate, with no one winning."

The professor added, "It's not quite that bad. Remember, the House votes as states, not as individuals. Thus, the outcome might be determined in one or two rounds."

Manders continued, "According to our findings, and addressing Grover's point, there are twenty-six states and the District of Columbia that have laws that require their electors to vote for a pledged candidate.[ii] Of those states, in the recent election, fifteen of those pledge-requiring states favored Faulkner. Those were, Alabama, Alaska, Florida, Mississippi, Montana, Nebraska, Nevada, New Mexico, Ohio, Oklahoma, Oregon, South Carolina, Virginia, Washington, and Wyoming. So, Anne Marie, are you saying that, due to the 1952 Supreme Court case, the 135 Electoral College votes from these fifteen states will have to go to Faulkner, despite the fact that he is dead?"

After a short pause Fishkis said, "Yes, according to the ruling in *Ray v Blair*. Unless someone from one of those states has a successful Supreme Court case that overrides *Blair*, 135 votes will be guaranteed to a dead man, leaving the vote, interestingly enough as, Ryan 268, Faulkner 135, and Martinez 135!"

---

i. Wikipedia http://en.wikipedia.org/wiki/Corrupt_Bargain December 29, 2012.

ii. www.archives.gov/federal-register/electoral-college/laws.html

CHAPTER 27

The Sleepless One near Seattle

Bellingham, Washington
Monday, November 16, 2020
3:07 A.M.

Just as meteorologist Jeannie Hospie had predicted, at about 3:00 A.M., severe winds and heavy rains hit the western half of the state of Washington, winds gusting so strong that they were able to wake Erin Morgan from her usual sound sleep. As she turned to her right and saw that her husband Bill wasn't in the bed, she was not surprised. Slowly pulling the covers off of herself, she slipped on her robe, and started walking down the darkened stairs that led to the first floor.

As she reached the last step, she walked toward the door that led to the garage. Barely opening the door a crack, she peered in and saw her husband doing what had become a nightly ritual, restoring his recently purchased yellow 1969 Ford Mustang, attempting to bring it back to its original luster.

"Bill," she said, surprising her husband, "I told you that if in the middle of the night if you wanted to tinker with something, that all you had to do was stay in bed, turn to your left, and wake me up. You don't have to come all the way down here."

Bill, who was known for his appreciation of a good joke, laughed heartily, his belly shaking like Santa's. "Honey, the Mustang's motor didn't hum like yours can." She smiled, and then reminded him, "Bill, this is the third night in a row that you were not able to sleep, eventually finding your way down here."

Slowly walking toward her husband, ever mindful of the tools on the floor, Erin reached out her hands to him. Receiving the hug she wanted, she said, "I know that you don't want to hear me say this again, but why don't you call Davida. She's great, she's willing to help and she owes us a favor."

But her husband, as he had done for more than a week, insisted, "I can get through this myself."

"You're aware that you've had your hands on the car's chassis more than you've had them on mine. Bill, it's not going well. You're not handling it well. You need some guidance and Davida is the one you should speak with. She's not going to say anything to anyone about your conversations.

"You watched Leah Manders's panel on television last night. There's a great deal of confusion out there. No one knows what to do with this thing. Just because you're the mayor of Bellingham doesn't mean that you are supposed to have all of the answers. I know that you haven't spoken to any of the other electors either. You should get an idea of their thoughts too. Now, let's go upstairs and you can check out what's under my hood."

With those words the intensity of the hug increased and the couple held hands, quickly walking back up to the bedroom.

The next morning, from his City Hall office on Lottie Street, a still-reluctant Morgan looked up the phone number of Davida Shepherd. Dialing the number, he made an appointment.

In the midst of another heavy rainstorm, several hours later, arriving at her office, Bill found that the elevator was out of service. With his huge six-foot four-inch, three-hundred-fifty-pound frame, he was not accustomed to walking up four flights of stairs, but climb them he did. Arriving at Davida's office door, he took several deep breaths to try to recover from the first exercise that he had done in several months. Walking into the office, he was greeted by the receptionist, Holly Carcich, who recognized him and said, "Mr. Mayor, could you please pass a law requiring elevators to be fixed within twenty-four hours? This one's been out for almost two weeks, and I've taken more steps than Ginger Rogers!"

"I hear you. My feet feel like Fred's danced on them for a couple of hours."

"She's on the phone talking to Olympia, probably another ten minutes or so. Can I get you some cold water?"

"You don't have to ask me twice," said the still-panting mayor.

After what seemed to Bill to be a short twelve minutes, an apologetic Davida walked into the waiting room. "I am so sorry to have had to keep you waiting!" said the diminutive lawyer. "Thank you for coming here. It kept me from lugging all of my heavy materials over to City Hall."

Hearing Davida's greeting, Holly looked at the hulking frame of the mayor and wondered about his ability to "lug his big frame" over to her office. She was going to ask, but chose not to, noting Davida's glance in her direction and reading the mind of her boss.

"Here, step into my office, Bill."

After a short discussion about Erin and the rest of his family, Davida said, "So, Bill, Erin has enlightened me regarding this matter and how much it's bothering you."

"Yeah, to be honest, I really don't know what to do."

"So let me make sure that I've got this correct. You're one of the twelve Republican electors for the state of Washington."

"That's correct."

"Since President Faulkner won the election here in Washington, you and the other eleven have won the right to vote in next month's gathering of electors in Olympia. Correct?"

A still slightly tired mayor nodded his head in agreement. Continuing, Davida added, "But he's dead. And you want to vote for anyone other than a dead man, correct?"

Again the big-boned mayor nodded his head in agreement, this time while drinking his fourth glass of water.

Davida had never seen such a display of water drinking in her life. Amused, perhaps inspired by his blue-striped suit and light blue shirt, in her mind she made comparisons of Bill and large blue whale. She waited for the moment until he put down his glass, and before he could pour himself another, she looked at her notes and then blurted out, "But state law, let's see, here it is, REW 29A.56.340,[i] the one that requires you to vote for the pledged candidate, is confronting you. I looked it up, the fine is $1,000. That's a bit steep."

Bill, having finally quenched his thirst completely, caught his breath, said, "The money isn't the issue. You know that Erin and I are doing very well; her dermatology practice is going very well. You know she opened her fourth office? This one's in Ferndale. So money isn't an issue. It is the principle of the thing. I want my vote to count for something. I feel as if I am being forced to be part of a travesty. Voting for a dead man, indeed! Who the hell wants to vote for a guy in a coffin? And what if he wins? This nation will be the laughing stock of the world."

Davida smiled and while searching through the folder marked "Bill the Mayor" said, "You want to know something, I happen to agree with you. This would be a travesty, and I didn't know anything about it until your wife informed me. So, I looked into it, and I think I have figured out a potential solution. That is, a solution if everything goes our way."

Bill's interest increased. He leaned forward in his chair, signaling to Davida that she had a big fish on the line, one that she might be able to ride to fame and fortune, although she already had the fortune—her law firm of Katz, Kleinberg, Goldberger, and Shepherd, was among the most prestigious in the state, called by many a "hot firm" that was receiving many high-powered clients.

"Bill, my entire law firm will be behind you. We'll have everyone working on this."

"Don't worry about the costs. My family's fishing business is doing well. Let's just get this done."

Having talked about the financial side of the case, Davida started to talk about the case itself. "First of all," she said, "Our federal government isn't going to want to look foolish. The issues that you are facing are being faced by electors in other parts of our state and electors in many of the twenty-eight other states that were won by Faulkner. That's a great many people who, I am sure, don't want to be part of something that makes them or the nation look foolish.

"But it's late in the game, and we need to get the ball over the goal line quickly. We need to advertise this problem across the nation, or at least in the several states where Faulkner won. We need to get rid of the main culprit, which is the 1952 Supreme Court of the United States case of *Ray v Blair*. Once we get to the Washington Supreme Court, knowing its makeup, it will be difficult to find a state law unconstitutional."

"All I know about the issue is what I've seen on the Leah Manders special. But I trust your judgment. So let's get it started. What'd we do first?"

"Okay, we have to bring the case to the Thurston County Court. That'll get the ball rolling."

"Do we have a good chance of winning there?"

"Of course," said the spirited five-foot one-inch lawyer. "That's why I'm taking the case. But, if we lose, we can appeal it. My staff and I will draw up a declaratory judgment stating that the law shouldn't be enforced. We'll aim it at the Secretary of State, Lisa Fitzgerald."

---

i. James Pharris, email message to author, July 12, 2011

Chapter 28

The Court Speaks

Thurston County Courthouse
Olympia, Washington
Friday, November 20, 2020
9:00 A.M.

Davida Shepherd had had several prominent athletes as clients, and she had asked each one of them the same question, "Are you nervous on the day of a championship game?" Today those conversations seemed pertinent to her, as her nerves were acting up, the several deep breaths that she had taken previous to her arrival to the courthouse notwithstanding.

Over the previous couple of days and nights she had gotten very little sleep. She had spent many hours working alongside several of her associates trying to put together her case. As she looked down the table, two of her partners, Jerry Katz and Leo Simmons, were there. When he could, Katz, the senior partner of the firm, had been a huge supporter of Davida and had often spent time sitting in on her cases.

Of course, the main person of interest for Davida was Bill Morgan, who on this day had more of the appearance of a gray whale, dressed in a three-piece cardigan suit of that color. Although she had spoken to him several times since their meeting four days earlier, she hadn't been able to actually sit with him. His constant smiles concerned Davida, as she figured that they were a feeble attempt to cover up the nervousness that he must have been feeling. But who was she to be critical? She was as nervous as hell, too.

As she looked at the other side of the room, at the opponents' table, she saw the lawyer that struck fear in the hearts of so many other lawyers in the state of Washington, State Solicitor Attorney Bob M. Hertz. He was the only one in the room that made Bill Morgan look like an average-sized man, as his six-foot nine-inch frame was significantly muscled.

The former Seattle Supersonic power forward (of course, that was prior to the team's moving to Oklahoma City) had gained, during his NBA career, the nickname Bob *Mega* Hertz, a name that amply described him in the courtroom too. He was a larger-than-life opponent for most that came across him, known for the same aggressive and unforgiving style that had twice made him a second team NBA All-Star.

Upon the entrance of Judge Paige Schneider, who would be presiding over this bench trial, the complaint and instructions were read. Davida, taking several deep breaths, jumped to her feet and began to attack with her opening statements. She took some of the sting out of Hertz's position, acknowledging the existence of *Ray v Blair* and claimed that it would be the centerpiece of the state's case. However, she pointed out that the 1952 US Supreme Court case was aimed at keeping presidential electors from frivolously choosing candidates at will, perhaps making a mockery of the Electoral College system. Acknowledging this, she said, "Your Honor, what would be more frivolous than requiring our electors to vote for our deceased president? Was electing a deceased man to the office of President of the United States the intended purpose of the Supreme Court's 5–2 ruling back in 1952? I think not. Your Honor, with all due respect, you must rule in favor of common sense, freeing Bill Morgan and eleven other electors of this fair state from the unintentional consequences of a ruling that sixty-eight years ago had no foresight as to see a circumstance like we have before us today."

As she turned to regain her seat, she was passed by the one and one-half foot taller Hertz. Sitting down, she was congratulated by everyone at the desk. Hertz started his argument by thanking Davida for her reference to *Ray v Blair*, as "It is, as the plaintiff's lawyer suggested, the heart of our case. Your Honor, the justices upon that day in 1952 officially defined electors as agents of their respective states, not free agents who are selected to speak their minds and vote as the wind blows them. Rather, their decision ended any possible attempt at cronyisms.

"Your Honor, you may question why the state of Washington is so eager to defend law REW 29A.56.340, requiring electors to vote for the candidate to which they are pledged, especially under the sad circum-stances of the death of our president. We are fighting to keep this law alive so that Bill Morgan and the eleven others, who are pledged to the state of Washington, won't be able to make the mockery that Ms. Shepherd seems so worried about. If you allow their complaint to be judged favor-ably, what would keep Mr. Morgan from voting for, let's say, his Aunt Colleen? And he does have an Aunt Colleen who lives in Spokane. No, your Honor, the justices of the 1952 Supreme Court knew exactly what they were doing. With all due respect, your Honor, please do not con-sider ruling in favor of the plaintiff, rather preserve the ruling that was so carefully created by the justices in Washington, D.C.

"And, please keep in mind, your Honor, that REW 29A.56.340 will keep order for future elections, too. Upholding its merit will keep order in terms of future electoral voters."

The actual case was heard until 6:35, some ninety-five minutes past the regular closing time. But Judge Schneider, knowing the national importance of the case, the time she would need to make a decision, the time needed to gain an appeal for whichever side lost, and the upcom-ing Thanksgiving holiday that was only six days away, ordered the sides to finish their arguments that day, calling all witnesses (including Mr. Morgan) to the stand and expediting the case as quickly as possible.

Upon hearing the closing arguments of each side, the crusty thirty-eight-year veteran of the bench promised, "Despite the important intra-division contest between our Seahawks and San Francisco 49ers, I will have a decision for you on Tuesday. All interested parties are due back in this courtroom at 9:00 A.M. on Tuesday the twenty-third of this month." The pounding of her gavel ended the proceedings of the day.

The weekend seemed to fly by for Bill Morgan, as he and Erin spent Saturday at the Bellis Fair Mall followed by trips to Costco and Wal-Mart, all in preparation of the Thanksgiving holiday, which for the third straight year since the passing of Bill's mother would be held at their home. Ironically, on Sunday, Bill attended the Seahawk game that Judge Schneider was missing due to the case. On Monday, Bill went to his City

Hall office, but the anticipation of the holiday and the decision made it impossible for much actual work to be done.

That night, at a few minutes before midnight, Erin again caught Bill working on the Mustang, only this time she sat with him and talked about the next day's events.

"I see that you are at it again."

"I can't sleep, honey. I'm thinking about tomorrow."

"Honey, Davida did a good job you're going to win. Now let's go back upstairs."

"But what if we lose? I can't vote for a dead man!"

"Don't think that way. She's going to win it for us. Now, let's go back to sleep."

On Tuesday at 8:30 A.M., Davida arrived at the Thurston County Courthouse, meeting Bill and Erin who had arrived twenty minutes earlier. Seeing Davida, Bill said, "Thank you so much. No matter what happens we feel good about having you on our side."

"It's been my pleasure. Let's go inside."

They entered the courtroom and, after several short discussions, became silent as the entrance of Judge Schneider was announced. As she spoke, everyone in the courtroom listened, "The case before me is one of the more interesting cases over which I have had to preside, as each party has made salient points, which have had my attention all weekend. In essence I must rule between two ideas, the law of the state of Washington and the complaint for what has been referred to as the sensible alternative, that being siding with the plaintiff, Bill Morgan. Though I see the issues that face Mr. Morgan and his eleven co-electors, I must consider what the laws are in this state and in this nation."

Nervously, as Judge Schneider cleared her throat, Bill Morgan reached for his second glass of water. He bit his lip as Judge Schneider said, "It would be simple for me to rule in favor of Mr. Morgan, citing what his attorney calls 'a frivolous act,' that being, voting for the deceased president. Attorney Shepherd suggested that it wasn't in the mindset of the United States Supreme Court to vote as they did; not knowing that one day a case like this one might be brought into play. Yet, in my research and through my calls, I have not heard, nor have I read, any suggestion that the justices of 1952 *didn't* know that this unique circumstance might arise. Thus, it would be an assumption on our part to think that they didn't, and I can't let speculation overrule what is fact. Therefore, because of the ruling of *Ray v Blair*, I must uphold Washington State law REW 29A.56.340 and I instruct Mr. Morgan, as well as the other electors to vote as they have been pledged, for the late President James Augustus Faulkner. The Court has spoken!"

Bill Morgan was not as devastated as he thought he might be, but after shaking hands with Bob Hertz, Davida seemed to have enough devastation for the two of them. "I am so sorry," she said to the Morgans, as Erin had joined them at the desk. "This is not an excuse, but I had the feeling that she was going to rule that way. Judge Schneider has been around this state a very long time, and I am sure that she wasn't going to allow a state law to go down.

"But don't worry, as soon as I get to my car, I will call my office, and the staff is set to work all through the Thanksgiving holiday to get the appeal set for the Washington State Supreme Court. I will head there on Friday to file the appeal."

"Working through the holiday?" suggested Bill. "Why not eat with us? We have plenty of food."

Davida declined. "The Boston Market on Harrison Avenue is on notice. They will have dinner ready for the thirty of us who will be at our Olympia office on Thursday."

By 10:15 on Friday morning, the staff had finished the appeal, and Davida, after thanking each one of them, put it in her briefcase and drove to the Washington State Supreme Court where she went to file the appeal. The clerk, Jasmine Wilson, seeing that it was 2:45, kiddingly said, "I expected you an hour ago. What took you so long?"

They shared the laugh and Davida, after filing the appeal, exited the courthouse and headed back to her office. On the way, she called her favorite mayor. "Bill, the appeal's been filed, and we'll have to wait for word from the Court as to if and when they'll take the case."

That statement prompted Bill to ask a basic question, "Do you expect them to hear it?"

Without hesitation Davida told him yes, "The importance of this case with its implications for the nation will be too much for them to pass on. I wouldn't be surprised if I heard from them later today. Your case is that important. Listen, much to do—I'll get back to you as soon as I hear something."

Later that afternoon, Davida's premonition proved to be correct, as the motion for appeal had been accepted, and the case had been placed upon the docket for Tuesday, December 1st, just four days away.

Again, her staff was on notice, with the entire office participating in the process of getting in order all of the materials that Davida would need. When she felt that everything was complete, she sat in her office, alone, and prayed for a miracle, one that would help her win the case.

The solitude did feel good, as she had instructed her secretary to tell all callers that she was in "trial preparation" and that they should call back afterward. Enjoying the first quiet moments in what seemed to be a month, Davida sat back and thought about her presentation. Fifteen minutes later she had her solitude interrupted, when her secretary Holly Carcich buzzed her, "Pick up Line 3."

"Holly, I thought I told you that I wanted no calls."

"I think you'll want to hear from this person."

"Who is it?"

Holly, still excited said, "It's some guy from New York who says that he has information that will win your case for you."

"Please get his name."

A moment later Holly said, "It's a Professor Tyson Joseph."

"Tyson Joseph! *The* Tyson Joseph! Please put him through immediately."

"This is Davida Shepherd, do I have the pleasure of speaking to Mr. Tyson Joseph, the famed lawyer from New York?"

"Famed? I'm not so sure about that. And pleasure is debatable too. But this is Tyson Joseph from New York. I know that you are very busy, but I thought I could be of some help."

"Well, help is always welcomed. Thank you for the call, and, like you said, I am very busy, but never too busy to hear from you. How can I help you?"

"Rather it is I who can be of help to you. So let me get straight to the point. I've been following every word of the trial and I am anxious for your appeal."

"Thank you. It's an important issue out here. Please, go on."

"Hey, it's an important issue everywhere. You might be aware that besides having my law practice, I teach at Columbia University. While all of this has been going on, I thought about a few elections and asked my staff to look into something. I made a few statements on the air and further research by a few of my clerks has uncovered an item that I am sure will win your case for you.

"As it turns out what I said on Leah Manders' panel was incorrect. The research supports that I made a huge mistake. I read about Mr. Morgan's case in the *New York Times* and instead of going public with the newly found information, I thought that I would provide it to you for use in court."

"I'm impressed. I'd love to learn more about it."

"So, you had a good argument, but I promise you if you are armed with what I am about to tell you, that you will come out a winner."

"Sounds great. What is it?"

"Okay, either get a pen or record what I'm about to tell you."

"I'm all ears. I have a pen, and I'm ready to go."

For the next thirty-five minutes Tyson outlined the strategy that Davida should employ, one that he predicted would have flawless results. As the conversation was about to come to an end, she asked Professor Joseph, "This is so appreciated. Why did you step forward with the information?"

"Look, it's simple, Davida. I'm on the side of the little guy and what's best for the nation. I can promise you that maybe a handful of people in the nation are aware of those details; I am willing to bet that Mr. Hertz and his team don't know a darn thing about it. Use it and win. Good luck."

"Thank you, Professor, and let me tell you that I'm a big fan of yours."

"Win this case and your fan base will grow tenfold. Go get 'em, Davida."

The super-excited Davida got on the intercom, called her paralegals, and said, "All of you—get in here now!" Once inside she told them, "I just got a call from New York and received a big tip that I think will win this thing for us. But we have to move fast. The first person to get me the information that I need will receive a large bonus."

Fifteen minutes later, holding a large book, Bianca Moss ran into the office asking, "How much is that bonus worth?"

"It'll pay for half of the sports car that you saw on the street two weeks ago." Reading it over, Davida came to the same conclusion that Professor Joseph had reached: She couldn't lose. She thanked Bianca and excitedly called together the entire staff, briefing them on the new "can't lose" strategy. She couldn't wait to get to court.

The first day of December was a rainy Tuesday in Olympia. As Davida entered the Supreme Court she put down her umbrella, took off her raincoat, took her last sip of Starbucks, and greeted those in her party. The last people that she saw were the eagerly waiting Bill and Erin Morgan.

Bill looked at her and reminded her that she was the best lawyer in the West, if not the entire nation. "Thank you, but today, I just want to be the best lawyer in this courtroom."

As they entered the Halls of the Supreme Court, Davida thought about her last time arguing before the justices, a 2016 defeat at the hands of none other than Bob Mega Hertz. As she prepared her papers she saw Bill Morgan drinking from the water fountain, which reminded her of their first meeting about the case.

Upon the entrance and seating of the nine Supreme Court Justices, the Chief Justice, Juliana Nuriddin, greeted the parties and reminded them, "Due to the factoring in of time and the constitutional and national implications of the case, the Court has accepted this case on an expedited basis, skipping the Court of Appeals, and will be hearing this case directly from the Thurston County Superior Court. If there are no questions, let us begin."

Davida, speaking strongly and more determinedly than she had in

Thurston County, began: "Your Honors, please let me remind all of you that, in essence, at stake here is the electing of a dead man to the office of the President of the United States. In my arguments before Judge Schneider I included the fact that as an elector, Bill Morgan, by Washington State law, is required to vote for the person who the people, based upon their votes in November, have indicated they want to be president. Mr. Morgan was placed in the position as an elector because people in his party thought that he would represent the interests of the party and the interests of the people of Washington State. I offer to you that all electors in each of the fifty states and the District of Columbia all have the same responsibility, and some are not bound by state laws mandating their respective votes. All of these voters are considered to be equal in the eyes of the American people, a voter from Washington State having the same power as an elector from New York. Yet, the elector from New York is free to vote for whomever he or she wants, not bound by state laws. I suggest that this disparity might be considered an infringement upon the Fourteenth Amendment's equal protection clause."

Justice Seamus O'Rourke, with his thick Irish accent, stated, "*Ray v. Blair* answered that question—allowing each state the right to require their prospective electors to take a pledge and that this process does not interfere with the equal protection clause of the Fourteenth Amendment. I suggest that in the years that have passed that nothing has changed."

The nods of agreement by several of the other justices suggested that, while she still had time, that she play her trump card.

"Your Honors, supporting the Thurston County Court decision in this case is a recipe for disaster, one that would have perilous results in the very near future."

Smiling, thinking about the passion with which Professor Joseph had put forth the forthcoming information, she continued, "Previously I have argued against the merits of State Law REW 29A.56.340 in general terms. Your Honors, if I may speak in specifics, let us say that you uphold the decision reached at Thurston County. If you do, with all due respect, you will be rendering the vote of Bill Morgan and his eleven fellow electors useless."

Justice Liza Lopilato asked, "Just how could that happen?"

"Justice Lopilato, there is precedence for a matter like this, one in which a presidential candidate dies during the time period between the people's vote and the vote of the Electoral College. And, at this time, I would like to introduce some new evidence to the Court."

Veteran Justice Barry B. Cox, who was routinely referred to by the media as "the crusty, seasoned, senior-most" of the justices, quickly interrupted, "Counselor, you are aware that this is an appellate hearing, one in which the presentation of new evidence is frowned upon."

"Justice Cox, if you and your fellow justices will allow me the latitude of introducing this key piece of evidence about which I have just learned, it would allow me to correctly represent my client—"

"Why should we allow this evidence? Won't it bring prejudice to the state's case?"

"Not at all, Your Honor. Rather, it is information that will shine a new light on the entire case and will help the esteemed members of the Court make the proper decision. If I may say, it is the obligation of everyone present here today to make sure that Mr. Morgan, his fellow electors, and the millions of voters in our fine state are aware of all the facts that will help this Court reach the proper decision, even if these facts laid dormant in the history books for years. I am certain that prior to rendering your decision on this most important case, Your Honors will want to have all of the pertinent facts that are available."

Not impressed, Cox stated, "And why weren't these facts presented to Judge Schneider in Thurston County?"

"Your Honor, at the time of that hearing I was not privy to the information."

"It sounds to me like sloppy preparation, counselor. If it is to be brought into evidence here, why not then? And just how did you learn of this so-called *important* information?"

"I received a phone call from a lawyer in New York who is an expert in this particular area. Upon his advice, my staff and I realized how important this information is to my client and to the people of our state. And so, I am asking this Court to allow me to present it. Upon hearing it, Mr. Hertz will hardly be able to claim prejudice. Further, Your Honors, I claim that, indeed, if the state is aware of this information, then it is I, representing Mr. Morgan, who might be able to claim prejudice."

Still not impressed, Cox said, "And just who was this New Yorker who helped you with this valuable information?"

"Your Honor, the call came from Tyson Joseph, the famed lawyer and professor of American History at Columbia University who was kind enough to present me with this obscure detail in our nation's history, a fact that is known to few but will affect the millions of voters in our state and those of several others."

After looking at her fellow justices, and receiving a nod of approval from all, Chief Justice Nuriddin said, "Well, if the esteemed Professor Joseph feels that this is of importance to millions of Americans, let it be noted for the record that this Court will not stand in the way of its presentation. Proceed with this new evidence, counselor, but be forewarned that if we feel that it is not of substance, that you will be stopped in mid-sentence."

"Thank you Madam Chief Justice. I will continue."

Now, with posture that suggested a new confidence, Davida furthered her cause, "If your Honors would allow me to go back into American History, in 1872 Horace Greeley, the Liberal Republican Party's candidate for president, received the majority of votes in several states, enough so that he was able to receive 66 Electoral College votes. His untimely death on November 29th of that year, a few weeks previous to the vote of the electors, left the Congress with a problem that had not been seen before and hasn't seen since, at least not until James Augustus Faulkner passed away last month.

"As many of you are aware, the official reading of the electors takes place before a joint session of Congress. The 1873 joint session allowed 63 of the 66 voters for Greeley to vote for other candidates. But it is the plight of the other three voters that I suggest is of foremost importance to this Court, to my client, and to the electors all across this fine nation. You see, your Honors, the three voters, all from the state of Georgia, unlike their fellow electors, chose not to switch their votes to other candidates, but rather chose to remain loyal to the deceased. And so they voted for Greeley, despite the fact that he had been buried weeks before. In the joint session, upon the reading of Georgia's vote, there was an objection made by Representative Ebenezer Hoar of Massachusetts and the members of the Senate were asked to leave the House chamber, so debate could follow.[i] The Official United States Congressional Record shows the result of that debate, the Georgian votes were disallowed because, and I quote,

> That the votes reported by the Tellers as having been cast by electors of the State of Georgia for Horace Greeley, of New York, cannot lawfully be counted, for the reason that said Horace Greeley, for whom they appear to have been cast, was dead at the time said electors assembled and cast their votes, and so not a person within the meaning of the Constitution, this being a historic fact, of which the two houses may properly take notice.[ii]

As a completely hushed courtroom awaited her next words, Davida confidently offered, "Your Honors, the votes for Greeley were disallowed because at the time of the Electoral College vote, he was dead, disqualifying him from receiving votes. Now, if we push that idea ahead 147 years, to our present election, that would bring us to the same scenario, only with James Augustus Faulkner being the person in question.

"Thus, with this precedent, I respectfully submit that any votes cast for James Augustus Faulkner shall, too, fall victim to his not being viewed as a quote, 'qualified person' by the House of Representatives and thus the votes will not be allowed. I strongly suggest that if you allow the previous ruling of this case to stand, then, just as their counterparts did in 1873, the members of the House of Representatives of 2021 will void the votes of electors, this time, the votes being those of Mr. Morgan and his fellow electors—meaning, in the end, that the great state of Washington will have all of its votes disqualified just like those votes from 1873, and thus, our state will have no say in the election of the president. This, Your Honors, would create a situation in which nearly three million voters of our fine state will have their voices silenced, disenfranchising their votes. Is that logical and foreseeable result in the best interest of the people of the state of Washington? If this honorable court sides with the state in such matters as law REW 29A.56.340 suggests, then, are you not setting up a scenario that would result in the votes for James Augustus Faulkner being considered as dead as is he? Only you, your Honors, can prevent this miscarriage of justice from occurring. Please side with Bill Morgan, his fellow electors and the voters of the great state of Washington. Let the electors vote their minds, and not be required to throw away their votes, as well as the votes of the people of Washington.

"Thank you, Your Honors."

As she prepared to sit down, she glanced at Hertz, winking at him. Hertz looked as if he had either been hit by a freight train or been blind-sided by a Charles Barkley pick. For several minutes the once-confident solicitor spoke to the justices, but it appeared that, by their questions for him, on this particular day, his efforts were going to allow him to receive a silver medal, with Davida winning the gold.

"I want to thank each team for their legal arguments," announced Chief Justice Nuriddin. "Our ruling will be announced in a few days. We stand adjourned."

As a much-relieved Davida and her team left the courtroom they discussed the events that had just transpired, confident that they had been successful in overturning the previous decision. Meanwhile, Bob Hertz's team was hearing a different message, as he told them, "Don't wait for the ruling; start preparing for the paperwork for the state to seek certiorari in order to get the case to the Supreme Court of the United States."

---

i. Steve Davenport, Reference Librarian/American History Specialist, Main Reading Room, Humanities & Social Sciences Division, Library of Congress. Email to author with attachment of 1872 Congressional Record showing the debate over votes.

ii. Ibid.

Chapter 29

The Dinner

Sylvia's Restaurant
328 Malcolm X Blvd
Harlem
Thursday, December 3, 2020
6:25 P.M.

For the tenth time Dominique looked at her watch. "Where is he? He's never late for anything," she thought to herself. "And tonight of all nights!" As her waiter, Alejandro, walked toward her for the fourth time, she shook her head, indicating that she still hadn't heard from Tyson. "I'm starting to get worried about him. He's always on time," she told the expressionless waiter.

"Would you like to have some more water?"

Just as she was about to answer the question, she saw Tyson hurrying toward her. "I'm sorry that I was late. The meeting went a few extra minutes, and I had to make some arrangements."

"You know, Tyson," an angered Dominique said, "Sometimes I think that I'm an afterthought to you—school, cases, philanthropy, and television appearances. You have so many things going. I always understand. But tonight I wanted an evening just for us.

"It's a special night for us. I asked you to pick a restaurant near the Apollo, and I would get the tickets for the new play about Stax Records and Isaac Hayes. It's a special night, Tyson, and as always, it seems to mean more to me than it does to you. Six o'clock, you're half an hour late. You couldn't call?"

"No, my phone is dead. I couldn't call."

"Tyson, no one else had a phone? Do you even know why this is a special evening for us?"

"Dominique, first of all, I didn't realize how late it was. And I was late because I was making some final arrangements. And, yes, I know that it is a special night for us—that's what the arrangements were for."

"Tyson, what are you talking about?"

"Can I borrow your phone for a second?"

"I don't believe it, we're having an important conversation and you have to call the office?"

"Please, just let me borrow it for just a second."

"Here," she said indignantly. "Take it."

Reaching for her iPhone, he took it and pressed seven numbers, listened for a person to answer and then said, "Now!"

Hanging up the phone, he handed it back to a now-puzzled Dominique, telling her to look at the door. A moment later, three men and two women entered the dining room, all dressed in tuxedos. Concentrating intently upon the people, Dominique failed to notice the cart that was behind them that had upon it four violins and a cello.

As the group gathered around the couple's table, each reached for his or her instrument. Just then, Alejandro walked over to the table carrying a wireless microphone. His announcement rang throughout the entire room: "Ladies and gentlemen, may I interrupt your dinner for a moment? Thank you. I want to introduce the restaurant's manager, the best boss in the world, Mr. Lamar McCormick."

Taking the microphone, the smiling manager proudly said, "Ladies and gentlemen, I am honored to announce that seated here at table 17 are Ms. Dominique Dalton and Professor Tyson Joseph. Mr. Joseph has been a friend of mine and a friend to this restaurant for more than ten years. My wife Lucy is walking out with something special for Ms. Dalton."

At that moment Mrs. McCormick brought out a beautiful bouquet of twenty-four red and white roses, which she cheerfully handed to Dominique, the latter giving Tyson a "I-can't-believe-you-did-this-and-I'm-so-so-very-sorry-I-doubted-you" look. As Dominique took time to smell the flowers, Lamar continued, "Dominique, it has come to our attention that your favorite singer is Lionel Richie."

With those words the violinists put their instruments to their chins, while the cellist sat in a nearby chair, her bow drawn. Suddenly, they started to play the opening notes to one of Dominique's favorite songs, when Lamar said, "We have a special artist to sing the lyrics of this song, so ladies and gentlemen please look at the door to the lobby."

All heads, including Dominique's, turned toward the door wondering who the guest singer would be, and no one saw Lamar hand the microphone to Tyson. As the professor rose from his seat, he began singing the opening verse of "Endless Love." As he finished the last line of the first verse, in his beautiful voice, he said, "Honey, I think I did a good job, but you deserve the very best. So, ladies and gentlemen, here to sing the rest of the song is the one and only Lionel Richie."

As Lionel entered the dining area, he was met with a standing ovation, one he acknowledged with feverous waves. Walking over to the couple's table he gave Tyson a high five and a hug and then gently kissed Dominique's hand. Dominique, now crying, said, "You got me good. You got me real good."

Tyson looked at the crowd and announced, "Please look under your chairs. The words to one of Ms. Dalton's favorite songs are taped there. Please help the three of us sing Dominique's favorite song, 'You Are the Sun, You Are the Rain.'"

The string section introduced the song, and Lionel himself led the first verse, others, including the kitchen crew and all of the waiters, joining in along the way to finish the second and third verses of the Richie hit. Tyson turned to Dominique and said, "Yes, as you can see, I remembered that today is the five-month anniversary of our first date."

"You are too much. You couldn't do anything to top this. I love you so much."

Just then, reaching into his side jacket pocket, he pulled out a small black box. As he opened it, he stood up and then went down to one knee, showing Dominique the six-carat, pear-shape diamond ring that was inside. Pulling the ring from its velvet surroundings, he reached for her left hand, which she eagerly extended toward him. As he placed the ring upon her finger he reached for the microphone and asked, "Dominique, this may seem premature, as we have only been together for five months. But these have been the best five months of my life. I cannot imagine life without you, and I want to live the rest of my life as your husband. Please marry me."

With tears streaming down her face, Dominique asked for the microphone. "Tyson, first of all, thank you for the very special evening that you have put together. Mr. Richie, I don't know how he got you here, but thank you for being part of one of the most special nights that I have ever had. Tyson, you are forgiven for being late—at least, this time. You are a special man. By the way, you used the term 'premature' and let me tell you and everyone else in this room, that that is not a word that I have ever associated with you."

Hearing that, their fellow diners, having had a huge laugh, quickly quieted as Dominique signaled for silence and continued. "Tyson, seriously, you are the most romantic man that I know. I want to say yes to you, but I want to do it my way."

A perplexed hush fell upon the patrons as they watched Dominique stand up and walk over to Lionel, whispering in his ear. In turn, the singer walked over to the cellist, telling her to gather her fellow string members together, leading them to nod their heads feverishly. Then, on the count of three, they started playing another song, and Dominique stood, and with less-than-perfect timing and pitch, she began to sing, "My Love," another one of her favorites by Richie.

After the first few lines, she handed the microphone to Lionel who, upon completing the song, hugged the tearful Dominique.

As Tyson stood up to kiss her, with the crowd clapping enthusiastically, the smiling Dominique said, "Tyson, of course I will marry you."

Her new fiancé joined her on the microphone, Lionel sitting and applauding with every note.

As the song finished, an enthusiastic Tyson told the crowd, "Dominique and I want to thank the McCormicks and all of their staff for hosting this affair tonight. We want to thank Akina Matsui and her string section. And, of course, thank you, Lionel; you are the best, my brother. As for all of the rest of you, we want to thank everyone here for being with us tonight, on our special evening, and for playing the important role of our backup singers." A tremendous laugh was heard, followed by a loud round of applause. "Please continue with your meals—they're on us tonight." The announcement created the loudest applause of the evening.

They thanked the string section, and Tyson handed each an envelope that contained five one hundred dollar bills. The McCormicks were next, the hugs given to each indicative of the high level of appreciation that the couple had for their efforts.

As Lionel left, he kissed Dominique and asked if he could sing at their yet-to-be-scheduled wedding.

"Are you out of your mind? Of course you can," was her energized answer. "We'll try to book it around your schedule. Thank you so much for being here with us. You made a special evening even better."

After everything had calmed down, Dominique gazed at her ring and then asked, "You are so amazing. Tyson, how did you pull this off? And how come you didn't hand Lionel an envelope?"

"Dominique, it was easy. I planned it with love. Besides, do you remember ten years ago, the restaurant was sued for a million dollars by a couple who claimed to slip on water near the kitchen?"

"Vaguely."

"Well, I represented the restaurant and I proved that the couple, Earl and Delores Zelnick, had pulled off the same trick in Toronto, Paris, Zurich, and Tokyo, settling each time for about the equivalent of $550,000. So, Lamar has forever been grateful to me for that. So when you suggested to me to pick a restaurant in Harlem, of course, I picked this one.

"As for Lionel, I hope you didn't mind. He's a client slash friend. He happened to be in town and told me that he'd love to help out. He did it for free and next time I do some work for him, it'll be pro bono."

"Mind? You are too much, you really are. But thank you, honey. I have to call Desiree to tell her about tonight."

"Oh, honey, just wait until we finish eating; we have to hurry to catch the show."

Agreeing, Dominique rushed through her meal, suggesting that they skip dessert and coffee. After asking for the bill, Tyson walked over to the bar to settle the tab. But Lamar intervened, "Your money is no good in this restaurant. Please consider this our gift to the happy couple. No argument, either. What is done is done. It's already been paid. Besides, for all that you've done for us—let's consider ourselves even—you saved me many times the combined amount of these dinners for all of tonight's customers."

"Thank you. What about the staff—can we leave the tip at least?"

"Didn't you hear the part about your money is no good in here? They will be taken care of, although I am sure that they would all say that they'd do it for free."

"Call me the next time—"

"No need to finish. I will. Take care of yourselves and, Dominique, if you need help keeping this guy in line, just call."

"Oh, believe me, I will."

The couple walked out the door and a few minutes later were a block away from the Apollo. As they were about to cross the street, the hand-holding couple stood in the crowd that was waiting for the light to turn. As the signal changed, others started walking, but Tyson noticed something strange and pulled the arm of the forward-advancing Dominique, keeping her from proceeding.

"What are you doing, honey? We'll be late."

"Look at that cab. He let the other cars go and he just sat there."

"So—"

"He's had a green light for almost twenty seconds, and he's in the middle lane. A polite cab driver in New York City? No, I don't get it."

Suddenly, with the horns of those behind him blaring, the car's engine revved up, tires screeching, and the yellow vehicle sped toward the crowd, dozens jumping out of the way. Making a sharp turn onto 125th Street, the rapidly-accelerating taxi reaching a speed of about 50 miles per hour, quickly turned into the spillover crowd that was awaiting entry into the musical, hitting dozens of unsuspecting theatre goers. Then, before most of the onlookers could figure out what had just happened, the car exploded, its deadly packaged bomb blowing the car apart, spitting its life-ending shrapnel throughout the hundreds who, by chance, found themselves in harm's way.

The blast threw Dominique and Tyson off their feet, the shattered glass from the storefronts luckily missing each of them by inches, while hundreds of others were not as fortunate.

"Dominique, are you okay? Are you okay?" a near-panicked Tyson cried out. His speechless fiancée had trouble hearing him, since the boom of sound made her momentarily deaf. Tyson, speaking loudly told her, "Stay here. It looks safe. I want to see what happened."

As the sounds of approaching rescue vehicles could be heard in the distance, Tyson slowly raised his head, the setting eerily similar to the famed scene of gathered Confederate bodies in the Atlanta rail yard from *Gone with the Wind.*

"Oh, my God! Oh my God," was all that Tyson could say. "They're dead. Hundreds of them." Slowly he was able to stand, his legs still wobbly, the falling facades making him realize that their location was not as safe as he had first imagined. "Dominique, get up. Get up, we have to move," he cried. But Dominique lay there motionless. He strained to pick her up. While evading bodies and debris, he was able to slowly walk across the street and into the intersection, an area that had been sought out by others. As dozens of bewildered onlookers sat in shock, many having their wounds attended to, a groggy Dominique was able to gain full consciousness, asking Tyson what had happened.

"A car bomb. The bastard deliberately drove into the crowd. I think there are hundreds dead. There are bodies everywhere. I knew it. I freaking knew the 'N' stood for New York City. Now it's happened here in Harlem. Someone has to do something about this crap."

Several blocks away Kingsley had heard the explosion and tried to call the professor's phone, not knowing that the phone was dead, like hundreds of people around it. Earlier that evening he had driven Dominique into the city and was supposed to take the couple back to Westchester after the play. Not hearing from his boss, he chose to go on foot, looking for the couple. With each block bringing more and more carnage into view, unsuspectingly, Kingsley was able to make his way to within several feet of the couple.

Tyson, standing to rip his shirt sleeve to help stop Dominique's bleeding leg, saw a familiar face, calling to him, "Kingsley! Kingsley! We're over here."

Despite the noise from the sirens and the screams and moans that surrounded him, somehow Kingsley was able to recognize Tyson's voice. "Boss, are you two okay? What the hell happened here?"

Explaining what he had seen and what he had concluded, Tyson asked Kingsley if he could help him carry Dominique. The two men were able to get her on her feet, she, all the time, pleading with them to let her walk. Slowly the trio walked the ten blocks to where the car had been parked. Able to get out of the garage, Kingsley chose to drive east, avoiding the understandingly congested Westside Highway.

Some four hours later, in Mount Kisco, the couple watched as Leah Manders reported, "At the latest count there are three hundred thirty-eight confirmed dead, thousands more injured, all believed to be the work of a lone assailant who was armed with a yellow cab, supposedly, but not confirmed to be, filled to the brim with explosives.

"So many people were out and about on a beautiful December night in New York City, temperatures hovering around fifty degrees. Mayor John Brathcher of New York commented, 'The city is in shock, but the investigation of the crime has begun and those, besides the dead driver, that were responsible, would be hunted down and captured.'"

Both Dominique and Tyson struggled to hear the broadcast, as there was still a ringing in their ears. So, after turning up the volume, they heard Leah say, "Senator Carlton Byrd of New York called the action, and I quote, 'Gutless, senseless, and beneath the level of acceptability expected from decent humans,' end quote."

"Details are still sketchy, but WGDC is reporting three hundred thirty-eight confirmed dead in New York City tonight as a yellow cab has exploded on 125th Street in front of the Apollo Theatre, which was packed with people who were about to see the new musical *Stax*."

Suddenly Tyson stared at the screen. There in the background, just before the explosion, he saw the two of them on the corner.

"There we are," pointed out Tyson.

"Oh, my God, that is us. We were very close to the cab."

"Yeah, a few yards over and we probably would have been killed."

"Turn it up, honey."

As the volume increased Manders said, "The president has called in Homeland Security to aid in the investigation, and I am sure that they will investigate other videos from the many cameras that are in the area. There certainly will be more information available and we will provide it to you as soon as it's made public."

Looking at Dominique, who was falling asleep in his arms, Tyson was thankful that they had been fortunate enough to have been able to escape most of the evening's mayhem. He was saddened to hear the estimates about those who had died and were injured. But he was relieved that they, themselves, had been seconds away from being among them.

Chapter 30

The Next One

The White House
Washington, D. C.
Friday, December 4, 2020
9:08 A.M.

The president's executive assistant, Darlene Flowers, walked into his office and quietly announced, "Mr. President, while you were meeting with Mr. Furry and the rest of the committee, you've had several calls. In order, they're from the mayors of Orlando, Oklahoma City, Ocala, Odessa, Omaha, and Oswego, New York."

"Oswego, New York?"

"Yes, Sir. He's concerned too—New York State's been hit more than once. Then you had calls from the governors of Texas, California and Florida. Governor Martinez wants to know how you are going to handle the news about New York.

"And, Mr. President, please don't forget that prior to the meeting you had received calls from New York City's mayor and from the governor of New York."

"Okay, get me the last two on a conference call. I have to deal with them first."

Moments later, there was a call from Darlene, "Mr. President, the governor and mayor are ready on Line 1."

"Thank you. Gentlemen, I won't say good morning, 'cause I know that it's not. What do you have for us?"

Mayor Brathcher in a somber voice said, "It's bad, Mr. President. Really bad! The level of destruction is beyond belief. The death total is up toward four hundred, and the hospitals are full of individuals who are missing limbs. The persons responsible for this knew what the hell they were doing."

"Mr. Mayor, I just met with Director Furry. The FBI is examining what's left of the store cameras and should have some answers shortly. Is there any truth to the idea that the real driver of the cab was found dead somewhere in Queens?"

"Yes, the person who was the cab's legal driver had picked up a person at JFK. The cabbie's body was found near Citi Field. He had been shot in the back of the head."

"Okay, the FBI is looking at the videos from the airport. Perhaps we can see if we can see the person getting into the cab."

The governor added, "Thank you for the help, Mr. President. Just having the national presence there has eased the situation to a degree. And your speech this morning offering funds for businesses and individuals was reassuring to the public. But, Sir, it's a mess. A real mess."

"I know, Governor Berenberg. I promise you that we will get the people who are responsible for all of this."

The three politicians spoke for another six or seven minutes before Hathaway told them that he had to speak to Director Furry again. "Chip, what's going on?"

"Mr. President, you aren't going to believe this, but Oakland has been hit by an attack."

"What the hell is going on? When?"

"Ten minutes ago."

"What happened?"

"At rush hour, a Cessna Skyhawk, flying from west to east, flew over the Yerba Buena Tunnel and then crashed into the Oakland neighborhood of North Oakland."

"Why there?"

"I don't know, but I have someone looking into it. Maybe because it's the black section of town. Anyway, he must have been carrying explosives. Untold damage. The fire ball was incredible."

"Casualties?"

"Countless, at this point.

"How do we know that it wasn't just an accident?"

"Mr. President, he dropped leaflets prior to the crash."

"Leaflets? What did they say?"

"Death to the last panthers."

"What? The last panthers? It doesn't make any freaking sense."

After a moment's pause he exclaimed, "Wait, I got it. Northern Oakland was the original home of the Black Panther Party. Clearly this is keeping with the theme of hitting black areas."

"Sir, then written vertically were the words 'Succumb America Now', with each letter having the name of the city that was attacked. And, Sir, the 'O' in Oakland had a bull's eye, while next to the 'W' the words that were written were 'Where do you think.' I think it's going to be D.C."

A glum President said, "Interesting thought. We'll talk about it."

"The city's like a fortress, no way to get explosives in here. We'll beef up security some more, sir. Meanwhile, we've had two major incidents in two days."

"I don't need a freaking scorecard. I can see what the hell is going on. Get me some answers—where the hell did he take off from."

"Not sure yet; only know that he buzzed the Bay Bridge before his attack."

"Well, get back to me when you have some freaking answers!"

President Hathaway stood up and walked to the mirror, looking sadly at himself and said, "I need some help here, Lord. Please, Lord, help us, I beg you."

CHAPTER 31

The Three Southern Gentlemen

The White House
Sunday, December 6, 2020
9:49 A.M.

Elgin Hathaway, sitting in the Oval Office, was aware that the electors would be voting soon and that there was a remote chance that come January 20, 2021, he'd find himself behind the Resolute desk again. After all, the Supreme Court had freed the electors to vote for whomever they wanted, although the likelihood was that Faulkner's votes would be cast for Vice President-elect Maria Martinez. He figured that he would have about a month to put forth an agenda, one that would represent his short tenure in office.

Of course one of the items that had to be considered was his conversation with Professor Tyson Joseph. Should he as the president react to the facts that his former teammate had reported? They were true, he knew, because the papers from the Wilson Administration, which were now in his possession, authenticated them. Should he ignore them like so many of his predecessors had done, or should he go public with them?

He realized that if the latter were to be chosen, all hell would break out in our nation. After the recent death of Faulkner and what was certain to be a controversial Electoral College vote, could the nation be ready for another dramatic issue such as the one that Tyson had placed upon his shoulders?

In his mind Hathaway constantly heard the voice of his late father, the lawyer, who had repeatedly told him, "The truth is the truth, no matter how old it might be." The president had remembered those words and had used them often to guide him through life. Hathaway's decision, in part, might be influenced by the spirit of his late father.

A buzz from Darlene interrupted Hathaway's focus, a message reminding him that the three guests scheduled for 10:00 had been waiting for him. Hathaway realized that it was now 10:07 and that he had a busy day scheduled.

The president was looking forward to the meeting, since with all of the issues that had been swirling around the White House, a meeting with three religious figures from the South might be able to provide him with some heavenly guidance.

The three men entered the room. The first to shake Hathaway's hand was the tallest of the group, Reverend Reginald T. Emerson from Savannah, Georgia. He might have been the only person born in Savannah after 1865 who shared a middle name with the infamous General William Tecumseh Sherman. A famed orator, Emerson was instantly recognizable by his long, flowing, slicked back, white hair and short-cropped white beard. Impeccably dressed, he was one of the most respected religious figures in the nation.

"Pleased to meet you, Mr. President."

"The pleasure is mine, Reverend."

Walking two feet behind him was Hattiesburg, Mississippi, native Reverend Antonio Tillman, who wore a three-piece, dark grey suit, with a lavender shirt and black tie. He, like Emerson, was a highly respected speaker, whose addresses from the 14th Avenue Baptist Church were watched by millions each Sunday. As he shook hands with the president, Hathaway thought Tillman's handshake the strongest that he had ever experienced.

"Thank you for having us, Mr. President."

The last person to enter the room was Reverend Beauregard Ivy of Charleston, South Carolina. The shortest of the group, he was the least-well known nationally. However, at his Hope Methodist Church he was a legend; people would often travel hundreds of miles to hear his sermons. His appearance was just the opposite of that of Reverend Emerson, as Ivy had a bald head and was beardless.

"I am honored to have the three of you here," said the president.

Hathaway continued, "Thank you for coming. Let me first say that it is my pleasure to have the three of you here. Hopefully your arrival will usher in a calming period in our city. Over the last few months, this has been a wild place."

"Mr. President, I know our time with you is short, so, if you don't mind, we will get right to our point," said a smiling Reverend Ivy. "Mr. President, we are here for three reasons. First, we want to welcome you to the White House and to the presidency. Second, we want to introduce you to G.O.D. And finally, we want to give you the names of the three people responsible for the carnage across the nation."

Before the president could respond, Reverend Emerson interrupted, "Yes, welcome to the office. We have been fans of yours for some time. As my friend Reverend Ivy has suggested, we are here to tell you about G.O.D."

An amused Hathaway said, "I am well aware of God. I went to church when I lived in White Plains, New York. And I was taught at home too."

"I beg your pardon, Mr. President," said Emerson with a smile, "The G.O.D. of which we speak stands for Guardians of Dixie, an organization that is responsible for the violence and death."

"The Guardians of Dixie? I never heard of them!"

"It's a small Southern-based group, not many of them, perhaps a few dozen."

"What the hell, excuse me, what the heck, do they want?"

"Simple, to preserve the Southern way of life."

"By killing innocent people with car bombs?"

"In their minds they're doing what they think is necessary to preserve their ideals from the past."

"Most northerners don't know anything about them," replied Tillman. "But the files of the FBI are filled with their actions. There are just no perpetrators attached to the crimes. Fact is, many crimes are related—they're done by G.O.D. to protect the South, but only recently have they acknowledged their own participation in these acts."

Emerson told the president, "I am positive that there is no mention of G.O.D. in the files of any of the government agencies. It has been a secret of the South. From what we have recently learned, when some people in the South say 'It's G.O.D.'s Way,' their meaning is one that no northerner could understand."

"So, please, enlighten me, but before you do, how could you three men support an organization that perpetrates violence and death?"

Emerson, with a raised voice quickly answered, "Sir, under no circumstances do we condone the views of this group. We have learned about the organization only within the last two weeks. We contacted each other, and we each researched the dealings of G.O.D., um, that would be the organization, in our areas. We compared our findings, and that's why we are here."

"Besides, Mr. President, you couldn't understand," said Ivy. "Your roots suggest a heritage that in the 1860s and 1960s had events that enhanced your people. On the other side of the coin is the Southern heritage, one that during those same periods of time had the Southern lifestyle stripped of some of its dignity."

"You're saying that there was dignity in owning other human beings or in later years keeping other human beings from obtaining the same rights that others in our nation often took for granted? Where's the dignity in that?"

Tillman interrupted, "We're not saying that. But many of our ancestors were. They overtly fought for that type of life in the Civil War, and many have covertly fought for that type of life ever since. That is what G.O.D. is all about."

Reverend Ivy interrupted, "We have learned that since 2008 there has been a new leadership group, one with a more militant outlook, who feared that the nation had lost its way. You know, electing Obama didn't sit well with those folks. Then you were elected vice president, and even before the two of you were in office, there had been two black Secretaries of State—Powell and Rice. Then Obama had Holder as Attorney General, and you could see how some of their members became worried about what they called 'The Blackening of America.' They became convinced that the interests of the South were being ignored. There were random acts during the Obama years, as most of the group's efforts were directed into the political arena; you know, funding candidates and getting some members of Congress to block his actions. But in 2016, when the trend seemed to indicate that a black man would continue to hold at least one of the two top offices in the nation, the new leadership of G.O.D. called for more action. However, some of the members have decided to take matters into their own hands—to a level that most of the group dared not consider."

"You're saying that G.O.D. is responsible for the murders," said the president.

Emerson followed with, "Yes, in part. A few of its radical members are."

"Who are they?"

"In a moment, Mr. President. In a moment," said Emerson. "It seems that you have been investigating some ideas that have their roots from the nineteenth century. There is a person on your staff who has given this information to G.O.D., and the organization is fearful that you'll publicize it. Clearly, that information would bring harm to the South."

"For God's sake, they're killing innocent people. Who are they?"

Taking a piece of paper out of his jacket pocket, he handed Hathaway the names of three men.

"How did you come across these names?"

Ivy said, "The wife of one is a member of Hope Methodist. She told me that her husband is the owner of a large landscaping company who has been using phony invoices to supply his fellow criminals with the materials that they need to make bombs. After finding out and confronting him, she could not live with him, nor could she live with herself if she didn't tell someone. So she told me."

"Why you and not the police?"

"She was confused and needed guidance. Once she told me the story, I sought an audience with you. I didn't trust some of the police down there with this information, fearful that I might be telling ears that were connected to the hands behind some of the crimes. She told me about the other two men, and I knew that they were in the cities of Reverends Emerson and Tillman. Besides, I want you to get credit for this. Get these three men and start to chisel away at the foundation of G.O.D. You and your administration will get the credit for it."

"Thank you, but I really don't care about the credit—I just want to see these crimes come to an end."

"Capture these men and the crimes will end."

Chapter 32

The Chosen One

The White House
Monday, December 7, 2020
8:04 A.M.

Anyone who knew Robert Vasquez would speak highly of him; he had led a distinguished life. The former special ops agent had been raised in a poor section of Newark, New Jersey, the third child of Maritza Vasquez, who alone had raised him and his two sisters, Nicole and Yulitza. A good student in school before choosing to enter the Marines, he had become a standout basketball player at the hometown St. Benedict's Prep School. He quickly rose through the ranks, a tribute to his dedication and out-standing service in Afghanistan. Upon his retirement from the service, he became trained as a United States Secret Service Agent, eventually landing a position at the White House. After five distinguished years of service there, he was picked by the Faulkner administration to replace the retiring Tevin Johnson as lead agent for the protection of the president. Upon Faulkner's resignation, Vasquez was assigned as the lead agent to protect President Hathaway.

Before Faulkner's death, Vasquez had gained a tremendous amount of respect for Hathaway, as the two had often spent time together. He was pleased to see Faulkner leave the White House, not fond of the president's late nights and extramarital affairs. Indeed, he respected the wholesomeness that Hathaway brought to the White House. Their mutual respect and fondness for each other allowed Vasquez to speak to the new president in a manner that he would never have been able to address the now-deceased Faulkner.

"Mr. President," said a concerned Vasquez, ""Director Furry will be here soon."

"Good, we have many things to go over."

Just then, there was a knock on the door and FBI Director Chip Furry walked in. "Mr. President, I ran those three names into the system, and they all had priors. In fact, they've all done hard time in the past. We checked phone records, and they've been in contact with each other; I guess they didn't think that we'd be on to them. We can apprehend them any time that you want, but I'm fearful that none of them will go down without a fight."

The president wasn't interested in hearing about their welfare, "I want these three men before tonight—do whatever you have to do. Give them the same chance for survival that they gave to their victims—none at all. Bring them in alive if you can, but don't take any chances. Get it done, or heads are going to roll around here."

Elmer Valentine's landscaping business was Charleston, South Carolina's largest, and was an excellent cover for a person who wanted to use fertilizer for bombs, a purpose for which, for more than three years, Valentine had used it. On this particular Tuesday afternoon, at about 3:00, he was in his office doing some paperwork. He hadn't heard the vehicles pull up and was caught by surprise when several FBI and ATF agents, all brandishing automatic weapons, burst into his office. "Elmer Valentine, you are under arrest. You have the right to remain silent and anything you say may be used against you . . . ."

At the same moment, on Interstate 95, in the southbound lanes near Fayetteville, North Carolina, those same words were being spoken to Bobby Hall, the owner of a trucking business, who had had his eighteen-wheeler pulled over by ATF agents. Likewise, in Opelousas, Louisiana, Hank Edmonds was hearing the same exact sentences, as agents had raided his gun shop.

In fact, dozens of others across several Southern states had been rounded up and taken into custody, all allegedly having been part of the network of renegade members of G.O.D. who had taken it upon themselves to terrorize the nation.

By 9:15 that night President Hathaway was able to speak to the nation.

"My fellow Americans, I am addressing you tonight to announce that FBI and ATF agents have arrested thirty-six individuals for their alleged connection to the string of bombings that has caused the deaths and injuries of far too many Americans. The men and women will be facing various charges, ranging from illegal possession of weapons to murder.

"We are certain that we have taken a huge bite out of the network of criminals who have chosen to kill innocent Americans, crippling the organization that they have notoriously represented. During the next few days more details will be available to you. I want to thank the brave agents of these two law enforcement agencies, the officers of state and local agencies, plus the dozens of citizens who helped us put an end to this reign of terror. Good night and again, thank you to all who were responsible for these arrests."

One hour later Director Chip Furry, Secretary of Homeland Security Kitty Niles, and CIA Director Dennis Peluso were in the Oval Office, being told by Hathaway to investigate G.O.D. and all aspects of it, including its possible foreign ties. He congratulated Furry for his fine effort and asked all of the directors to get back to him the next day to provide him with updates.

The next morning, as Hathaway looked at the three people seated around him, he knew that he was in good company. To his immediate right was Secretary of State Virginia Loving, among the most highly respected people in the nation's capital. Her background was outstanding: Stanford Law School and the creation of one of the largest law firms in the nation—Loving, Myers, and Schwartz of Los Angeles. Her ties to Washington included service to four prior administrations, all with distinction.

To Loving's right was seated Speaker of the House Pierce Allen, from Kansas. Like Loving, the Speaker's credentials were impeccable, having been a decorated Vietnam War veteran.

The final person at the table was Senator Benjamin Hayes of Virginia, a man, who in private, was referred to by the president as "The Prick from Portsmouth" and was the President pro tempore of the Senate. Voted by his colleagues as "the most powerful man in Washington," he had a reputation for disliking everyone. Often he was referred to as the "Anti-Lincoln," one who had malice toward all. Although he was disliked by many in the D.C. area, he was respected by almost everyone. It was said that items didn't get passed without the consent of Benjamin Hayes.

Hathaway started the meeting by thanking each of them for being on time for the hastily created meeting. After a discussion of the current political climate in D.C., the president asked for silence and said, "Folks, let me assure you that my next idea is being presented to you with a clear mind and after much consideration. With so much happening with the election, we have a politically charged electorate, one that has the capacity to do almost anything. I have worried about the safety of those of us in the political arena. The vibes are not good; there is discontentment everywhere. With the election results uncertain, I fear that the nation is worried about the condition and stability of the government. The FBI is worried about my safety and with no vice president, we face a potentially perilous situation. If something were to happen to me and with no apparent winner of the election in sight, well, I suggest that we make sure that everything is set up for the reading of the Electoral College votes a month from now."

His audience of three sat motionless, stunned to speechlessness. Of all of the possible topics that were up for discussion, not one of his distinguished guests would have figured that this would be discussed. As the silence became awkward, Senator Hayes found fault with the idea. "Well, Elgin, with all due respect, it seems a little early to worry about all of this. The system has worked well over the years—some two hundred of them—and with Pierce and I there as leaders, we'll be fine. Don't worry about our end of things. We have the Congress well in hand. So you just worry about the things that are on your plate—we'll worry about ours. Okay, Elgin?"

The others listened silently, stunned by the senator's tone. Hathaway, who had expected some negative reaction from the senator, stood and said, "Senator Hayes, do you recall the first time that we met?"

A surprised Hayes looked quizzically at the president and said, "No, Elgin, I can't say that I do."

The president calmly said, "I didn't think you would. But I do, so let me remind you. It was January, many years ago. I was a first-term congressman, and it was my first day in the Capitol Building. I was lost inside that huge structure, and I needed to get to a meeting fairly quickly. Someone pointed out where I had to go, and I used my sprinter speed to try to get there on time.

"As I went around a corner, I bumped into you, knocking you over. After helping you regain your footing and helping you gather your papers, I apologized and then realized who you were. I said, 'Benjamin Hayes! Wow, you are an important person around here.' You coldly looked at me and then at my nametag and said, 'Hathaway, you will learn that in this building you refer to me as *Senator* Hayes. You are in my building, and you make sure you know your place around here.'"

Hayes sat silent, with a that-was-you look on his face. Before he could react, the president, walking in the direction of Hayes, pointed his finger at the senator's nose and said, "Now you're in *my* house, and your place around here is to call me Mr. President. Do you understand me?"

"Yes."

"Yes, what?" the president said with authority.

After a momentary pause, the Senator, unaccustomedly squirming in his seat and without making direct eye contact at the president softly uttered, "Yes, Mr. President."

The president looked around the table, at all of his silent guests and said, "Okay, now that we have all been properly introduced, perhaps we can now get down to the people's business."

He repeated his request for more security, looking for any potential snags to what he considered to be a perfect reading of the ballots.

"On January 6th of next year, we need someone in whom the people have confidence to stand in front of Congress and read the results of the votes by the electors. There is the potential for a great deal of confusion on that day, and we need a stabilizing force, one in whom the people have a high degree of confidence and trust. Pierce, as Speaker of the House, that person would be you. Are you prepared for all of the additional pressure of the day?"

"Mr. President, pressure is my middle name! I will be as ready as ready gets. If I'm re-elected Speaker I will serve you well."

"That's the point—I want you re-elected."

"It's been said that I should get the nod—so I'll be ready."

And who on Earth could question Allen's statement? He had had a pressure-packed life. Born and raised outside of Topeka, Kansas, the six-foot five-inch Pierce Allen quickly became a legend in the Sunflower State. In basketball seasons that later made many think of the movie *Hoosiers*, during his junior and senior years, he led undersized and underdog Alf Landon High School to State Championships each year.

Upon graduation he attended Wichita State University and turned the program around, twice leading them to a berth in the round of the NCAA Tournament's Elite 8.

Although much was expected of the team during his senior year, he made national headlines, stating that he was leaving school so that he could join the Marines to fight in Vietnam. Although the basketball community was highly disappointed, nearly every person in Kansas respected his decision to avenge the death of his older brother who had been killed in a Vietcong sniper attack.

During his tour of Vietnam, Allen rose to the rank of captain. He was a hand-to-hand combat specialist who gained the respect of the people in his command. He had it all going for him, but his fortunes turned on April 11, 1968, when the platoon of the twenty-five-year-old wandered into a small village in North Vietnam, where they met with fierce resistance from the enemy. As the Marines scrambled to retaliate, they took defense behind a series of nearby huts. Shooting at an enemy that had gathered to their northeast, the company seemed to be winning the heated exchange, but as Vietcong reinforcements gathered, the battle took a turn for the worse and at least a dozen Marines were killed. Suddenly three grenades landed in the area in which the Marines had been positioned. Allen grabbed two of the grenades and flung them back toward the enemy. Running twenty feet and dodging the enemy's rounds of fire, he reached for the third grenade just as it exploded, throwing his limp body some fifteen feet into the air. His mangled body landed with a thump, and the unconscious marine was dragged to safety by two others in his company.

His once magnificent body, now torn to shreds, was minus its left leg. He was bleeding profusely, his life in the hands of a first-year medic. Allen, who had saved the lives of twelve of his brethren, now needed someone to save his, forever to be thankful to Nathaniel Mannarino, the first-year medic who stopped the bleeding and was able to keep him alive until better, more complete medical care could be provided.

Returning home, and after a two-year rehabilitation, Allen returned to Wichita State and gained a prelaw degree, eventually becoming a lawyer. His reputation as a great lawyer was his springboard into politics. He easily won his district's race for Congress, spending many exciting terms in the House of Representatives.

The Chairman of the Finance Committee, Allen became a national favorite, liked by colleagues of both parties. People respected the man who championed the cause for the physically challenged, and he had become the most beloved person in Washington.

"Mr. President, I truly respect your question, but since I was sixteen years old, there hasn't been a day in my life without pressure. I am up to the task."

"Great, Pierce. We are fortunate to be in a position to have you lead us. So that being said, I don't have any concerns for the big day in January. I thank you all for coming."

Chapter 33

The Final Decision

United States Supreme Court
Washington, D.C.
Friday, December 11, 2020
10:00 A.M.

On Friday, December 4th, the Supreme Court of the State of Washington had overturned the decision of the Thurston County Superior Court, allowing Bill Morgan and his eleven co-electors the right to vote for a living person, absolving them of the requirements of having to vote for the deceased president.

Morgan's in-court hug of Davida had been met with her caution. "Prepare for a trip east. He is appealing this to the US Supreme Court, I'm sure."

On the following Monday Davida received the call, the papers followed shortly, stating that the United States Supreme Court had agreed to hear the arguments and that *Fitzgerald v Morgan* would be heard by a very interested Court on Thursday, December 10th, the expediency necessary because the electors were due to vote the following Monday, the 14th.

Again her staff put in late hours, and armed with their findings Davida, her partners, and the Morgans boarded a flight bound for the "other Washington." Although Bob Hertz had argued several cases before the highest court of the nation, this would only be the second time Davida had been in the building; the first time she was on a tour as a seventh grader. She was so thankful that four years earlier that her local bar association had sponsored a group admission to the Court—little did she envision that one day she'd be called before the justices.

By the time the case was to be heard, the national media had swarmed upon the nation's capital. Outside the courtroom were camped dozens of media outlets, including members of the national networks. This was no longer a state issue, as it had evolved to become one that affected electors in several of the states.

Despite countless hours of research into every known aspect of the 1872 election, Bob Hertz and his state staff had failed to uncover anything that could remotely counter the arguments presented by Davida Shepherd in Olympia. And so, when the smoke cleared and the night had turned into day, on Friday, December 11th, the nation heard the unanimous voices of the United States Supreme Court.

As Davida sat in the nation's highest court she wondered, "Did I really pull this off? Had the justices here taken the same interest in my statements as had their brethren in Olympia?"

She thought, too, about her late father and just how proud he would be of her. And then, when Chief Justice Owen S. Alfonso read the Court's decision, one could hear a pin drop.

Loudly clearing his throat, he read, "In the Case of *Fitzgerald v Morgan*, the Court had many facts to consider, of which, the most prominent is that the results of this case from the state of Washington have a bearing on our entire nation.

"Seldom in our nation's history has a state case had as many important national implications as has this one, as it serves to determine for whom the members of the Electoral College could vote. It is with these paramount implications in mind, and with a very hurried timetable of events before us, that we carefully scrutinized the case.

"When our Founding Fathers framed the Constitution, the basis of our government, unlike today, the majority of our citizens lacked what has come to be known as a formal education. Most were farmers who were separated by miles from the rest of society; even many of those who were city dwellers, lacked this so-called formal education. It was for that reason that the Fathers lacked trust in the ability of these citizens to be responsible enough to elect the person who would become the leader of the nation, the President of the United States. And so, a system was set up, allowing the people to vote for a group of knowledgeable people, who would, in turn, vote for the president; the birth of the electoral college. Whether right or wrong, the creation of this set of intermediaries put the responsibility of the election of the president solely on their broad shoulders, with no parameters set before them.

"Although over the years, the process has been refined, the original concept has endured; the electors have the interest of the people in mind, taking their interests to heart before rendering their Electoral College votes.

"In its wisdom, the Constitution has allowed each state to have its own set of procedures, which set up the qualifications for the selection of and the rules governing the behavior of those who become electors in their respective states."

At this point, as her stomach was knotting up, Davida did not know in which direction the Court was leaning.

The Chief Justice continued, "At the heart of this case is whether a state or a group of states, despite having the power to set up the qualifying standards of electors, has the power to determine how the electors shall vote.

"If one were to look at the election process in our nation, one would see that one or more candidates seek office, hopeful of receiving enough votes to secure a victory for the office of their choice. The people are free to vote for any of the qualified candidates who have had their names placed on a ballot, or in some cases, they may vote for those for whom names can be written in by the electorate. However, in no case, in regard to those who are qualified to receive votes, are there restrictions placed upon those who are qualified to vote. On the national, state and local levels, we as a society trust that those who qualify to vote can be trusted to vote their consciences—the only restrictions being their limitation of one vote and their responsibility to vote for qualified candidates.

"Does this concept lose out when one is an elector? In some states this Court sees evidence that it does, as restrictions are being placed upon electors, restrictions that are not in place for those who they represent. In 1952, in *Ray v Blair*, the Court ruled that these restrictions were fair, as they supported the views of the individual states. This Court, however, in light of the dangers brought forth by the unfortunate and unforeseen circumstances left to us by the death of President James Augustus Faulkner, cannot agree. Implicit in these laws is the requirement that the electors should be robotic, voting for the pledged candidate of their party, blind to circumstances that might arise between the time the people vote in November and the time that the electors are to vote in December. In the view of this Court, these laws turn a blind eye to the possibilities of scandal, mishandling of votes and, in this saddest of cases, the death of a candidate. Precedent has shown that our elected leaders are wise enough to overcome these potential obstacles, just as they did in 1873 when the House of Representatives disallowed the votes for presidential candidate Horace Greeley who had died, claiming that he no longer was a qualified candidate. It is with this precedent in mind that our Court's members have decided upon this issue."

Was Davida hearing what she thought she was hearing? Her inner voice said, "Finish, dammit. Finish. Don't drag this out—did we win?"

"Thus, this Court rules unanimously," continued Chief Justice Alfonso, "Nine to zero, that Washington State Law REW 29A.56.340 and all laws like it in all of the other states requiring electors to vote a certain way, are immediately null and void and that Mr. Morgan, the other electors of Washington State and electors all across the nation are *not* required to vote for the deceased candidate, but, in turn, are free to vote for any qualified person they shall see fit to choose."

Davida stood motionless. Was this a dream, or did she hear what she thought that she had heard? The elation on the faces of Bill and Erin made it clear that she hadn't been dreaming. Realizing that she had won, she used every inch of her sixty-one-inch frame to jump up and give each of the embracing couple a high five. She jumped up and down several times before suddenly remembering that she was in the Supreme Court.

Straightening her clothing, she quickly slicked back her hair and regained her composure. She walked across the aisle and shook the out-reached hand of Bob Hertz, congratulating him on his efforts. He returned the compliments, saying, "Davida, you were brilliant! Well done. What you have done will be discussed in law classes for years."

"Thank you, Bob. Coming from a person like you makes it even more rewarding to hear. You were great too. See you back home."

Davida shook his hand, turned and walked toward the very-excited Morgans outside the courtroom.

Waiting on the steps of the Court was a large contingent of cameras, microphones, and reporters. Bill was asked the first questions, all of which he handled like the veteran public speaker that he was. With each answer he gripped Erin's hand tighter and tighter, a sign of his excitement.

Then Davida took center stage. There were more than thirty reporters attempting to get questions answered, making Davida's head spin like that of an owl. Finally, after what seemed to be more than three dozen questions, Davida waved her hand, indicating that the question session was over for the day.

As the overjoyed group was about to get inside of their waiting limousine, Davida asked Bill and Erin to stand outside for a minute so that she could get a picture with them using the Supreme Court as a backdrop. After several pictures had been taken by her driver Louie, a reporter, Ayan Gelston, handed her an iPad that had the CNN website loaded. The headline made Davida burst into laughter. Above a picture of the victorious, smiling Shepherd shaking hands with the much-taller Hertz was printed in the headlines, "Davida Slays Goliath."

CHAPTER 34

The Bad Guys

FBI Headquarters
Washington, D. C.
Friday, December 11, 2020
4:15 P.M.

"The FBI Headquarters is the appropriate setting for me to make the following announcements," stated a serious-speaking President Elgin Hathaway. "For years, the men and women of this agency have served our nation with class and dignity, and at no time finer than they've done during the last few days, when they investigated and then arrested sixteen people from an organization named the Guardians of Dixie, the members of which were determined to carry out the destruction of American lives for their own selfish goals. Members of the organization, which has roots tracing back to the 1840s, were hell bent on wreaking havoc across parts of this nation, causing a path of destruction and panic on a scale previously unknown in America. Throughout their recent history, they have caused Americans in several of our cities to fear for the safety of their loved ones, schools, businesses, and homes.

"Director Chip Furry and his team of agents have carefully scoured the nation, turning clues into evidence against those who wished harm against Amcrica. The ongoing investigation has netted several key figures who wished to harm our people, individuals who are presently under arrest, many of whom have been charged with the murders of or with conspiracy to murder more than five hundred people. Others are pending charges and have been detained."

Pausing for a moment, the angered but under-control Hathaway continued, "Topping the list of the thirty-six detainees are Elmer Valentine of Charleston, South Carolina, a person with a long list of previous convictions, Hank Edmonds of Opelousas, Louisiana, and Bobby Hall of Fayetteville, North Carolina, each of whom is facing multiple charges. All of those arrested have had numerous convictions in the past, and we are certain that the charges against each will stand up. It is at this time that I will introduce Director Furry to provide further comment."

As the director stepped up to the microphone, the president listened, then took a few steps back and reflected upon Furry's comments. After the director spoke of specific charges and provided the names of the other detainees, the president resumed his comments, thanking all members of the agency for their support.

Answering questions for the next fifteen minutes, the president and the director provided the media with several of the details that they requested, although, due to the pending investigation, some of the details could not be released.

Among those in attendance was Leah Manders who, afterward, told her audience, "The gathering of all of these individuals is a fine showing for the Hathaway administration, one that could provide fodder for some additional consideration regarding the December 14th voting of the Electoral College. There are many in the media who are speculating that the original 270 votes that were to be declared for President Faulkner will be split between Vice President-elect Maria Martinez and President Hathaway. Just how those votes will be split, if, indeed, they are, won't be revealed until early January, but these arrests might be able to garner some additional considerations for the president, who, to this point, has not commented upon Monday's vote of the Electoral College."

As the camera zoomed in, she continued, "Although there is no way to know for sure, several in the media have suggested that the two Republicans might split the late president's Electoral College votes, resulting in a situation in which no candidate would receive a majority of those votes, causing the 2020 election to go to the House of Representatives. Time will tell, but in terms of possible Electoral College votes, today's announcements certainly don't hurt the president.

"This is tied in to the other big story coming out of the nation's capital today, as the United States Supreme Court upheld the decision reached by the Supreme Court of Washington State, allowing the electors across the nation to vote for anyone that they want, rather than being tied down to the results of the states' popular votes. If all of the 268 voters who are pledged to Governor Robert Ryan remain loyal, and if he were to receive two additional votes, then the governor would become the next president of the United States. Stay tuned.

"The question yet to be answered is what will become of the 270 votes thought to be originally gathered by the late president. Who will receive those votes?"

Staring into the camera for a brief minute she concluded with, "Our coverage of these two important stories will continue in a moment."

Chapter 35

The Conference

The New Sheraton Hotel
Mount Vernon, New York
Saturday, December 12, 2020
6:33 P.M.

Dominique walked to the podium, listening to the loud applause that greeted her from the four hundred fifty people in attendance.

"Ladies and gentlemen, I am honored to host the first event of this beautiful new hotel. I thank the management of the Sheraton of Mt. Vernon for allowing our conference to be its first scheduled event. And I want to thank all of you for being part of our evening entitled, *The Women's Vote—One Hundred Years Later.*

"Our meetings this afternoon were all very enlightening, and I want to thank our speakers for their insights that they presented. Can we give each of these women a collective round of applause? Imagine, each of them is a descendant of or is related to some of the legendary women in our nation's history. Today you were able to visit with women who have in their family trees such people as Abigail Adams, Maya Angelou, Clara Barton, Rachel Carson, Shirley Chisholm, Geraldine Ferraro, Dolores Huerta, Barbara Jordan, Lucretia Mott, Eleanor Roosevelt, Harriet Beecher Stowe, and Harriet Tubman. Each of their sixty-minute discussions brought new light to their famed family members and the specific period of time in which each lived, highlighting the contributions that were made by each of them. When my committee and I organized the speakers, I knew that we'd be presenting many excellent choices for you."

Dominique paused as the audience stood in appreciation of the speakers, and after the several moments of cheering finally subsided, Dominique was able to continue, "Speaking of choices, tonight is just two days removed from the day upon which the Electoral College will make its historic vote for president. As the electors vote in their state capitals, the future direction of our nation will be determined. But tonight I want to concentrate upon an election that took place one hundred years ago, on November 2, 1920. It was Election Day, but it was an Election Day like none that had preceded it, as it was the first time in our nation's history that women were allowed to vote in all of the states. Imagine the euphoria of that day, as millions of women cast their votes for the very first time.

"The result of the Nineteenth Amendment's requiring that women be allowed to vote nearly doubled the popular vote of the previous election in 1916. This was due to the power of the woman's vote, a power that has been growing ever since. In fact, since the election of 1960, women have been the majority of voters in each presidential election."

Another round of thunderous applause followed those words, and Dominique waved her hands, attempting to silence the crowd. Finally, she was able to say, "Women are not only a powerful force in the ballot booth, but they are also a powerful force receiving votes too. Since 1975, when Ella Grasso of Connecticut became our nation's first elected woman governor, we have had thirty-two women governors in this nation.[i] In 1938 Gladys Pyle was elected United States Senator from South Dakota, and since then we have had forty-one women elected to that high office.[ii] And, since November 8, 1916 when Jeannete Rankin first represented Montana, we have had nearly three hundred women serve in the House. [iii]

"Of course we cannot leave out the achievement of Sandra Day O'Connor who was the first woman on the United States Supreme Court, followed by Justices Ruth Bader Ginsburg, Sonia Sotomayor, and Elena Kagan. And finally, you may ask about the Executive Branch. Two days from now Maria Martinez may be elected as our first Latina president!"

Those words brought the loudest applause of the evening and for the next fifteen minutes Dominique dazzled her audience with her discussion about the role of women in US politics and government. Afterward, the standing ovation warmed her heart.

As she left the stage she waved to the supportive crowd and walked to the room that had been set up for the conference speakers. There she shared stories with all of the women, who, earlier, had shared their stories with those who had attended from across the nation. Two hours later, as she drove home, the smile hadn't left her face.

---

i. Wikipedia article: List of female governors in the United States. http://en.wikipedia.org/wiki/List_of_female_governorgovernors_in_the_United_States October 4, 2014

ii. Wikipedia article: Women in the United States Senate. http://en.wikipedia.org/wiki/Women_in_the_United_States_Senate October 4, 2014

iii. Wikipedia article: Women in the United States House of Representatives. http://en.wikipedia.org/wiki/Women_in_the_United_States_House_of_Representatives October 4, 2014

Chapter 36

The Electors Vote

Richmond, Virginia
Monday, December 14, 2020
10:59 A.M.

Leah Manders stood outside the Virginia State Capitol Building waiting for her cue. It was a very cold, snowy day in Richmond, and she wanted the network feed to start quickly so that she could get back inside the production truck for some steaming hot coffee and the warmth that it would provide.

Receiving her cue, Manders began, "Good morning everyone. At this moment in South America there is a solar eclipse occurring.[i] In ancient times, many of our ancestors thought of such events as the end of the world as they had previously known it. Today, here along the East Coast of the United States, we are viewing events that could signal the end of the election process that we had previously known.

"I am standing at Capitol Square here in Richmond, Virginia. The building that you see behind me is the beautiful State Capitol of the Old Dominion State, built in 1788. It is a cold morning, about twenty-three degrees, and you can see that I am dressed for it.

"It has been snowing for several hours, more to come tonight, probably heavy, with upwards of some six to eight inches predicted. Yet, the weather, as bad as it might become, is the second biggest story in town today."

Turning to look at the building behind her, with her breath visible to all who were watching, Leah continued, "We are here in front of the Capitol because in less than an hour, the thirteen Republican members of the Electoral College from Virginia will cast their votes for president. In fact, here in the Eastern Time Zone, at that same exact moment, twenty-four states plus the District of Columbia will have their electors vote for either Democratic Governor Robert Ryan of Indiana or, well, *that* is the question! For whom will the Republican electors cast their respective votes?

"That same question will be asked and answered, in part, later today, in the several states farther west. I say in part because, as most of you are aware, the votes are cast today but will not be revealed until the joint session of Congress meets on January 6, 2021. That's correct. Although the votes will be cast today, we will have to wait more than three weeks to find out the results. But under certain scenarios, even after a wait of three weeks, we still might not know who the winner will be."

Several people, all on their way into the Capitol, passed Leah's location, with one young man shouting, "Go get 'em, Leah. Richmond loves you."

Unaffected by his attempt to distract her, Leah said to her audience, "Why are we here? In all my years of journalism, the day of the elector voting has never been one that has been seen as particularly newsworthy. After all, in every presidential election within memory, the results were assumed to have been known based upon the popular vote of November. Therefore, the day upon which the electors voted just arrived and passed by, seen by most as just a formality of sorts, few really paying close attention to it. Even in the year 2000 . . . Wow, can you believe that that was twenty years ago? Once the United States Supreme Court had ruled in favor of George Bush, we knew that that year's meeting of the electors would be an anticlimactic finish to a very exciting election.

"But here, in 2020, some very unusual events have led us to conclude two things; first this will be no ordinary meeting of the electors, and second the only thing that we can conclude is that we cannot conclude anything. We will be back after this brief message."

The brief commercial break lasted long enough for Leah to have several sips of her coffee and to reposition the hand warmers that she had placed inside of her black gloves. Upon getting the signal to continue she said, "So let us start off with some facts. Governor Ryan, according to the standard practice, seems to have received an Electoral College vote of

268, one vote short of a tie, and two short of a victory. The late President James Augustus Faulkner received 270 votes, but he is no longer with us, having died on, of all days, Friday the thirteenth of November. To remind you of some of the other events that led up to this moment, I turn to correspondent Liza Lovitch who is on the floor of the Virginia Capitol.

"Liza, I'm sure that you are a little warmer in there than I am out here."

"Yes, the temperature in here is a balmy seventy-one degrees, Leah. As for the events that led to our being here, shortly after the president's death, Bill Morgan, a Republican, Mayor of Bellingham, Washington, and a presidential elector, brought suit against the Washington State Secretary of State, Fitzgerald, in an attempt to declare a state law null and void. This law would have required the mayor and the other eleven electors of his state to vote for President Faulkner, as the state law requires electors to vote for the person who they are pledged to vote for based upon the popular vote of November.

"After three court cases, the last one at the United States Supreme Court, Bill Morgan and electors around the nation are free to vote for whomever they want; state laws requiring voters to vote a certain way have been rendered null and void by the Court.

"Leah, that brings us to today and the fifty-one sites at which electors will cast their votes."

"Thank you, Liza. Ladies and gentlemen, today is the first Monday after the second Wednesday in the month of December, making it, according to the Constitution, the day upon which the Electoral College members in all of the states go to their respective state capitols to vote.[ii] So why are we in Richmond? From our D.C. studios, this is the closest state capital of a state in which last week's Supreme Court decision would have an effect. Virginia law number 24.1-162 states that the electors 'shall be expected to vote for that person for whom the popular vote was won.'[iii] We're going to talk with people here, to see their reaction to the recent events that have rocked our political process."

After showing four interviews by other correspondents, all with state office workers, the network broke for a short commercial break. When the broadcast resumed, Manders was standing next to veteran reporter Laura Peters, who had covered several elections of the past. When Manders asked her what we could expect, Laura smiled and said, "As you correctly stated, Leah, we will not know who has actually won until January 6th, the date the Constitution calls for the joint session of Congress to meet and review the electoral votes. I am positive that although we know the identity of each elector, each of them will remain silent regarding the nature of his or her vote. I know this for a fact, as I have attempted to interview each of Virginia's electors—all politely refusing to answer any questions.

"That aside, the most interesting aspect of this issue concerns itself with the Supreme Court decision. It might be safe to assume that Governor Ryan will retain all of his 268 votes; his electors really have no reason to change their minds. But, based upon the Court ruling, it appears that none of the 270 electors for Faulkner will be required to vote for him, so they have to change their votes to someone else.

"If two switch to Ryan, he wins. But if all of the 270 switch to the same person, that person would win. The two likely recipients of those votes would be Maria Martinez, who was running for vice president, and Elgin Hathaway, the sitting president. In either case, 270 would give that person the win.

"The election would enter a fascinating level if some of the 270 Faulkner electors vote for Martinez while others vote for Hathaway, or someone else, creating a scenario in which none of the three, including Ryan, has reached the magic number of 270, causing the election to go to the House of Representatives. That, Leah, is a place into which a presidential election hasn't ventured since 1824!"

"Once there," Leah said, "The states would vote, one at a time, until one of the candidates receives the majority of states, that being twenty-six states. So Laura, the history teachers and professors are gearing up for what could be a major addition to the history books."

As the bells on a nearby church rang in the 12:00 hour, Manders continued, "It is noon here in Virginia and along the East Coast. At this moment behind us is a scene that is being repeated in several other locales across the nation. Shortly each elector will reveal his or her choice and, afterward, the Secretary of State for each state will seal the election results—results that eventually will find their way to the nation's Capital. There, a joint session will, on January 6th, reveal the winner of the 2020 election.

"There is a great deal of uncertainty out there, but of one thing we are certain. The winner will be someone other than the late President James Augustus Faulkner."

---

i. TimeandDate.com http://www.timeanddate.com/eclipse/list.html October 4, 2014

ii. Wikipedia article: Electoral College. http://en.wikipedia.org/wiki/Electoral_College_(United_States) December 30, 2012

iii. Virginia law 24.1-162   http://www.archives.gov/federal-register/electoral-college/electors.html

CHAPTER 37

The Presents

The Dalles, Oregon
Friday, December 25, 2020
9:00 A.M.

It was the first time in forty-two years that Caroline Faulkner woke up on Christmas Day without her beloved Jimmy next to her. For several minutes she struggled to get out of bed, but after a few bouts of tears, finally she was able to lower her feet to the floor and say, "Oh, God, please help me to get through this day." Pushing herself up, she walked into the bathroom, looked in the mirror and told herself that she was ready to face whatever would come her way.

As she walked to the kitchen to have her first morning cup of coffee, she passed the corner of the living room where normally the Christmas tree would have been standing. Instead, the corner was bare; save for three presents, all from the president, wrapped and labeled, "From your loving husband—wherever I am." Looking at them, she instantly burst out in tears, crying out, "Jimmy, Jimmy, I miss you so much."

After pouring herself a cup of hot coffee, she brought it back into the living room and walked toward the presents, which had been there since Election Day. That was the day upon which the president had asked her not to move the presents until she opened them on what he called, "Our last Christmas together." She was so saddened by her loss, yet despite her noticeable weight loss, she had been able to persevere through her many lonely nights.

She picked up the red present, marked with a label that said "One," only to think that her late husband had always been so organized. She marveled at how light the toaster-sized box felt. Pulling off the paper, she opened the carefully sealed box, and after moving around the tissue paper found an envelope that was fastened with the presidential seal. On the front, written in his handwriting were the words, "To my wonderful Caroline."

Wiping away more tears, she saw a piece of paper inside, which she unfolded. "Caroline, I probably am in a different place right now. I want you to know that there was no place on Earth that I liked better than being here on the farm with you. Despite all of our worldwide travels, and all of the wonderful people with whom I have had contact, there is no one person I'd rather be with than you. Yours in time, Jimmy."

She read the letter three times, each time having more difficulty trying to keep her tears from flowing. She looked up toward Heaven several times, proclaiming her love for him and reminding him that this was her favorite place, too.

Her hands shaking, she placed the letter and envelope on the floor next to her and looked at the second present, which was wrapped in white paper. This box was much heavier than the first one and was wrapped more tightly too. It was about the size of a bicycle. Struggling to remove the paper, she finally let out a shriek, "Dammit, Jimmy," then frantically tore the paper, removing large portions at a time. The sealed box had to be cut, which she did with the scissors that she had on hand. But the box was too heavy to lift, so she slid it from around the contents. What seemed like millions of Styrofoam fillers started to spread all across her body and the area surrounding her. But once she removed the box, she shouted out, "You didn't!" She was staring at the four-foot-tall glass bottle that the president had sit on the floor behind his desk in the Oval Office. The former candy jar—he had always liked to snack on almond M&Ms— was filled with soil from the ranch. Etched into the glass were the words, "Can't Wait to Get My Feet Back on the Soil of the Flying Faulkner Ranch." Through her tears, she said, "James Augustus Faulkner, nice touch, but I think you now have that soil all around you." Allowing the huge bottle to sit on its side, the cap sealing the precious soil in the container, she set her attention upon the last of the three gifts. Appropriately wrapped in blue paper, this one seemed almost as light as the first one. Opening it quickly she found a picture frame that had three five-by-seven pictures of the couple, the one on the left taken at their prom, the one on the middle taken on their wedding day, while the one on the right was taken a week prior to the most recent election night. Attached to it was a Post-It Note® that read, 'Together from the beginning to the end, Love, me." She looked at the picture for several minutes until tearfully saying, "Forever, darling. Forever!"

It had been a tough month for the former First Lady. Not only had she lost her husband, but she had had only one day to move out of the White House. The move back to Oregon had taken its toll upon her; despite the months of knowing about the president's illness, the quickness of his resignation and death left her so unprepared.

Choosing to spend the holiday alone on the ranch, the previous night she had received two telephone calls, both from her mother Tess. Other than that, she expected no other calls, choosing to brave the holiday alone, just as she had told others that she wanted to do. So lost in thought was she, that she never heard the first three rings of the phone. Finally realizing that the phone was ringing, Caroline jumped off the floor and rushed to answer it. Instantly recognizing the number, she picked it up and said, "Hello, Mr. President. How are you?"

"Caroline, Merry Christmas to you! I hope you are well."

"I am as well as can be expected," she said, wiping away the last of that round's tears. "It certainly is a different kind of holiday."

With each attempting to console the other, the conversation centered upon their deceased spouses. They talked about the good times in their lives, reminding each other that better times were ahead. As the topic drifted back to the deceased president, Caroline asked, "So how is the job?"

"I guess it is what I expected; some things easy, and a new challenge every day."

"I guess Jimmy left you quite a mess at the White House."

"Caroline, he did no such thing. Your husband will always be remembered as a good man who worked hard to make this nation a better place for all of us. Remember, the people have twice elected him to the highest office this nation has to offer. He left behind millions of adoring fans, including me."

"Thank you, Elgin. Although he seldom showed it, he thought the same about you. Jim was complicated like that—seldom showing appreciation for those he respected the most."

"Yeah, I knew that about him. Right now, I don't feel like I am anyone's hero, and during the next twenty-five days, I will probably have people think far less of me."

"Well, you'll always have a fan here in Oregon. I hope you don't mind that the funeral was a private affair; Jim didn't want any ties to the government. He wanted just me, my mother, and his siblings to be involved."

Proving to be a great politician, Elgin transformed his original thoughts of, "It's a good thing—half the audience would have consisted of attractive forty-year-olds from across the country, all making us wonder which of the group had been Jim's lovers," to a subtler, "That's okay, Caroline. Your husband was a man who was able to reach out and touch the insides of so many people from coast to coast. He's in the hearts and minds of countless people. He will be missed by people of all ages."

She then told the president about all of the funeral's details, and with each sentence, she wiped away tears. After several minutes of description, the emotionally drained former First Lady paused, "You know, his leaving has put me exactly where I always feared that I'd be—alone here in The Dalles."

"I feel for you, Caroline."

"I've known my Jimmy since we were kids, when his father would bring him around to deliver cherries to my grandmother's grocery store."

"That was Quinella's. Correct?"

"You've heard of it?"

"Certainly. Jim spoke of it fondly, saying that that place changed his life."

"Mine, too. His dad brought him around to learn the business; we were maybe twelve or thirteen years old. I was stacking cans of soup in an aisle when our eyes first met. Elgin, I'm not sure if, at that age, I knew the definition of the word hot, but he's defined it for me ever since."

"That's a great story."

The former First Lady paused, wiped away a few tears then continued, "We started dating not long afterward. He had a way about him. He'd call me 'Car-Line' and always say that he was saving the 'O' for when we were in the throes of passion. I was so in love with him, even after the day I saw him kissing a cheerleader.

"That was a beginning of the cycle, his infidelities followed by forgiveness on my part. But he was a charmer, Elgin. He knew that I didn't want to work at that store for the rest of my life, even though it was destined to be handed down to me. I'd read all of those labels on those cans and bottles and see all of those faraway places knowing that I would never visit them—I'd be stuck in The Dalles the rest of my life."

"But it's beautiful there."

"It certainly is; don't get me wrong. I love it here—it's the most beautiful town in the most beautiful state in the union. But Jimmy promised to take me places and, boy, did he deliver. Paris, London, Barcelona, Rio, you name it, we were there. I put up with all of his crap over the years because he allowed me to see the world—he got me out of the freaking grocery store. If years ago I'd left him, like so many suggested that I do, I would have spent the rest of my life in Quinella's. Was I wrong?"

"Caroline, I'm so sorry for what you had to go through. Hearing that story has given me a new level of respect for you."

"Most people think that I was a doormat, just letting him do whatever the hell he wanted to do with those bimbos. They don't know—I was using him to see the world. Now, I'm back in The Dalles—alone, just like I always feared I'd be."

"Listen, Caroline, we all have to do what we have to do to survive. As for being alone, you're not. You have your Bolognese pups."

"Yes, de Niro and Pacino are always with me. And I love 'em to death, but you know what I mean."

"Of course. I was only kidding. But you have so many people in your corner. What's happening with the store?"

"My mother still owns it, God bless her. But when I went off to see the world, she brought in a manager to take care of the business. It's booming."

"Great, so all you have to do is sit back and watch the money come in."

"Yeah, I guess that would be right."

"Caroline, would you excuse me if I had to run?"

"Of course, I know how that is. Business calls?"

"Yea, even on Christmas."

 "Merry Christmas, Elgin."

"You too, Caroline. "

Chapter 38

The Trio

The White House
Monday, December 28, 2020
10:36 A.M.

"Of course you want him to reveal the information, Leah. It has tremendous news value for you," said an agitated Tyson. "You would be able to cover the topic for years."

"Don't go there, Tyson," answered the angered journalist. "How dare you personalize this! That doesn't have a damn thing to do with it."

"Will you two please simmer down? Both of you, cut it out!" said President Hathaway. "Listen to yourselves, dammit. Now consider the emotions that millions of people will have over this idea. Imagine what's going to happen in this country."

Still upset, Tyson stood up and walked around the table. "Okay, I see Leah's point. This is an issue that has been concealed since the 1860s. It should be brought to light because so many unsuspecting people have the opportunity to gain so much. But look at the other side of it—there are other unsuspecting people who will have the opportunity to lose so much. Do you think that they're just going to sit back without a fight? And it's the word 'fight' that frightens me the most. Elgin, you could set off another Civil War—or a race war of some kind."

"That's why I have brought the two of you here. If I sit back and do nothing, then I'm as guilty as Grant, Hayes, Garfield, and the rest of those nineteenth century guys. It's the twenty-first century; if not now, when?"

"The law expires in 2065, Mr. President," said Leah. "If it's revealed too much later than now it'll run its course and die in the courts.

"Mr. President," continued Leah, "I know that this is tough on you, and I'll support you either way, but speaking from the news side of things, you'll eventually be lambasted for covering it up, if, indeed, that's what you choose.

"And if your presidency goes just one more month and you hand the information over to the next president, and he or she reveals it, how will that make you look?"

"Yeah, you're right, dammit," said Hathaway.

"Honestly, Sir, something like this will make you more than a piece of trivia in the future, as in 'Hathaway was the one who filled in for Faulkner after he died.' Rather this gutsy move would put you at the forefront of one of the major pieces of legislation that the nation has ever seen."

"Thank you, Leah. That's something to think about, although I am not worried about being trivialized. And Tyson, I see your side of it too. The lawyers will have a field day, as it will get real messy.

"I appreciate both of you for coming in to see me. You'll be the first to know my decision."

Chapter 39

The Magnolia Mixer

The Capitol Building
Sunday, January 3, 2021
11:00 A.M.

The Twentieth Amendment of the United States Constitution states that the first day for a new term of Congress shall begin at noon of the third day of January. For veterans who had gathered on that day, it was the beginning of a new term. But for those many newly elected members of the 117th Congress, this was the day about which most had dreamed, a day filled with a mixture of joy and anxiety. Among that group was Karla Kalkut from the Second Congressional District of Mississippi. The thirty-six-year-old, Jennifer Hudson-look-alike from Yazoo City was, perhaps, the most nervous of Capitol Hill's forty-three new representatives.

Also, she may have been the proudest. A successful lawyer, she had descended from a family of slaves and sharecroppers, living most of her life in poverty. Her last name, which was Jewish, was from her paternal great grandfather, Aaron, who had been a New York City merchant who had traveled to Mississippi to sell diamonds. He had fallen in love with his future wife, Sally, who was a house servant to the Magnolia State's richest man, his biggest client.

Graduating first in her class from Yazoo City High School, Karla attended Columbia University prior to graduating from Penn Law School. Afterward, for several years, she practiced law in Jackson prior to developing her own firm in Yazoo City. Her helpful handling of cases for so many of the poorer citizens of that city made her one of the area's most popular figures, so popular, in fact, that hundreds of her clients urged her to run for the House.

Reluctant at first to take their advice, corruption allegations against her would-be opponent led to an almost guaranteed-to-win status for Kalkut. Her eight-point lead in the summer polls eventually swelled to a landslide of seventeen points by Election Day, propelling her to Washington, D.C.

She had secured herself an apartment on Connecticut Ave NW in the Wakefield section of town, and she quickly learned her way around the city. Although she missed Yazoo City, she told everyone, "Hey, this is D.C., Baby! I love it here."

The agenda for the first day in the House of Representatives had been set. At noon, the clerk called the House to order, Karla finding her seat, listening as the quorum call was taken. Shortly afterward, nominations for Speaker of the House were taken. How proud she was when she cast her vote for Republican Pierce Allen of Kansas, who, as the eventual winner, at 2:25, would take the oath of office.

Kalkut listened carefully as the rules of the House were brought forward to the floor. As they were voted upon, Karla, the great granddaughter of sharecroppers Mattie and Oscar, teared up as she cast her affirmation vote. Looking around the chamber, she couldn't help but think of the history that had transpired in the room. She was amazed as, in her head, she rattled off names of dozens of famous legislators who had preceded her inside the room. She looked at the other four hundred thirty-seven members and thought how proud Mattie and Oscar would have been of her.

There were several other orders of business to conduct, but before she could catch her breath, the day had come to a close, the first day's session adjourning.

As she left the building she glanced back, as if to say, "Was I really in there? Was it a dream?" Taking the subway home, she quickly showered and changed her clothes into something more casual. She called a taxi, and upon its arrival, she asked the driver to take her to 1990 M St., NW, the address of Vidalia, one of the city's top spots to get Southern meals. Upon arrival, some ten minutes late, she walked into the restaurant seeking the rest of her party. Seeing them on the far side of the room, she walked toward them, their smiling faces making her feel somewhat at home.

She was led to a beautifully decorated table, at which three gentlemen were waiting, all colleagues from Capitol Hill, all from Mississippi. Silver-headed Ronald Davis of Biloxi (the Fourth District), a five-term representative, was the first to greet her, his eyes feasting upon his fellow Mississippian, who was some forty years his junior. Next to rise to greet Karla was Victor Polk, the George Clooney look-alike, from Tupelo, of the First District. He was the veteran of the group, a seven-time elected member of the House, perhaps the most powerful and popular politician in the Magnolia State—a person who, it was thought by many, aspired to higher office. His warm smile greeted Karla, and then he reached for her hand. As Karla extended her hand to shake his, the always debonair Polk turned his wrist, exposing the back of her hand, gently kissing it and saying, "You look exquisite." Karla thought, "Oh, you are a charmer, aren't you, but I've heard all about you." Finally, to his left, was another newly elected representative, Curtis Howard, who had known Karla for many years, having been a law school classmate of hers. Howard, from the Third District—he hailed from Natchez—had been the object of Karla's imaginary affection for several months. Likewise, he had had strong feelings for her too. Their embrace made the other two gentlemen look at each other, nod their heads, and smile.

After the four representatives had been seated, Polk said, "Welcome to the meeting of the Mississippi Congressional Caucus, or as I like to call it, the Magnolia Mixer. Karla, as the only Democrat you're outnumbered three to one, but we'll let you get a word in every so often. Seriously, both Ron and I want to welcome both of you to our group."

Karla smiled, "Thank you, Mr. Polk. I'm sure at some point I will try to get a word into the conversation. But it's a dream come true to be here representing the people of my area of the state."

"I'm equally honored to be here," said Curtis. "And I'm not afraid to talk at all."

After several minutes of discussion about a possible House vote on the presidential election, the economy and, of all things, the recent rare snowstorm that had hit northern Mississippi and Alabama, the conversation turned toward House business. Again Polk took the lead. "So, Mr. Howard and Miss Kalkut, since Mr. Davis and I have more experience in the trenches, I thought that we would fill you two, please excuse the term, rookies, in on what you should expect. Is that okay with you all?"

"That would be fine," said Karla. "We're here to learn."

For the next thirty-two minutes, as drinks, appetizers and salads were presented by their waiter, Salvador, Polk and Davis discussed the responsibilities of their jobs, the persons whom they could and could not trust, and several other items of pertinence. Both Karla and Curtis felt privileged to have had the evening with the veterans, who seemed to enjoy having their younger, admiring colleagues there to listen.

As they were finishing up their coffees, Davis asked if there were any other questions that the freshmen representatives might have.

Karla, who had had a couple of glasses of wine, tapped Curtis on the shoulder and told him to ask Polk the question that the two newcomers had previously discussed.

"Mr. Polk," asked a reluctant Curtis, "With all of the coverage of the election results, what is the likelihood that we will have to play a role in determining the next president?"

Polk smiled, looked at Karla and said, "My dear Congresswoman Kalkut, you should never hesitate to ask a question. In our business we have to know what is happening around us and be prepared to react to anything. It is the unasked question that can cause the most trouble. Please, for your own sake, don't let this happen again." Then, for emphasis he emphatically asked, "Do you understand me?"

Sheepishly Karla nodded her head, acknowledging her mistake. Afterward Polk continued, "Now, for the answer to the question! On January 6th at noon, the actual votes from the Electoral College will be read. With the Supreme Court ruling behind us, we basically have 538 free agents out there. They can vote for anyone, so the projected numbers that were reported back in November are all out the window. Well, at least many of them will be. It will be interesting to see who comes out of this thing with a victory.

"We would get involved if no one gets the majority and quite frankly, the way I see it, that's a likely scenario. If Martinez gets all of the votes that were intended for Faulkner, she will win. But if some of those votes are siphoned off by another candidate or candidates, look out. We could be headed back to an election like they had in 1824! But to explain the potential process, I'll turn it over to Ron, who has in the past taught a class that centered upon the election of 1824."

Ron Davis smiled, "Yeah, I taught that class for ten years. So here's what would happen. It's quite fascinating. First the Speaker would direct a roll of the House to be called by the states. Then the members of each state would sit in the order that the states are to be called, starting with I guess, Alabama. The roll would then be taken, and the delegations of each state would each be handed a ballot box by the Sergeant-at-Arms. The Speaker would indicate that the voting was to take place, with each representative placing his or her ballot inside their respective boxes."

"That sounds interesting," said Karla.

"Oh," continued Davis, "Then it gets heavy. After each representative deposits his or her ballot, each delegation then names a Teller who moves to the front and sits at tables with other Tellers. Then at each of the tables a sole representative is appointed to read the results from that table and when it is his or her time they'd say something like, 'Mr. Speaker, the results at this table are Candidate X has received this number of votes, Candidate Y has this many, and Candidate Z has this many.' After all of the results from all of the tables are announced, the Speaker, who has been keeping a tally, would say something like, 'Candidate X, having a majority of the votes has been elected president of the United States.'"

After glancing at Curtis and Karla, Polk could see by the look on their faces that, just like kids in a candy shop, they were eating this up. Thankful that he was working alongside people who took an interest in their responsibilities he commented, "We will know if we're needed as soon as the results from the first couple of states are announced. Once the results from Alabama, Alaska, and Arkansas are read, if they are split, watch out. If the vote is split, buckle up your helmets 'cause we're the next ones in the game.

"I think this will be historic. And Karla, please don't be afraid to ask any questions."

Chapter 40

The Votes Are Read

Capitol Hill
Washington, D.C.
Wednesday, January 6, 2021
10:40 A.M.

"Imagine, in less than ninety minutes we could possibly know the outcome of one of the most interesting presidential elections in our nation's history," said a warmly dressed Leah Manders to her viewing audience. "I am standing in front of where all of the action will take place, Capitol Hill, where, shortly, there will be a call from the Tillman of the House of Representatives to have the members of the Senate join them for the official reading of the Electoral College vote from last December.

"We are aware of a few things heading into that reading, the first being that the 270 electors who had voted for the late President James Augustus Faulkner have been forced to vote for someone else or else risk having those Faulkner votes nullified by the House of Representatives."

Manders turned to look directly at the Capitol, before saying, "We know that the Supreme Court has freed the electors to vote for anyone that they choose, eliminating the restrictions that had been placed upon many of them due to state laws that required them to vote for pledged candidates. It's fair game out there today; anyone could receive votes.

"We know that Governor Robert Ryan, the Democratic candidate from Indiana, had 268 votes pledged for him, but even those are not guaranteed. But if he collects those 268 and gains two others from the deceased candidate, he will be our next president."

Again, Manders paused, again looking back at the Capitol.

"We know that if no one receives the needed 270 votes for a majority, then the election will be in the hands of the House of Representatives.

Remember, that is the new House that was sworn in a few days ago, one that has a Republican majority.

"And finally, we know that the Speaker of the House Pierce Allen will be the person presiding over the entire scene. Some have suggested that, due to his outstanding record, he might be, despite his age, considered a compromise candidate. We'll have to see if the well-respected Kansas native receives any support."

Manders started walking toward the Capitol when she stopped and said, "In just one moment I'll be reporting from inside this historic landmark. Meanwhile, here is a list of people who are most likely to receive votes. Clearly Governor Ryan will receive many, if not all, of the votes that he thinks he has gotten. Maria Martinez, the potential vice president-elect will most probably get her share of votes, too. She could receive some of the votes that were originally headed to her running mate, the late president. Speaking of presidents, will President Elgin Hathaway receive some of the votes, even though he was not part of the ticket? Since the capture of the domestic terrorists, the president's approval rating had risen to new personal high levels. But keep in mind; these votes were cast seventeen days ago. Will there be votes for someone else whose name hasn't even been mentioned? And of course, will there be votes for President Faulkner, even though he's dead and the votes could be nullified?

"Then there is the House of Representatives possibility! The bookmakers in Las Vegas are giving the odds at one to three that the election will go to the House. Wow, you can bet on anything in Vegas.

"With so many scenarios, it is little wonder that some people are calling this the 'Most Intriguing Election in History,' while others refer to it as the 'Nightmare Election of 2020.' During the next few minutes we will recap the events which have led us to this exciting moment."

Manders was joined by several correspondents who reported on the various events of the election season. They recapped the primary season, the nominating conventions, the campaign, election night, the death of James Augustus Faulkner, the Supreme Court case, the December 14th vote of the Electoral College, and the soon-to-be reading of the votes.

Toward the end of the presentation, after several guests had made interesting points, Manders said, "So there you have it, America. Those are the facts and events that have led us into the most sensational election in our nation's history. No matter what happens during the next hour or so, I predict Americans will be talking about this election for the next two hundred years!

"We will now remain silent; there will be no commentary. The next voices that you will hear will be from the House of Representatives. The United States Constitution states that the vice president of the United States, in his duty as President of the Senate, and the Speaker of the House will preside over the proceedings and the reading of the ballots. But since there is no vice president, President pro tempore Benjamin Hayes will preside. The voice of Pierce Allen should be the next voice that you hear. Oh, there's the feed now. Enjoy, and at the conclusion of the reading of the ballots, we will be back to provide a summary of the afternoon's events, commenting upon the winner—the next president of the United States."

A smiling Pierce Allen took the gavel, pounded it upon the Speaker's platform and began the much-anticipated process by saying, "Members of Congress, pursuant to the Constitution and the laws of the United States, the Senate and the House of Representatives are meeting in joint session to verify the certificates and count the votes of the electors of the several states for president and vice president of the United States.

"After ascertainment has been had that the certificates are authentic and correct in form, the Tellers will count and make a list of the votes cast by the electors of the several states.

"The Tellers on the part of the two houses will take their places at the clerk's desk."[i]

After a momentary pause, to allow the two senators—one Republican and one Democrat—and two representatives—likewise, one Republican and one Democrat—to take their assigned places, Speaker Allen continued, "Without objection, the Tellers will dispense with reading formal portions of the certificates.

"After ascertaining that the certificates are regular in form and authentic, the Tellers will announce the votes cast by the electors for each state beginning with Alabama."[ii]

With those words, the moment for which millions of Americans had been waiting began. Television sets all across the nation were tuned in to watch this event, an event that seldom provides the public with any substantial interest. Who would be the next president of the United States? The moment was here at last.

Roger Potoma, a Republican Senator from Missouri, was the first Teller to rise out of his seat and walk to the podium in front of and below Pierce Allen, who handed him the first envelope. Potoma, a soft-spoken, six-term senator, adjusted his microphone and said, "Mr. Speaker, the certificate of the electoral vote of the state of Alabama seems to be regular in form and authentic and appears there[iii] from that Maria Martinez of the state of Florida has received four votes for president and five votes for vice president; Elgin Hathaway of the state of New York has received five votes for president and four votes for vice president."

With those words, a hush fell across the chamber floor, as the results indicated to all of the members of the joint session that this election was headed in a direction that none of the previous fifty-eight presidential elections had ever been. From the sampling of one state, it appeared that the Electoral College, not bound by any state laws, could be headed into uncharted waters. Many in the chamber thought that if several other states were to take the lead put forth by Alabama, then there would be no predictability to this election—any man, or, for that matter, woman, was capable of winning.

As Potoma sat down, the second Teller, a Democratic representative from Memphis, Tennessee named Russell Michaels stood and walked toward the microphone.

"Mr. Speaker, the certificate of the electoral vote of the state of Alaska seems to be regular in form and authentic and appears there from that Elgin Hathaway of the state of New York has received three votes for president and Maria Martinez of the state of Florida has received three votes for vice president."[iv]

"Normalcy," proclaimed Suzie Greenbaum, a third-term Republican Senator from Florida, as others around her agreed with pleasure. However, the situation quickly changed as the third Teller, Democratic Senator Dee Dee Guarino of Maryland said, "Mr. Speaker, the certificate of the electoral vote of the state of Arizona seems to be regular in form and authentic and appears there from that Elgin Hathaway of the state of New York has received ten votes for president and one vote for vice president and Maria Martinez of the state of Florida has received one vote for president and ten votes for vice president."

Greenbaum, unable to speak, just shook her head in stunned disbelief. "They are going to make a shambles of this process. You watch! I'm telling you that this is going to be messy."

As Greenbaum spoke with her colleagues, the fourth, and final Teller, Republican representative Victor B. Dougherty of Oklahoma, who slowly walked to the podium and was handed by Speaker Allen the results from the state of Arkansas. "Mr. Speaker, the certificate of the electoral vote of the state of Arkansas seems to be regular in form and authentic and appears there from that Maria Martinez of the state of Florida has received six votes for president and Elgin Hathaway of the state of New York has received six votes for vice president."

Greenbaum, who, had a pad of paper on her lap to keep an unofficial score looked at her nearby colleagues and said, "This is crazy. He's got twenty votes, she has seven. It's maddening. But at least all of the votes are for our side."

That quickly changed as the first Teller, Roger Potoma, appeared again at the microphone, "Mr. President, the certificate of the electoral vote of the state of California seems to be regular in form and authentic and appears there from that Robert Ryan of the state of Indiana has received fifty-five votes for president and Taylor Bishop of Minnesota has received fifty-five votes for vice president." In fact, the next four reports from Tellers were all favorable of the governor and his running mate, Bishop, as it was stated that they had won the states of Colorado,

Connecticut, Delaware, and the District of Columbia.

It was time for Michaels to make his third appearance at the podium, and he announced that Martinez had gathered all twenty-nine presidential votes from her home state of Florida, Hathaway gaining the same number for the vice presidency. She almost shut him out in the next state, too, gaining a fifteen-to-none advantage in Georgia, with a lone vote going, to, of all people, Governor Robert Ryan—a gift from the now-deceased mayor of Macon, the Honorable Noah Pryor; the vote pleased Governor Ryan and his assistant Bob Gittings, both of whom were watching the results in Indiana, and Gittings thought, "I love that man from Macon. We should get at least 269 votes now—we're in for at least a tie."

After a Ryan victory in Hawaii was announced, Hathaway was announced as a three-to-one victor over Martinez in Idaho. Ryan then won the next three states, Illinois, Indiana, and Iowa, gaining a total of thirty-seven votes from the Midwestern trio of states. However, Kansas supplied a little surprise, as Hathaway captured five of the six electoral votes; the other went to Speaker Pierce Allen, which made him smile and whisper to those around the podium, "Hey, I only need two hundred sixty-nine more of those to win the damned thing."

The Democrats watched as Hathaway defeated Martinez in Kentucky and Louisiana; Hathaway won the former by a five-to-three score and the latter by a seven-to-one score. Then, as the multitude of "M" states were being announced, Ryan surged, winning, in order, Maine, Maryland, Massachusetts, Michigan and Minnesota, for a total of fifty-one votes. But in the last group of "M" states, the Republicans rallied, gained a total of nineteen votes from Mississippi, Missouri and Montana. (Hathaway received a total of nine votes, while Martinez gained ten.)

Halfway through the alphabet and more than halfway through the states and the District, the Republicans were down—and worried. It would have been a huge task to defeat the popular Ryan with the incumbent President Faulkner, but they were now trying to defeat him with two candidates—one, yes, the sitting president, but he had been sitting for only about a month. And to make matters worse, he was losing votes to another Republican. At this point Suzie Greenbaum's unofficial tally was: Ryan 170, Martinez 69, Hathaway 49, and Allen 1. Her concern centered upon the fact that the two, make that three, Republicans in the race were being outgunned by Ryan. Her other concern was that Ryan was exactly one hundred votes shy of winning the election! She was hopeful that the second half of the alphabet would shine a more favorable light upon her party.

Indeed, things started well for the Republicans, with Hathaway winning Nebraska's five votes and then winning five out of the six that Nevada had to offer (Martinez winning the other). But Ryan was victorious in the next two states, New Hampshire and New Jersey, placing a total of eighteen votes in his bank. Although Martinez was able to capture the five votes from New Mexico, Ryan gained victories in New York and North Carolina, taking with him their forty-four votes.

Greenbaum looked at his colleagues, "Damn, Faulkner screwed this up for us. He shouldn't have run in the first place."

But she became more pleased as Hathaway won North Dakota's three votes, signaling the beginning of a mini-run for the Republicans, as they also took all of the "O" states; Hathaway defeating Martinez sixteen-to-two in Ohio and four-to-three in Oklahoma, before seeing Martinez sweep Faulkner's home state of Oregon and its seven votes. But Greenbaum cursed as Ryan pulled farther away with wins in Pennsylvania and Rhode Island, gaining their combined twenty-four votes. With only eleven states remaining, things were looking down for the Republicans.

"We have to stop this guy before he wins the entire election," said Greenbaum. "Crap, he's going to win the freaking presidency."

Greenbaum's anxiety was calmed a little as Hathaway proved to be victorious over Martinez in the next three states, winning South Carolina six to three, South Dakota three to zero and Tennessee seven to four. But, although everyone knew that Texas was going to be placed in the Republican column, it was the ease in which Martinez defeated Hathaway that made some people take notice, winning thirty-six to two.

As the states trickled down to a precious few, despite a five-to-one victory in Utah for Hathaway over Martinez, Republicans grew more concerned with the prospect of a Ryan victory. The Democrat's victory in Vermont placed him three votes closer to winning. And even after Hathaway's thirteen-to-nothing victory in Virginia, and twelve-to-nothing victory in Washington State, when Ryan was declared victorious in Wisconsin, Republicans gasped as the governor was within one vote of winning. Only Wyoming stood in his way.

Suddenly, in Indianapolis, Bob Gittings stood up and said to Governor Ryan, "This is the moment we waited for. If Gabby Cook comes through for us, we win!"

The governor, looking confused, asked him what he was talking about.

"She's the representative that told me to put money in her account in case she switches her vote. If she switches to you, you'll have your original 268 votes, plus Noah Pryor's vote and hers—giving you 270 and the presidency!"

Now realizing the situation, Governor Ryan joined Gittings, each standing and pacing around the room, focused solely upon the television set.

Maryland's Dee Dee Guarino stood at the podium and read, "Mr. Speaker, the certificate of the electoral vote of the state of Wyoming seems to be regular in form and authentic and appears there from that Maria Martinez of the state of Florida has received three votes for president and Elgin Hathaway of the state of New York has received three votes for vice president".

Hearing Guarino's remarks, a furious Gittings, head bowed, proclaimed, "Crap, it looks like we saved ourselves three hundred thousand freaking dollars."

Meanwhile, the decibel level in the House Chamber rose tremendously, causing Speaker Allen to bang the gavel several times. Handed the results he said, "Members of Congress, the certificates having been read, the Tellers will ascertain and deliver the result to the President pro tempore."[v]

Approximately one minute later, with a saddened look upon his face,

Potoma read the following, "The undersigned, Mr. Roger Potoma of Missouri and Dee Dee Guarino of Maryland, Tellers on the part of the Senate and Mr. Russell Michaels of Tennessee and Victor B. Dougherty of Oklahoma, Tellers on the part of the House of Representatives, report the following as the result of the ascertainment and counting of the electoral vote for president for the term beginning on the 20th day of January, 2021."

A somber Pierce Allen then spoke. "The state of the vote for the president of the United States as delivered to the President pro tempore and the Speaker of the House is as follows: The whole number of electors appointed to vote for president of the United States is 538 of which a majority is 270.

"Robert Ryan of the state of Indiana has received for president of the United States 269 votes.

"Elgin Hathaway of the state of New York has received for president of the United States 135 votes.

"Maria Martinez of the state of Florida has received for president of the United States 133 votes.

Pierce Allen of the state of Kansas has received for president of the United States 1 vote."

After a slight delay, during which there was much conversation amongst the combined audience of senators and representatives, Allen continued, "The state of the vote for the vice president of the United States as delivered to the president of the Senate is as follows:

"The whole number of electors appointed to vote for vice president of the United States is 538 of which a majority is 270.

"Taylor Bishop of the state of Minnesota has received for vice president of the United States 269 votes.

"Maria Martinez of the state of Florida has received for vice president of the United States 136 votes.

"Elgin Hathaway of the state of New York has received for vice president of the United States 133 votes."

After some discussion in the chamber, Speaker Allen, after regaining everyone's attention said, "This announcement of the state of the vote by the President pro tempore and the Speaker of the House shall be deemed a sufficient declaration of the persons elected president and vice president of the United States each for the term beginning on the 20th day of January 2021 and will be entered, along with a list of the votes on the journals of the Senate and the House of Representatives. Thus, in the case of both the elections for president of the United States and the vice president of the United States, it be there upon declared that no person having reached a majority of the whole number for either office, an election for either office had not been effected; that for the office of president of the United States Robert Ryan of the state of Indiana, Elgin Hathaway of the state of New York and Maria Martinez of the state of Florida were the three highest on the lists of electoral votes and for the office of the vice president of the United States, Taylor Bishop of the state of Minnesota and Maria Martinez of the state of Florida were the two highest on the lists of electoral votes; and that it devolved on the House of Representatives of the United States to choose from these persons a president of the United States; and that devolved on the Senate of the United States, as provided in the Constitution, to choose from these persons a vice president of the United States.

"I declare the joint committee to dissolve and to reconvene upon the selection of both a president of the United States and a vice president of the United States."[vi]

Upon hearing the solid sound of the gavel hitting its mark, amidst much discussion, the one hundred senators left the House chamber and relocated to their own, where they quickly approved a motion to elect a vice president from the choices of Taylor Bishop and Maria Martinez.

WGDC's Leah Manders, reporting the outcomes of the elections, stated that this would be the first time that the House would choose a president since 1824, a fact that had been repeatedly mentioned in the media. Then she added, "This would be the first time since the election of 1836 that the Senate would choose a vice president. It was in that year that the Democratic nominee for vice president, umm, Richard Johnson, was elected by the Senate after he failed to receive the majority of electoral votes due to Virginia's twenty-three electors refusing to vote for him, as it was rumored that he had previously lived with and had fathered children with an African-American woman. Due to those allegations, he missed receiving a majority of the Electoral College vote by one vote but won the office by means of the vote of the Senate.

"Although the circumstances are much different, some one hundred eighty-five years later, we are headed back to the Senate for a vote."

After the motion was resolved, as prescribed in the Constitution, the vice president would be elected based upon a majority of the vote of each senator, who would be called in alphabetical order to declare his or her choice.

Rolf Kohlman, the Secretary of the Senate, called upon Senator Sue Adamson of Maine for the first vote. Adamson, with a loud, piercing voice, shouted out the name "Maria Martinez." Thus, the process had begun and during the next several minutes, the senators voted for their respective choices. To no one's surprise, upon hearing the vote of the last senator, Kaleigh Zaferatos of Washington, the close vote favored Maria Martinez by a slim margin of six as she had defeated Taylor Bishop fifty-three to forty-seven. Thus, the first female vice president of the United States had been elected!

Meanwhile, at the exact moment, in the House of Representatives, as prescribed by the Constitution, a motion had been passed calling upon the representatives to select a president. The procedure in the House differed from the Senate's procedure, as in the House there were three candidates (Ryan, Hathaway, and Martinez) from whom to choose. Also, the method of voting was different, as it was to be done by state, not individually.

Thus, California's fifty-five representatives would have a single voice, one equal to the one vote by Wyoming's lone representative, Paul Davison. Although constitutional experts had argued that the practice gave an unfair advantage to the smaller states (California's population of nearly forty-two million would receive the same single vote as Wyoming's population of 622,360), it had never been challenged successfully since the system, in 1824, had last been called into action. Perhaps during a future debate a constitutional amendment might change it, favoring a process by which the representatives would vote as individuals, as do their fellow politicians in the Senate. But that debate was for a future date.

Upon the acceptance of their task, just as it had been described at the Magnolia Mixer by Ronald Davis, the members of each state were seated, by state, with some having a short but spirited discussion. The Mississippi delegation started poorly, as Curtis Howard was late joining his colleagues and was admonished by Victor Polk, "This is the most important vote that you've ever made in your life and you're freaking late for it!"

"I'm sorry," said the highly embarrassed Howard. "I really had to go to the bathroom."

Slowly shaking his head in disgust, Polk added, "Well, I guess when nature calls, one has to go.

"Fortunately, I think that this will be pretty open and shut. Karla, you're probably voting for Governor Ryan, while the rest of us are voting Republican. If I might add, the three of us should vote for Hathaway; we *have* to vote for Hathaway."

Remembering the advice that Polk had given her earlier, Kalkut bristled. "Wait, are you suggesting that we can't vote for Martinez? Why not?"

"I have my reasons," Polk told her.

"Well, those reasons better not include the fact that she's a woman or a Latina," Kalkut said. "I hope you're not bringing any twentieth-century biases here."

When Polk was slow to answer, Kalkut stood up and shouted, "You are, aren't you? I guess the only reason why I should be here is to be mopping up the floors, huh?"

Polk glowered at her. "You can't speak to me that way!"

"I can and I did! Don't you get it? We're twenty years into the twenty-first century and you're still armed with eighteenth-century ideas!"

"I just don't think that we're ready for a woman president, that's all."

"Not ready? Not ready?!! It's 2021; exactly one hundred years ago, women got their first opportunity to vote in a national election. How fitting would it be for the nation to elect a woman in this year? Get with it! You know, people have a great deal of negativity toward our state, and it's people like you who perpetuate those feelings."

Glaring at Davis and Howard, she said, "Look, I'm voting for Ryan, but I hope you two will vote with your own minds. If you choose Hathaway, let it be for the right reasons. Who are you guys voting for, anyway?"

Davis and Howard assured her that no bias was influencing their vote.

"Thanks," she told them. "Listen, I'm sorry for my outburst."

The group awaited the arrival of the ballot box, where each would deposit his or her official ballot.

Speaker Allen, after gaining the attention of the entire body, announced, "The ballot boxes will be here soon. It is time to take a roll of the members."

A few minutes later, after it was established that all of the members were present, Allen said, "Sergeant-of Arms, please distribute the ballot boxes."

The process of giving each of the delegations their ballots and their boxes took several agonizing minutes, but after the process was complete, Allen said, "I now instruct the members of the House of Representatives to vote for one of the following candidates: Elgin Hathaway of New York, Maria Martinez of Florida, or Robert Ryan of Indiana. Afterward, you are to place your ballot into your state's ballot box."

After seeing that the Sergeant-of Arms had collected all of the boxes and that all of the boxes had been placed in alphabetical order on several tables in front of the Speaker, Allen said, "From your delegations, I need one of your members to come forward to assume the role of your state's Teller, to read the official tally."[vii]

A short discussion followed and eventually fifty representatives found their way to the seven tables in the front of the chamber, each having been appointed a Teller. After several minutes each state indicated that their votes had been counted, signaling the Speaker to ask for the results.

Representative Hamilton D. Osborne of Arizona, who had been nominated to read the vote by the other Tellers at Table 1, who were from Alabama, Alaska, Arkansas, California, Colorado, and Connecticut, stood and announced, "Mr. Speaker, The Tellers of the votes at this table have proceeded to count the ballots contained in the box set before them. The result they find to be, that there are—

For Robert Ryan of Indiana three votes,

For Elgin Hathaway of New York two votes,

For Maria Martinez of Florida two votes."

Linda Kahn of Delaware rose from the Table 2 whose other Tellers were from Florida, Georgia, Hawaii, Idaho, Illinois and Indiana to announce, "Mr. Speaker, The Tellers of the votes at this table have proceeded to count the ballots contained in the box set before them. The result they find to be, that there are—

For Robert Ryan of Indiana four votes,

For Maria Martinez of Florida two votes,

For Elgin Hathaway of New York one vote."

Mark Shine of Louisiana rose from Table 3, whose other Tellers were from Iowa, Kansas, Kentucky, Maine, Maryland and Massachusetts and stated, "Mr. Speaker, The Tellers of the votes at this table have proceeded to count the ballots contained in the box set before them. The result they find to be, that there are—

For Robert Ryan of Indiana four votes,

For Elgin Hathaway of New York three votes,

For Maria Martinez of Florida no votes."

Lorraine Maguire of Minnesota rose from Table 4, whose other Tellers were from Michigan, Mississippi, Missouri, Montana, Nebraska and Nevada, and loudly proclaimed, "Mr. Speaker, The Tellers of the votes at this table have proceeded to count the ballots contained in the box set before them. The result they find to be, that there are—

For Elgin Hathaway of New York three votes

For Robert Ryan of Indiana two votes,

For Maria Martinez of Florida two votes."

Karla Kalcut chuckled to herself, "Poor Polk, that bigot had to choose between a woman and a black man—and he voted black!"

Four of the seven tables had reported their votes, and presently Ryan led with thirteen votes, followed by Hathaway's nine and Martinez's six. With the winner needing twenty-six votes (a majority of the fifty states), Ryan was halfway to achieving the presidency.

David Altman of New York stood tall at Table 5, whose other Tellers represented New Hampshire, New Jersey, New Mexico, North Carolina, North Dakota and Ohio, stood and said, "Mr. Speaker, The Tellers of the votes at this table have proceeded to count the ballots contained in the box set before them. The result they find to be, that there are –

For Robert Ryan of Indiana four votes,

For Elgin Hathaway of New York two votes,

For Maria Martinez of Florida one vote."

A moment later, at Table 6, whose representatives hailed from Oklahoma, Oregon, Pennsylvania, Rhode Island, South Carolina, South Dakota and Tennessee, Julius Jordan of the Keystone State announced, "Mr. Speaker, The Tellers of the votes at this table have proceeded to count the ballots contained in the box set before them. The result they find to be, that there are—

For Maria Martinez of Florida four votes,

For Robert Ryan of Indiana two votes,

For Elgin Hathaway of New York one vote."

Representatives were counting the accumulated votes, as were millions of Americans at home watching via C-Span's coverage; among them were Robert Ryan and Bob Gittings, who were watching the proceedings at the governor's office. Each was fixated on the television. Alma Levine, a representative from Virginia, stood at Table 7, whose other representatives were from Texas, Utah, Vermont, Washington, West Virginia, Wisconsin and Wyoming, and announced, "Mr. Speaker, The Tellers of the votes at this table have proceeded to count the ballots contained in the box set before them. The result they find to be, that there are—

For Elgin Hathaway of New York three votes,

For Maria Martinez of Florida three votes,
For Robert Ryan of Indiana two votes."
With a disgusted look on his face, Gittings hung his head.
"Why are you so down?" said Ryan with a smile, "By my count we're up with twenty-one votes."
"Yeah, you're right."
"So, what gives?"
"Us! We give, as in 'Up'"
"What are you—"
"It's over, sir."
"Why? We're ahead."
"Sir, there was no majority on the first round—no one received the necessary twenty-six votes. You were close, but you're not going to get any more votes. We're tapped out. You watch, Hathaway has fifteen and Martinez has fourteen. The Republicans are going to talk about this and start to rally the wagons around only one of the candidates, and it ain't going to be you."
"You really think so?"
"Allen's calling for discussion now, allowing fifteen minutes of discussion. We'll see in what direction this thing is heading in a few minutes."
Several agonizing minutes followed and after being called to report, Hamilton D. Osborne's words proved Gittings to be correct. "Mr. Speaker, the Tellers of the votes at this table have proceeded to count the ballots contained in the box set before them. The result they find to be, that there are—
For Maria Martinez of Florida three votes,
For Robert Ryan of Indiana three votes,
For Elgin Hathaway of New York one vote."
Gittings reacted, "Okay, there's one more vote for Martinez. Let's see what happens at the second table."
A moment later, Linda Kahn proclaimed, "Mr. Speaker, the Tellers of the votes at this table have proceeded to count the ballots contained in the box set before them. The result they find to be, that there are—

For Robert Ryan of Indiana four votes,

For Maria Martinez of Florida four votes,

For Elgin Hathaway of New York zero votes."

"I think the trend is going in the direction of Martinez," said a despondent Gittings. And after hearing Mark Shine say, "Mr. Speaker, the Tellers of the votes at this table have proceeded to count the ballots contained in the box set before them. The result they find to be, that there are—

For Robert Ryan of Indiana four votes,

For Maria Martinez of Florida two votes,

For Elgin Hathaway of New York one vote."

Gittings said, "It looks like we'll have our first Latina president."

Table 4's vote remained the same—Hathaway with three votes and both Martinez and Ryan staying at two each, but gains were made by Martinez at Table 5 and Table 6, as she gained a single vote from Hathaway at each of the tables. Then at Table 7, Alma Levine announced, "Mr. Speaker, the Tellers of the votes at this table have proceeded to count the ballots contained in the box set before them. The result they find to be, that there are—

For Maria Martinez of Florida five votes,

For Robert Ryan of Indiana two votes,

For Elgin Hathaway of New York one vote."

Ryan, looking glum asked, "What's the count?"

"You stayed at your twenty-one. She has one more than you do, with twenty-two; Hathaway's down to seven."

"How many more—"

"For her, the third time will be a charm. This should be the last round."

Moments later, after Table 7's Levine announced that Martinez had gained six votes at her table, Gittings and Ryan sat with heads hung low as Speaker Allen stood at the podium.

With a smile on his face he announced, "The vote for President stands as follows,

Maria Martinez of the state of Florida twenty-eight votes.

Robert Ryan of the state of Indiana twenty-one votes.

Elgin Hathaway of the state of New York one vote.

I declare that Maria Martinez has won the majority of the votes and so she will be the next president of the United States, for the term that will begin on January 20, 2021."

A huge round of applause followed his words, and many of the representatives celebrated the victory of Martinez.

The festivity happened just after the Senate had celebrated the election of the first female vice president, Maria Martinez! By some unexplainable happening, the same person had been elected to both offices. No one ever thought that such a thing could happen, but in the election of 2020, nothing was surprising.

As is the custom, word of a winner in a chamber was sent by messenger to the other chamber. But as the couriers passed each other saying to the other in unison, "We have a winner," there was nothing to indicate that the proclaimed winners had been the same person.

As other envoys had been sent separately to Maria Martinez to tell her that she had won selection of the office, once each chamber learned of the other's choice, calls for another joint session were demanded.

The Constitution had been followed, the election had been long in nature, and the House had made their pick, as had the Senate. But the picks were the same person! Could the Constitution have an answer for this? The next few hours would determine the answer to that complicated, never-before-contemplated question.

---

i. You Tube Clip: http://www.youtube.com/watch?v=BcGt8hQZzg4 Electoral College Vote Count

ii. Ibid.

iii. Ibid.

iv. Ibid.

v. Ibid.

vi. The Register of Debates, February 9, 1825, Page 526. An email from the Office of the Historian – U.S. House of Representatives – April 14, 2015

vii. Ibid.

Chapter 41

The President-Elect Speaks

WGDC Studios
Washington, D.C.
Wednesday, January 6, 2021
3:05 P.M.

Leah Manders looked at the camera and told her viewers, "If I may borrow a classic line from a classic man, I would like to quote Yankee great Yogi Berra: 'It ain't over till it's over.' And let me add, that, according to what we just witnessed, it ain't over, yet!

"I am Leah Manders, and you and I have just witnessed something that I am sure the Founding Fathers had not foreseen. Ladies and gentlemen, I have assembled a panel to help us all, including me, understand just where we are, how we got here and, of most importance, where we will be headed, as the always-surprising, seemingly never-ending election of 2020 continues to put forth roadblocks prior to the eventual naming of its winner."

The camera angle was switched to show the entire panel.

"Along side of me we have Brittany Betancourt from Penn State University, a professor of Constitutional Studies; Elizabeth Logan, a professor of Constitutional Law at Georgetown University and we have brought back a regular panelist, Tyson Joseph, professor of American History at Columbia University, one of the nation's leading lawyers.

"So, Professor Joseph, how on Earth did we arrive at this place and indeed, does this show that there is something wrong with the Constitution? How did this happen?"

Professor Joseph looked into the camera, turned to look at Manders and upon turning back to the camera said, "Leah, as my man Marvin Gaye sang in 1965, 'Ain't That Peculiar'! But seriously, I think the results from today show that there are many things *right* with the Constitution. It's an amazing document, and both houses of Congress followed their instructions to a T. It says that the House is to pick from the top three candidates for president, and that's exactly what they did. It says that the Senate is to choose from the top two candidates for vice president, and that's what they did. Nowhere is it written that the two houses have to consult with each other to make sure that the same person doesn't get both positions. Remember, this is only the fourth election in which either house has had to use their methods for picking a winner; previously the Senate picked in 1836 while the House voted in 1800 and 1824.

"And what if they had consulted with each other? They can't ignore one of the choices—as the Constitution stipulates, each house must pick from those top candidates. Then it becomes a matter of picking someone in one's own party. Do you think a Republican or Democrat is not going to pick someone from their own party just to keep the same person from winning both jobs? I don't think so. It would have been political suicide for someone to vote outside of his or her party line. Besides, the two houses are working independently—unaware of what is happening with the other."

Professor Joseph's comments seemed to ring true with the other panelists, as viewers could see all of them nodding their heads in approval.

The professor continued, "Keep in mind, too, that the Founding Fathers and those who followed them have shown that they can plan for future events. From the very beginning, in the seven Articles of the Constitution, the Founders planned for almost everything, the Elastic Clause being a great example.

"But surprises do prevail, and our nation has dealt with them. A great example would be the reaction to the election of 1800, in which Jefferson and Burr tied in the Electoral College, and the response which followed—the Twelfth Amendment."

Professor Betancourt interrupted, "That's true, but was the Constitution prepared for anything like this? I mean, there has to be something wrong with the document if it can allow the same person to be elected to two offices at the same time.”

“There is nothing wrong with the document,” said Professor Logan. “I agree with Professor Joseph. The document is fine; it is the circumstances that were the problem. The situation led to the mess, not the document.”

“Please elaborate,” asked Manders.

“Certainly! Once President Faulkner chose to run for re-election, knowing that his days might be numbered, he set into motion a chain of events that were like a snowball rolling down the side of a hill, growing larger each moment. It got out of control. With all due respect to our former president, once he received the diagnosis of pancreatic cancer, he should have either resigned or at least refrained from running for re-election. Whichever of these choices he made, he would have avoided being a participant in the November election. The fact that he ran and won the popular vote in so many states started us on this slippery slope.

“That was the circumstance that led to the Constitution-challenging election of 2020. It’s a nightmare. Think about it, his resigning before the election would have meant that the Republicans would have gone into their convention and picked either Hathaway or Martinez and would’ve gone into the election with one of them.

“With that in mind, on a national stage, we would have never heard of Bill Morgan. There would have been no Supreme Court case and no freeing of the electors. The Constitution worked because it kept this runaway freight train moving along the tracks. Perhaps the destination wasn’t a clear one, but we knew that there was a final station out there somewhere into which the train could finally pull.”

“I agree,” said Joseph. “The Constitution has a provision for the death of the president-elect, but nothing for the death of the person who wins the popular vote but dies prior to the Electoral College’s vote.”

Leah asked, “Would you please clarify that for us?”

“Of course. If the American public learned anything, it is that the person who is perceived to be the winner in November might not be the person who wins the Electoral College in December. And once President Faulkner died, there was no provision for correcting the process.”

"So," asked Manders, "The Constitution wasn't prepared for this?"

Professor Logan shot in a comment, "But why would it be? This is only the second time in more than two hundred and thirty years that a candidate has died in the time period between the popular election and the elector's vote, the now-famous Horace Greeley being the first. Heck, at that rate, the next time this probably will occur will be in, umm, something like 2252. Our descendants will have to deal with it then. For crying out loud, this is the fifty-ninth presidential election that we have had. That's more than one hundred eighteen candidates. That's about a one percent chance of something like this happening. Let's not go overboard about it."

"Are you kidding me?" asked Joseph. "This can't be about how many times that it hasn't happened in the past. Rather this has to be about how many times it might happen in the future. What if this situation comes up four more times in the next ten elections?"

"Come on, is that likely?" asked Betancourt.

"Likely, no, but you can't guarantee that it won't happen. Can you?"

"No, I can't. But what are the odds?"

"Not good, but, then again, what were the odds that the same person would be elected president and vice president?" fired back Joseph. "Hell, it could happen again in 2024."

Manders, sensing that she should step in, asked Professor Betancourt, "Could you please sum up the chain of events that led to Maria Martinez's double election?"

"Of course," said Betancourt. "Once the Supreme Court ruled that electors were able to vote for whomever they wanted, the floodgates opened. I have always been against the state laws requiring electors to vote for prescribed candidates. My thought is that if people are trusted to get the position in the first place, then they should be trusted to vote in the manner that is expected.

"The problem here was that the Republicans had two viable candidates, President Hathaway and Governor Martinez. Note that even with the freedom for the electors, the Democrats stuck with their man,

Governor Ryan. The death of Faulkner is what set up the problem."

"Interesting," said an intrigued Manders. "Please continue."

"During the last century and a half, we have almost always had only two major candidates in an election, so the likelihood of someone not receiving a majority is basically off the board. But the strengths of Ryan and Faulkner made for a close election. And when Faulkner died, the party's electors were split between two camps. No one received a majority, and so the election headed to Congress. And with no one receiving a majority for vice president, either; well, here we are, Leah."

Professor Joseph, still upset from Logan's comments suggested, "But what else could the Supreme Court do? Were they going to uphold the state laws that would make electors in several states vote for a deceased man? Of course not, that would have created a shambles of things—the House would have rejected those votes."

Logan, who was still upset with Joseph, interrupted, "And it's not a mockery now?"

Manders, learning from their first exchange quickly intervened, "So, Professor Betancourt, what do you think President-elect and, I guess I should add, Vice President-elect Martinez will do?"

"Leah, you are among the most respected journalists in the nation. But let's say on the day that you were offered the job here at WGDC, you were also offered a job at a prestigious local station in, let's say, Upstate New York. Let's say that the latter was the job that you originally sought, but the bigger job came into the picture. Is there any question as to which one you would take? Of course not. The same thing happened to Maria Martinez. She will turn down the vice presidency. She will be the next president of the United States. On January 20th she will take the oath of office, and since she won't have a vice president, she will nominate one, just like the Twenty-fifth Amendment says that she can."

Professor Joseph nodded his head, adding, "I concur. Imagine the confusion if she were to turn down the presidency? Then what would we do? The House would have to vote again, this time between Ryan, Hathaway, and Pierce Allen, who received that single vote. If Ryan won—

and remember, he had the second most votes a few minutes ago, we'd be looking at a scenario in which we'd have a Democratic president and a Republican vice president—Martinez. Think about that for a moment. Imagine a situation arising in which she is the deciding vote in the Senate and she votes along party lines against the wishes of the president.

"Leah, she has to turn down the vice presidency and take the presidency—chaos would reign if she didn't."

Professor Logan nodded her head in agreement before saying, "This thing would never end!"

The discussion continued for several minutes. One thing that had become clear to Manders was that the tension between Joseph and Logan was escalating. During a commercial break she asked, "Look, you guys, I don't know what precipitated this ill-feeling between the two of you, but tone it down—you're detracting from the show, dammit."

After the commercial break, there were several minutes of dialogue, as the four panelists really hit their stride together. Manders asked, "So how do we guard against this happening again, Professor Joseph?"

"That's the easiest question of the day, Leah. Our electoral college was set up in the eighteenth century. Although many people call for its demise and want just a popular vote, I wish to retain it, as it gives validity to the voters of the smaller states."

"Please explain."

"In a popular vote only system, the votes of citizens from smaller states like Delaware and North Dakota would be combined with those votes from the larger states of California, Texas, New York, and Florida, losing their identity for sure. But under our present system, the smaller-state votes have a true identity and a candidate has to consider their importance. If Ryan had won either of the Dakotas or Wyoming, he would have won the entire election. The small states mean something.

"But what I *would* do would be to change the timing of things. The month between the general election and the vote of the Electoral College was created during a time when the votes were delivered via horse and buggy. For God's sake, it's the twenty-first century! It could all be done electronically, with the verified state results emailed to the Secretary of State, or sent via video conference to them, or at worst, overnight mailed to them. The college could vote a week after the general election—leaving enough time for any contested results to be settled.

"Yes, I realize that a candidate could also die within that one week's time that I have proposed, but it seems less likely to happen within a week than it would be within a month."

Logan interrupted, "Tyson, I like that. We could have the Electoral College vote in November, a week or ten days after the election, just prior to Thanksgiving. The results could still be revealed in January, although, imagine if the results were read in Congress in December, by the outgoing Congress. The incoming Congress would have to deal with any improprieties, but they'd have weeks to prepare for them."

"I like that. The election process would end with the outgoing Congress, sort of like it was on their watch—which was when the election happened in the first place," said Tyson. "And if there were any problems, they would be taken up by the incoming group. That has a nice ring to it—the old problem being solved by the new group—just like it is now."

"But," said Betancourt, "it still doesn't resolve the issue of a dead candidate. What happens if the winning candidate dies within that week?"

Quickly Joseph shot back, "There's a simple solution. How about a constitutional amendment that states that all electoral votes for a candidate who dies prior to January 20th are automatically transferred to his or her running mate? Then it wouldn't matter when the candidate died. If it had been in place for this year's election, Martinez would have received all of Faulkner's votes and would have won. That would fix the omissions of the Twentieth Amendment, and we wouldn't have had to go through this scenario with the law suits and court cases."

Logan added, "I like that. I like that a lot. One problem though, as I see it, what becomes of the vice president?"

"I guess there would be no problem," said a smiling Joseph. "We just invoke the Twenty-fifth Amendment and let the new Congress vote to approve the person who is eventually nominated by the president. Umm, that would be the person who was originally elected vice president."

As Tyson Joseph was about to make a point about Maria Martinez's legitimate claim to the presidency, he was interrupted by Leah Manders.

"Professor Joseph, I apologize for interrupting the key point that you were making, one, by the way that I liked, but I've been told that President-elect Martinez will address the nation in about ten minutes. I am sure that she will address the issues that this panel has so brilliantly discussed, possibly ending any speculation about her choices. Please stay tuned as WGDC will cover the statement live."

Several minutes later, Maria Martinez, dressed in a light grey, pin-striped suit, stood at a podium about to address the American public.

After the director pointed his finger to her, Martinez said, "My fellow Americans, I want to thank President Elgin Hathaway for allowing me this time to speak to you. He could have addressed the issue that arose earlier today, but he has allowed me to address you directly.

"I speak to you today as the president-elect and the vice president-elect of the United States. Many of you may ask if being elected to dual positions is constitutionally possible, perhaps conflicting with the Twelfth Amendment. The events of today prove that indeed they are possible—I am living proof that they are.

"As the Vice President-elect, I am honored to have been elected to the position that I had been actively seeking. The thought of serving this nation as the Vice President of James Augustus Falkner would have been a dream come true. Together, our vision for a greater America would have been fulfilled. His untimely death has prevented President Faulkner from moving ahead with this vision, so I will take the responsibility to make that happen. I am here to announce that I will accept that challenge. So, at this time, I must respectfully decline the position of vice president—not accepting the position, as by doing so, that action would further compli-cate what has already been the most complicated election in our nation's history. For by refusing to accept the presidency, a scenario would be set up that would cause further delays in the electing of a president—delays that the American public should not have to endure. Therefore, without any hesitation, I will accept, wholeheartedly, the position of president-elect, and I will be honored to be your next president."

The gathered press began to shout out questions, "How long did it take for you to consider your choices?" "Does this decision finally end the election?"

"Please, give me a chance to finish.

"President James Augustus Faulkner is sorely missed. As his running mate, I endorse the same positive ideas and platform that were responsible for our November election by the American public. I am delighted to follow through with the plans that he and I shared for the nation and the world. I promise to be true to our agenda.

"However, there are two ideas that I must also address, ideas that will be associated with a new Maria Martinez administration. First, after much consideration, but as soon as possible, using the Twenty-fifth Amendment of the United States Constitution, I will place the name of a person for consideration by Congress to be the next vice president of the United States. I will take all deliberate time to make sure that the person that I nominate is the person who is the most outstanding candidate that there is, one who will work alongside me, fulfilling our goal of a greater America for all of us.

"Second, I will place before Congress a proposal to amend the Constitution so that we never have a repeat of the chaos that plagued this most recent election. I am hopeful that the new Congress will spearhead the effort to clarify the part of the document that led to the uncertainty, temporarily delaying the political process. Shortly after taking office I plan to meet with several members of Congress to discuss a constitutional amendment, one which might suggest a shortening of the time period between the votes of the people and those of the Electoral College."

There was a smattering of applause from the press corps, one of whom shouted out, "Hallelujah."

"So, my fellow Americans, the election and all of its complications are now behind us. During the next two weeks, with the help of President

Hathaway, I will put together a list of future Cabinet members for the consideration of Congress. I will keep these selections as transparent as possible, hopeful that each will be confirmed quickly."

As she started to address the press one more time, she paused and said, "Finally, one more thing. I must address the fact that I am the first Latina to be elected president. I am a proud member of that group, and it is an honor to represent it in the Oval Office. But just as John F. Kennedy was the first Roman Catholic president and Barack Obama was the first African-American president, although I am prideful of my background, I am hopeful that I will be judged for my performances as the president, not by my ethnicity or gender. And despite my desire to be like my predecessors in office, I do relish the thought of being called 'Madam President.'"

"My fellow Americans, together we will continue America along the path of greatness. I will see you on January 20th, as your next president of the United States. President Hathaway, again I thank you for your valued support. And to you, the American public, I thank you too. Together, I promise, we will create a tremendous bond. May God bless each of you and may God bless America."

As the red light went out on her close-up camera, Maria Martinez let out a loud sigh, clearly a sign that she was relieved that the election process had finally come to a close. She was certain that she had given herself a fine introduction to the American public, one that should receive good reviews and have the nation excited about the prospect of a Martinez Administration.

As she stepped away from the podium, the tall, soft-spoken, soon-to-be former governor and future president shook hands with dozens of well-wishers, each excited to be among the first to shake the hand of the nation's first Latina president.

CHAPTER 42

The Unexpected

The Oval Office
Sunday, January 17, 2021
10:08 P.M.

"Thank you for seeing me on such short notice," said a grateful Pierce Allen, as he hurried into the Oval Office. "It's been a week now. Who do you think she'll pick for vice president?" referring to the selection that Maria Martinez would soon be making.

Hathaway smiled and said, "I'm not sure, but I can tell you the names of two people that aren't being considered—yours and mine."

Allen laughed loudly, his famous laugh portraying itself in high volume. After collecting himself, he told Hathaway, "Listen, I'm certain I'm not on any short list that she might have, but you, my friend, you might be someone about whom there is much consideration."

"Are you crazy?" said Hathaway. "If the nation had a Latina president and an African-American vice president, the number of people moving to Canada would hit an all-time high—maybe doubling their population."

Pierce smiled. "I'm not sure, but I think she would be wise to nominate someone with whom the Congress is comfortable. She'll be the third president within a few months, and I think Congress and the nation will be looking very carefully at the first really big choice that she would make. I'm certain that it'll be a veteran politician, one who's trusted by the American public."

"Trust? That would leave out about 92 percent of Congress and a majority of the governors," said Allen with a smirk. "Mr. President, I want to thank you for allowing me to speak to the nation from the White House. It will be my way of saying so long to the citizens. I wanted you to have an opportunity to review the speech, so I brought a copy here with me."

"No problem, Pierce. I was so sorry to hear about your health complications. You've been at this for a very long time—going home has got to feel good."

Hathaway hefted the sheaf of papers. "Wow, this is pretty heavy. Just how many pages are there to this thing?"

"Quite a few, Mr. President," Allen admitted. "I might have gone a little overboard thanking you, the people of Kansas and the citizens of the United States. But I was going to cut it down some."

"Okay," Hathaway said. "Why don't you cut it, then give it to me to read?"

"How about this? Do you have time to read the first, let's say, three or four pages right now? That's the part that I really wanted you to read."

"Yeah, I can do that."

Hathaway placed the speech on a small oak table and pulled his chair up.

Allen approached him, pen in hand. "Mr. President, would you mind autographing and dating this draft? I'd like to donate it to the Kansas Hall of Fame collection."

Hathaway smiled. "Sure, where would you like me to sign it?"

"Would you sign in two places, one copy for Kansas and another copy for my personal files? Pages twelve and sixteen. Thank you, it'll be appreciated. Here, let me show you." Allen shuffled through the speech, found the proper page, then folded back a quarter of the sheet. "Put your John Hancock right here, Mr. President," he grinned, then quickly turned to another page, folding back another corner. "And here too, if you'd be so kind." Hathaway obliged a second time.

Hathaway wiped his eyes, which had dark hollows beneath them. "Look, Pierce, it's been a hell of a day. You were writing speeches before I knew how to speak. You certainly don't need my blessing on this." He handed Allen the stack of papers. "Here, take this back and enjoy speaking to the public."

"Oh, I will, Sir. I will."

Allen watched intently as the president turned back to the pile of papers on his desk. As Hathaway picked up the first of several reports, Allen silently placed the document on the floor behind him and slowly undid a zipper that ran along the inseam of his left pant leg. He then carefully reached inside his pant leg, feeling for the release switch that would open a hidden cavity inside his prosthetic leg. He reached inside for the a four-and-a-half-inch serrated stainless steel knife inside—an item that he knew would one day become as infamous as Lee Harvey Oswald's rifle or John Wilkes Booth's pistol.

"I appreciate your faith in me as a writer," Allen said. "Did you see where I wrote that I would do anything for the people of Kansas and the United States?"

"Ummm, yeah, yeah, I saw that part, yes," said Hathaway, concentrating upon a report in his hands.

"Good, so you'll know the action I'm about to take is for them!"

He then gripped the knife tightly, and then plunged it toward the right side of the president's neck, aiming for the carotid artery. Hathaway, however, had turned to his left to stare at his interlocutor, which caused the sharp blade to rip through his right shoulder blade instead of its intended target. As he was about to shout out in pain, Allen placed his left hand over his victim's mouth, silencing his cry of despair. Allen quickly drew the blade beneath Hathaway's jaw, opening up a huge gash across his throat, then plunged the blade quickly into his chest, just above the heart.

Hathaway fell onto the carpet, his blood pooling around him. His assailant's attacks continued. "Die, you bastard," Allen hissed. "Die. You'll never deliver that speech."

Hathaway looked up at Allen. "You won't be able to get away with this. You—"

The end of the sentence remained unfinished, as did the president's time in office. Elgin Hathaway had delivered his last earthly words, dying on the floor of the Oval Office.

His clothes stained red with some of the president's blood, Allen called out into the hallway, "Come quickly! The president's been attacked!"

Three Secret Servicemen rushed into the room to find Hathaway lying motionless in a pool of his own blood, Allen calmly standing next to the president's desk where he had stabbed the bloody knife into the wood.

"Hands on the desk, Mr. Speaker!" Robert Vasquez, the senior Secret Service officer yelled. "One move and I'll shoot." Turning to the other Secret Servicemen, he said, "Quick, check the president! Call an ambulance!" Vasquez quickly cuffed Allen, patting him down and finding no other weapons.

"Remove these cuffs at once!" Allen shouted. "That's an order from your new President of the United States." He nodded at the document he'd placed on the floor. "Here, read it yourself. Not only had Hathaway signed off that he was unable to fulfill his duties, but he pardoned me for my actions. Look on pages twelve and sixteen—you'll see it there."

Vasquez shook his head in confusion. "I have no idea what you're talking about, Mr. Speaker. All the reading that I'm doing is of your Miranda rights. You're under arrest, and I'll let someone with a higher pay grade take care of the details."

"I tell you, *I* am President of the United States, Vasquez! As soon as Hathaway died, I became president! The minute I get these cuffs off, these hands will sign the papers to fire you"

"Is he dead?" Vasquez asked the Secret Serviceman on the floor next to Hathaway. She shook her head. "I don't feel a pulse."

"Rider's on his way," said the other agent, Mark Mirabella. "Ambulance too."

"Seal off the room!" Vasquez roared. "No one, repeat, no one, gets into this room without me being there too. Understood?"

"Got it, sir."

Just then Brook Rider burst into the room, falling to his knees next to the president's motionless body with an anguished cry. "Jesus Christ! What the hell happened here?" He was still administering CPR minutes later when the medics arrived.

One of the medics, Susan Perri, after assessing the situation told the passionate Rider, "Forget it, doc. He's gone." A moment later, the tearful Rider watched as the body of the nation's leader was carried out of the building.

Leaving Allen sitting on a bench inside a lockup facility deep in the bowels of the White House, Vasquez waited for word from his superiors. He buried his face in his shaking hands, his only thought, "Mother of God, who's in charge of the nation now?"

Chapter 43

The Cabinet Dishes It Out

Washington, D.C.
Monday, January 18, 2021
2:35 A.M.

With Inauguration Day only two days away, all of the members of the Cabinet, dazed and in mourning, gathered in the office of Secretary of State Virginia Loving to discuss the president's assassination.

From the very beginning of the meeting, Secretary of the Treasury Nathaniel Geller, a resident of Topeka and a lifelong friend of Pierce Allen, defended the Speaker. "Before we get started, let me just say that Pierce Allen is innocent until proven guilty. It looks bad, but—"

"Looks bad?" interrupted Homeland Security Secretary Kitty Niles. "Hell, he's as guilty as anyone that I've ever seen in my life. He killed the president—case closed."

An angry Geller shouted back, "Who the hell are you to talk? If your agency had done a better job of protecting the president, he'd still be alive!"

"Hey, I'm in charge of the nation's security. The Secret Service is to blame for this."

Loving interrupted, loudly shouting, "Hey, enough, already! We have important business to take care of. We can discuss faults later."

"Like what?" asked Secretary of Labor Jodi Gewitz. "I can't imagine anything that the public might think is more important than providing justice for the president."

"He's freaking guilty," shouted an enraged Secretary of Energy Tim O'Connor. "That's the most important thing. We need to do something and do it fast."

"Crap, just execute the bastard," screamed Commerce Secretary Tomas Salvestrini.

"Yeah, I'd go for that too," said Jonathan Beaton, the newly-appointed Secretary of Defense.

"Enough!" shouted Loving again. "We have to determine who's in charge of the nation right now. The president is dead. With no vice president, according to the presidential Succession Act of 1947, the next person in line for the presidency is the Speaker of the House—meaning Pierce Allen would be in charge. But my question is 'Can we allow that to happen'? Let me quote the Act,

> (a) (1) If, by reason of death, resignation, removal from office, inability, or failure to qualify, there is neither a President nor Vice President to discharge the powers and duties of the office of President, then the Speaker of the House of Representatives shall, upon his resignation as Speaker and as Representative in Congress, act as President.

> (2) The same rule shall apply in the case of the death, resignation, removal from office, or inability of an individual acting as President under this subsection.

> (b) If, at the time when under subsection (a) of this section a Speaker is to begin the discharge of the powers and duties of the office of President, there is no Speaker, or the Speaker fails to qualify as Acting President, then the President pro tempore of the Senate shall, upon his resignation as President pro tempore and as Senator, act as President.'

So, according to the Act, Allen is in, because we have the document signed by the president stating that he's handing over his duties to Allen, but was that signed under duress? Allen might have had that knife to his throat forcing him to sign. Can we count it? Is Allen, his murderer, 'qualified' to be acting president as it suggests?"

"Do we have a choice?" Gewitz replied. "The Constitution says that the signed document is all that we need. I guess when they made the

Amendment they didn't consider a murder attempt and mutiny by someone who was in line for the office. But with him being locked away, it might be a non-issue anyway. Besides, Hathaway's death supersedes all that other stuff. Allen is next in line."

"What do we do? What *can* we do?" asked Niles.

Gewitz suggested, "We hand the thing over to Benjamin. As President pro tempore, he's the next in line after Allen." Jodi glanced over at Benjamin Hayes, who looked back gravely.

"Hold on there," interrupted Loving, "There are a couple of issues that need to be addressed. First off, is the Presidential Succession Act even constitutional? There have been claims made that as members of Congress, the Speaker of the House and the President pro tempore do not qualify under what Article II of the Constitution calls 'Officers of the United States', meaning that Allen and, sorry, Benjamin, don't qualify. Some would argue that due to its potential unconstitutionality, that the guideline to follow would be the Succession Act of 1886 in which Cabinet positions are given top priority."

"Madam Secretary," snapped Hayes, "If this is some veiled attempt on your part to do an end run and secure power for yourself, then I must protest. It's a known fact that the Act of 1886 names the Secretary of State as being next in line after the vice president—meaning that you would be the person to take over. Presently, until it is ruled any other way, the 1947 law is the law of the land—meaning that I will be Acting President."

"Relax, no such seizure is being attempted, Benjamin," Loving shot back. "Get hold of yourself. I am bringing to light a possible constitutional issue. Besides, we're only talking about being in office for a day and a half, and then Martinez will be inaugurated. Look, anything can happen in that time. Someone has to be in charge, and we need a ruling on this issue *now*."

Director Furry stood up and said, "I think all this is a moot point. My agent in the field, Vasquez, tells me that Allen has a pardon from Hathaway absolving him of all crimes. Thus, he is a free man, one who happens to be the Acting President of the United States."

A hush fell over the group. "What the hell!" shouted Loving. "That bastard thinks he has some legal footing to be in charge?"

"We can't let him do that," exclaimed Secretary of Agriculture, Peter Andrews.

"I agree," shouted Transportation Secretary Suzanne Molinar.

"Yes," answered Furry. "What's more, he claims that if he isn't released right away, he'll make another attempt at the courts for resolution."

"I don't know about the rest of you, but I say we let the freaking bastard rot in the basement," sputtered Secretary of Justice Robin Ashley. "Let him try to get another hearing over the next thirty-six hours. I'll make sure no court will hear him. There's no way Elgin Hathaway would have signed this document unless he was tricked or under duress. That makes it inadmissible!"

"In a court of law we couldn't prove the duress," said Gewitz.

"That means that whether he's under arrest or not, he's the Acting President," said Geller. "And one more thing—we have the signed pardon telling us that he is free and clear of any charges against him."

"Stop being his freaking ally," shouted a disgusted Secretary of Veterans Affairs Regina Hayes. "Somehow he's going down for this!"

Gewitz sighed. "As you all know, a pardon clears the recipient of any charges for a federal crime. My thought is that the attack took place on federal land, upon a federal official. Thus, it's a federal crime. The pardon would hold up. Any ideas now, folks?"

Hayes thought for a moment and then said, "We still have to deal with the pardon. If Allen is exonerated from any prosecution, then as you said earlier, Virginia, he is the Acting President. We can't get around that fact. We will have to release him, and he can go straight to the Oval Office for the next two days. He's got the ultimate 'Get out a jail free card'—the greatest in our nation's history. And although it *should* say something about it, the Constitution says nothing about keeping a mutinous person from taking control, unless . . . unless we try to attach the treason clause to his actions. How does that sound? Could we use treason against him?"

Loving pored over her copy of the Constitution. "Treason against the United States shall consist only in levying War against them, or in adhering to the Enemies, giving them Aid and Comfort. No Person shall be convicted of Treason unless on the Testimony of two Witnesses to the same overt Act, or on Confession in open Court." Loving paused. "Unless we got him to confess, with only the president as a witness, the Constitution's treason provision would not be applicable. And, our only witness is dead, let alone having two witnesses in hand."

The silence in the room, the type of silence that one hears upon learning about the death of a close friend, deepened as the occupants thought about possible solutions to their devastating problem. Then Secretary of Education Carrie Sussman raised her hand. "I think I have it! I think I have it! Okay, hear me out on this one. This might sound silly, but in what order did he sign the documents?"

"Why should that matter?" Loving asked.

"I think it might make all of the difference in the world," a jubilant Sussman responded. "If President Hathaway first signed a document stating that he was unable to discharge his duties, then anything that he did or signed afterward, including the pardon, should be null and void. Read the Constitution, only after he signs a document stating that he is able to resume his duties can he, well, for lack of a better term, resume his duties. If he signed the release first, we're golden. But if he signed the pardon first, then we're toast."

Loving digested the idea for a moment. The chatter of the others in the room suggested that Sussman might have come up with a very good point. But, a moment later a depressing look appeared upon Loving's face. "There are only two people who know the order of the signatures. One is dead; the other is his alleged assailant. It would be conjecture on our parts to assume that the pardon was signed second. Besides, looking at the two pages in question, the pardon was on page twelve and the release on page sixteen. So it appears that the pardon was signed previous to his transferring power to Allen.

"As for the previous point, according to the Constitution, the president is not considered to be incapacitated until he has conveyed the message to Robert and Benjamin. Now does that mean the vice president takes over as the president finishes signing the document, or upon the receipt of the message by the Speaker and the President Pro Tempore? We'd need clarity on that point!"

Sussman put forth another idea. "Clarity! God, please give us clarity. Who the hell writes these things in code, anyway? Suppose we follow the exact words of the Amendment. Look at Section Four; we here in this room represent the principal officers. Now, follow me on this. Let's assume that, after everything plays out, Allen has the authority to be the Acting President. But, we deem that he's unable to perform his duties, because he's incapacitated—the bars and the handcuffs causing the incapacity. Not to mention mental incapacity, because who else but a crazy man would try to kill the president? We require him to undergo a comprehensive examination with three psychiatrists. In the interim, Benjamin is the Acting President until Martinez takes over. We have, in essence, rendered him powerless. Now, using Section Four, we declare Allen unable to discharge the powers and duties of the office. Thus, we have put him out of office before he even takes over."

"Hmm. I like that plan," Loving said. "But it also says that the vice president should then take over as Acting President. Folks, we have no VP to assume those duties, unless, of course, we use the terms of the Succession Act of 1947. But I would add that President Martinez, upon taking office, should suggest an amendment that addresses this issue."

After a spirited discussion of Sussman's ideas, Secretary Loving called for a vote, "All in favor of using Article IV of the Twenty-fifth Amendment to question the mental capabilities of Pierce Allen, raise your hand."

All hands were raised.

"So be it," Loving said. "That will be the government's official position, and we will proceed with naming Benjamin the Acting President."

"Stop!" said Angelica Herzog, Secretary of Housing and Urban Development. She held a copy of the Constitution in her hands. "I just noticed this. I can't believe it!"

"What is it?" asked Loving.

"We went through all of this for nothing."

"What do you mean?"

"Reread this passage." Herzog handed Loving her copy of the Constitution.

She read it slowly aloud as Herzog had instructed her to do. "So what gives?"

"Don't you see?" asked Herzog. "Quote, '. . . then the Speaker of the House of Representatives shall, upon his resignation as Speaker and as Representative in Congress, act as president.'"

"Yeah? So what?" said Loving.

"So, did I miss it? Just when did he resign? The bastard never resigned."

Loving closed her eyes. Then with a beaming smile said, "Crap, you're right. He has to resign before he can assume his new position."

To the bewilderment of the Secret Service members that were congregated in the hall, a loud cheer emanated from the conference room.

A moment later Gewitz smirked. "Virginia, do you want to tell him?"

"Sure. In a couple of days, after Martinez takes over. Meanwhile, we'll use the inability to discharge his duties as our official position."

CHAPTER 44

The Lawyer Reacts

WGDC Studios
Washington, D.C.
Monday, January 18, 2021
12:37 P.M.

". . . Leah, the bottom line is that my client is being held illegally," said famed defense attorney Justin Dante Mathews. "There is no reason for him not to have been awarded bail."

"But Mr. Mathews, perhaps he is seen as a flight risk."

"That's asinine; the man is the Acting President of the United States. Where would he want to be other than in his constitutionally-awarded seat in the Oval Office?"

"Well, Sir, the Secretary of State has issued a statement from which I will quote, 'Pierce Allen, the alleged killer of President Elgin Hathaway, has commented that he is the Acting President of the United States, a stance he claims is backed by the Presidential Succession Act of 1947. An early morning meeting of the Cabinet has resulted in the federal government questioning the mental capacities of the alleged assassin, and so, until we are told otherwise from a panel of mental therapists, we are ruling, under Section Four of the Twenty-fifth Amendment, that Pierce Allen is unable to discharge the duties of the presidency, thus naming President pro tempore Benjamin Hayes the Acting President of the United States. This decision was reached by a unanimous vote of the Cabinet.'"

"Pure hogwash," he answered with his thick Southern accent. It is nothing more than a stall tactic being used by them in an attempt to derail my client from gaining his constitutionally approved position. He is deserving of his position as the president. Besides, how can they bring into question his mental capacities without a previous examination? There's no foundation!"

"But wait a minute. He killed the president."

"Allegedly, Ms. Manders. Allegedly."

"So, allegedly, why would he have done it—kill the president, that is?"

"Ms. Manders, I will not comment upon those outrageous speculative allegations, but I will promise you an interview with Mr. Allen as soon as he is correctly recognized as the president."

"Do you think that there's enough time for him to fight the charges for murder and be named Acting President?"

"Ms. Manders, those aren't the allegations we need to quickly overturn. We need immediate action to overturn the blocking of his rightful position as president. The alleged murder charges will be taken care of in due time."

"Thank you, Mr. Mathews. We appreciate your being available to us by phone."

Four hours later, Leah Manders reported to her audience, "The District of Columbia District Court ruled against Pierce Allen and his attempts to claim the presidency, ruling that it can be determined that he is unable to discharge his duties even before he is sworn into office! This ruling blocks the way for him to be considered Acting President of the United States. He is appealing the decision to the United States Supreme Court.

"Meanwhile, an unnamed source, who wants to remain anonymous due to his or her closeness to the situation, claims that the Supreme Court will not hear the case, keeping Pierce Allen from being able to proceed with his plan to appeal the District Court's ruling. Thus, Benjamin Hayes will remain in the position as the Acting President of the United States, while Pierce Allen will remain incarcerated."

Chapter 45

The Latest Development

Tallahassee, Florida
Monday, January 18, 2021
6:45 A.M.

Although the overflow crowd of media did not threaten Maria Martinez's path to her car, she was thankful for the sphere of protection that her Secret Servicemen provided. She attempted to be as polite as she could be, but there were just too many questions being fired in her direction.

She paused to address the shouts from the reporters. "What is your reaction to the Speaker, Madam Governor?" "Any word from the White House?" "Are you in touch with the Speaker or the Secretary of State?"

The still-shaken Martinez approached the rope separating the press from the president-elect. "If the allegations are true, then Speaker Allen has to be held responsible to the fullest extent of the law. In fact, he has to be held to a higher degree than any politician in history. If the reports are true, then he will be held responsible for his cowardly acts. Right now our major concern is for the family of Elgin Hathaway and for the welfare of the nation. Both are in my personal prayers."

"Will these latest developments make you postpone your plans for naming a vice president," yelled out CNN reporter Selma Crino.

"Yes! In a little more than an hour, I was to announce my nominee. But due to this emergency I will postpone that announcement. Now, please excuse me, as I must check with the Cabinet."

"One more question, Madam Governor. Is Pierce Allen the President of the United States?"

"I'll answer that question in two days after I'm sworn in. In the meantime, that answer is out of my hands."

"Should he—"

"Thank you, ladies and gentlemen. I'll see everyone in Washington."

Chapter 46

The Oath Is Finally Taken

WGDC Studios
Washington, D.C.
Wednesday, January 20, 2021
6:30 P.M.

"I . . . Maria Gabriella Rose Martinez . . . do solemnly swear that I . . . will faithfully execute...the Office of the President of the United States . . . and will . . . to the best of my ability . . . preserve . . . protect . . . and defend . . . the Constitution of the United States . . .. So help me God."

Leah Manders beamed into the camera. "With those words, earlier today, Maria Martinez was sworn in as our nation's forty-sixth president, the nation's first Latina president.

"Good evening, I'm Leah Manders, and on a picture-perfect, forty-eight-degree day here in the nation's capital, a crowd estimated to be between five hundred thousand and seven hundred thousand eagerly watched as President Martinez took the official oath, completing the most complicated election in US History.

"By now you are aware of the many controversies, the court cases, the votes of the House and the Senate, and the other too-numerous-to-mention details of the Constitution-challenging Election of 2020. Yet, here we are, having gotten past all of those pitfalls to witness yet another peaceful transition of power to a new president.

"In her powerful, carefully crafted speech of 2,352 words, a total of words which is said to have been designed to equal the average length of all fifty-seven inaugural speeches between the Washington and Obama Administrations, she described such topics as her modest upbringing, her path into politics, her years as Governor of Florida, her thoughts on the election and, of course, her goals for the new administration. The entire speech is available on our website and will be repeated tonight at 11:00, in its entirety, on these airwaves. Here are a few excerpts.”

Leah turned to another monitor as WGDC showed Maria Martinez making her first national address as president. “Thank you all, both here in the nation's capital and in your homes and offices around the nation. A special thank you goes out to the brave men and women in our armed services, who are keeping brightly lit the torch of liberty around the world.

“A special thank you goes to the men on this stage who have preceded me as president, I thank each of them for the dedicated years of service that they have provided to our nation. I would be remiss if I were not to mention and give a special thank you to my immediate predecessors, James Augustus Faulkner and Elgin Hathaway, each of whom has been missed by our nation and by me personally.”

Her words were greeted with a tremendous ovation from those in attendance.

“I am humbled to be here before you as your elected president, and I want to acknowledge the efforts of Governor Robert Ryan of Indiana, who contested an honest, hard-fought campaign, one that I respected for its integrity.

“I am also humbled to stand before you as the first Latina president of our fine nation. Although I am proud to represent this group, I am here to tell you that I will represent all Americans, Republicans and Democrats, males and females, transgender and gays, Latinos, blacks, whites and Asians, rich and poor, centenarians and newborns. Please make no mistake about it; I am here to represent you all.

“Progress abounds for our nation. One hundred years ago, a woman's role in a presidential election was to ask her significant other who he voted for. And most Latinos were relegated to picking the fruits and vegetables that would end up on the tables of voters. Today, I proudly stand before you showing that those days are behind us for good.”

“You can say that again, Madam President,” shouted one observer.

“Hell yeah,” shouted an older woman.

“Even some fifty years ago, in many states, a fine man like Elgin Hathaway would have been denied the right to vote for president, and the dream of becoming president was still unborn in the minds of African-American children. Yes, progress is being made, but there are still mountains to climb. But we will climb them together—with me at the front of the line!"

"We're behind you, Madam President."

Manders spoke directly to the television audience: "Later, the president addressed her modest childhood. Let's take a look at another clip."

The cameras showed Martinez speaking again: ". . . The spirit of America lives within its people, whether you are born into a wealthy family or, like me, born into a loving family that struggled economically. One should never be judged by the location of one's zip code but rather by the location one allows his or her dreams to take them. My family had little money, but I had rich dreams. I stand before you today as living proof that one's dreams are limitless. I promise you that if we all work toward a common goal, we Americans can do anything . . . ."

Manders added, "President Martinez also addressed her years as the successful governor of Florida. Let's look at another clip."

". . . The same progress that I helped to bring to my native Florida, I will bring to the entire nation. Under my administration, Florida saw its largest eight-year growth spurt in its history. We can achieve the same thing for people all across the country. Crime was reduced, too. And I promise to be tough on criminals all across the nation."

"Of course," said Manders, "Citizens across this nation wanted to know what Martinez herself had to say about the bizarre election of 2020." Manders cued up another clip.

"Americans all across the nation should be proud of the way we all handled the recent, complicated election, as we all were subjected to almost every possible scenario that could arise," intoned Martinez. "There was never a panic among our people, as we had confidence that the Constitution would overcome any obstacles, which it did. Whether it was challenges to the Twentieth or Twenty-fifth Amendments, involvement by not one but both houses of Congress, or the plethora of court cases, despite all of those impediments, we have had an orderly conclusion to the election, proving that the Constitution is the strong, viable backbone of this nation that we need it to be. Simply put, the system works . . ."

"And finally, she addressed the goals of the Martinez administration." Manders rolled one final clip.

" . . . Our economy will continue to grow, just as it did during the previous administrations. My administration will push forward legislation that supports American business and furthers the cause of the middle class . . .

"We will continue to negotiate for a peaceful coexistence with the world community, keeping them mindful that we are vigilant for any troubling winds that might blow our way. We are a nation of peace, which should not be misconstrued as being a nation of weakness. We will continue to support our allies and remind our foes that we are a nation of might.

"Technology has forever had its origins in the United States. Let us continue to support the efforts of our scientific community. And so, I am proud to announce that the Martinez Administration will push for us to safely land a team of astronauts on Mars and return them safely to our nation. Let us all strive to make this happen within the next few years.

"And speaking of space, we can no longer sit back waiting for news that a cosmic body is on a collision course with our planet. I will push for an international commission of all nations on the planet, led by the United States, that will intensify our efforts to identify, hunt down, and destroy any possible foreign intruders that could bring harm to our planet."

Similar to the chants for the former president, the crowd shouted out, "Mar-teen-ez . . . Mar-teen-ez . . . Mar-teen-ez."

"As Americans, we each have a dream for ourselves, for our communities and for our great nation. My dream is for a term in office that coincides with a prolonged period of world peace and high economic gains.

"Please help me make this America be an America that yet unborn generations of school children will read about in their history books and think, 'What a great time it must have been to live in the United States in the 2020s.' Let them look back to a second Roaring Twenties in American History. Yet, to achieve this hope for our unborn descendants, we, the Americans of today, must strive to make this a great place for all Americans now. We owe it not only to ourselves, but to those who will follow."

"Mar-teen-ez . . . Mar-teen-ez . . . Mar-teen-ez."

"It is our time, America. Let's do this correctly, with all of our might and with efforts that derive themselves from the very fiber of all of us. Let's taste the fruits of prosperity that we together will harvest, and upon reaping those treasured fruits, let's cherish every bite, now and forever.

"Thank you for this opportunity, America. I will not let you down. God bless this administration, God bless each of you and may God, as He has done since our formation, bless America."

Manders looked sternly into the camera. "With those words, the administration of Maria Martinez has begun. Her words brought countless applause and have been the recipient of praise from members of both parties. Again, the speech in its entirety can be viewed on our website and seen on this network tonight at 10:00 Eastern. We will be back momentarily with an esteemed panel who will dissect the president's speech."

Chapter 47

The Discussion

Founding Farmers Restaurant
Pennsylvania Ave., NW
Washington, D.C.
Wednesday, March 24, 2021

"Tyson, I've told you three damned times that that's the business that I'm in. News—that's what I do for a living," said an aggravated Leah Manders.

"Look, you told me, in fact you *promised* me, that everything that we discussed was off the record," Tyson Joseph shot back. "You gave me your freaking word."

"It's still off the record, for now, but when you and I had that conversation many months ago, I was promising to keep a lid on things to help protect Elgin. He's no longer with us, and I have no allegiance to Martinez, so why keep it quiet any longer?"

"No matter who's the president, it still has potential to be dangerous for the nation. Who knows what implications it might have? Do you want to be responsible for the kind of mayhem that might lead to rioting or worse?"

"But, Tyson, it's the law of the land, a very old one, indeed. It's my job to inform the public and bring light to newsworthy items. Besides, be honest. Ask yourself. Why did you give me the damned information in the first place? I'll tell you why; it was in case something happened to Elgin and to you. You wanted it in the hands of someone who would safeguard it and deliver it to those who needed to know about it. That, my friend, is why you came to me in the first place. So, Elgin is dead, and it's only you who is the keeper of the flame. And what if something happens to you? I've sat on this thing for months; I have a freaking job to do."

"Let's calm down for a minute," Tyson said. "You're right. You're right, dammit. Let's figure out how to handle this. I want this to come out too, Leah. I just don't want to do it irresponsibly."

"Okay, Tyson, where do we begin? Help me lay it out in a way that people will understand."

"Clearly we should start in 1862, during the War, when Lincoln signed the Second Confiscation Act, allowing the north to seize all rebel land, although his lack of support for it doomed its effectiveness—so some politicians wanted something stronger. Then we should mention that in 1865 the Radical Republicans took things into their own hands—for their own diabolical confiscation law."

"Right," Leah nodded. "Knowing that it wouldn't pass the entire Congress, they held a secret meeting, comprised of just enough members of Congress to have a quorum in each house. What was that date?"

"Leah, the date's an important part of the story—April 3, 1865. They proposed a bill that was far more reaching in its scope than anything else that had ever been proposed. It not only confiscated rebel land, but it gave it to the slaves and, even more diabolical, to any descendant who could prove that he or she was kin to those who served on that particular plantation. That's a tough stipulation, and when you add to that that they provided a two-hundred-year shelf life for the law, making it viable until the year 2065; you're talking about some major legislation, there."

"Yeah, and then you add to that that they made part of the law stipulate that the present owners of the land, no matter what the year, were responsible for all court and legal fees of those who made the claims, and you can see why the law has been kept under wraps for so long."

"Correct, Leah. So we must add that the bill passed both of the Houses that night, thus the Quorum's Child was born - the quorum being the majority of both houses needed to pass the law and the child being the law itself."

"But here's what I don't get, Tyson. How did it pass? Most of these guys were fearful of it."

"The Radicals told them that it would never be signed by Lincoln and that its real use was as leverage, to be used as a means to get the South to fear it enough to pass a future Fourteenth Amendment. Add to that the closeness of the vote, and they were certain that it could never override a Lincoln veto."

"Okay, I get that part, but the next part is confusing. You're the historian, please explain it to me."

"Certainly. There are three means by which a bill can become law. The most obvious is that it passes both houses and is signed by the president. The second is that after passing both houses, it is vetoed by the president, but the veto is overridden by a two-thirds vote of both houses."

"Yeah, those are the easy ones. It's the third one that gets me."

"That's because it's the least known. It's called a pocket veto and that happens after a bill passes Congress and it is given to the president, who keeps it on his desk for ten days without doing anything. Those ten days do not include Sundays. If it stays unsigned all that time, it automatically becomes the law of the land—even without his signature. That was the key to the entire plan. They gave it to the White House on April 5th. Then, on April 10th Lincoln met with the Speaker of the House and leading Radical, Schuyler Colfax, asking him about the bill and being told to wait until the morning of the 14th when more information would be forthcoming. With the euphoria of the end of the Civil War on hand, Lincoln agreed. All reports state that on the morning of the 14th the two of them were overheard having a loud shouting match. Schuyler returned to the White House at 7:00 P.M. that night, probably attempting one last time to have Lincoln sign the bill. But a few hours later, Lincoln was shot, dying on the 15th, the day that the Quorum's Child became the law of the land."

"Okay, I think I got it," Leah said. "The 15th was the tenth day, not including Sundays, and so using the provisions of the pocket veto, it was the law."

"Yes, and it can be concluded that the Radicals were behind the assassination so that the law would automatically become law, ruthlessness at its best . . . or worst, depending upon one's point of view. With all of the attention over Lincoln's murder, there was no attention given to this passed law."

"I get that, Tyson, but why didn't the Radicals push the issue?"

"One would have to think that they underestimated the public's reaction to the assassination. With a conspiracy-minded atmosphere, the Radicals didn't want any traces of a secret meeting going public—fearful, and rightfully so, that people would correctly conclude that the conspiracy had involved killing the president."

"Okay, so why not expose the law once things died down?"

"They got close! They impeached Andrew Johnson, and if he had been convicted by the Senate, they had one of their main Radicals in line to take over."

"Benjamin Wade?" asked Leah.

"Yes, but because he was so extremely radical, many of the senators who might have voted for impeachment chose to refrain, fearful that Wade was going to lead the nation in the wrong direction. In a famous statement, a newspaper covering the aftermath of the impeachment trial wrote, 'Andrew Johnson is innocent because Ben Wade is guilty of being his successor.'[i]

"With that opportunity missed, their next chance to release information about their law took place during the Grant administration, when none other than Schuyler Colfax became the vice president. Knowing that Grant, the war hero, was a neophyte politician, things seemed perfectly aligned for the unveiling of the confiscation law."

"One would think so. Colfax could have led Grant into a position where he would have supported it—especially Grant who had fought the southerners. So why didn't it happen?"

Tyson sighed. "Because Colfax got caught up in the nefarious activities of the Grant administration, one of the most scandalous in history. For Grant's second term, he wasn't asked to be part of the ticket. Then things got worse for the Radicals. As a response for his winning the presidential vote of a special 1876 election committee, Rutherford B. Hayes, the Republican candidate, promised to end Reconstruction and pulled the federal troops out of the South. That, coupled with the deaths of so many of the Radicals, dimmed the chances for the revival of the confiscation law. So it died, like many of those who had created it."

Leah nodded. "But then, in 1880, Radical James Garfield was elected and when he started to appoint some African-Americans to high positions, some of the remaining Radicals thought that the Garfield administration would finally shine the light on the then fifteen-year-old law. But an assassin's bullets, and some shoddy medical care, killed Garfield and the last chances for the Radicals. Right?"

"Right. And it remained undisclosed for the rest of the nineteenth century and then into the twentieth under McKinley and Teddy Roosevelt, who, like their predecessors, kept it under wraps."

"Tyson, that brings us to Woodrow Wilson, the first southerner voted into office since the Civil War. He called for discriminatory measures to be put into effect in the government. He longed for the days of Southern strength. Certainly, upon receiving the information from Taft about the still-secret law, he would have done anything to keep it quiet."

Tyson laughed, "That's something that he and his wife accomplished for more than one hundred years."

"So, do you think that Wilson passed it on to Harding?"

Tyson shook his head. "No. I don't think it was heard about again for years—Wilson successfully buried it—literally. In fact, I think it was kept under wraps for a long time."

"Well, we know that Elgin knew about it."

"Right, I told him."

"And how did Faulkner learn about it?"

"I think, and I don't know this for a fact, that it's tied into that time capsule. Maybe it was actually literally buried for one hundred years—Faulkner being the first to learn about it."

"Yeah, if Elgin knew, Faulkner had to know," Leah said.

"Okay, that might be. So what about Martinez?" Tyson asked.

"I'm not sure if Elgin had enough time to let her know. But she might." Leah paused for a moment. "Well, I'm going to find out. I'll ask her if she knows and if she doesn't, then I'll tell her."

"That could lead to trouble, Leah. You know that I've always been worried about the repercussions of letting that information go public."

Leah sighed. "I know you're right. You've convinced me. So, let's come up with a plan to ease the nation through it. Tyson, you're among the smartest people I've ever met. Figure out a plan that would keep the nation from blowing itself up. You do that, and I'll confront Martinez. How long would you need?"

"I wouldn't be able to finish it, I'd say, for three to four months, if I want to get it right."

"It's been hidden from the public for more than one hundred fifty years. What're talking about a few more months? Good luck with everything. Keep in touch, and let me know if there is anything that I can do to help you. We have a great many resources at GDC," Leah said.

"Sounds good." Tyson smiled at her. "Thanks for trusting me, Leah."

"Thanks for the exclusive, Tyson," she smiled back.

---

i. Institute for Historical Review http://www.ihr.org/jhr/v07/v07p175_Black.html October 4, 2014

Chapter 48

The Knot

Near Bar Harbor, Maine
Friday, April 23, 2021
4:30 P.M.

"Reverend Stogel says that the temperature tomorrow is going to be unseasonably warm," said Dominique.

"Good, I certainly hope so," answered Tyson with a smile on his face.

"Hey, it was *your* idea to do this up here."

"I know, but honestly, honey, I'd marry you anywhere. Here, Antarctica, the Amazon, Mars, anywhere. I'm the luckiest man in the world, and marrying you on a boat in Acadia National Park will be an honor of a lifetime. Look, it's getting late. Let me walk you back to the house, and then I'll head back to the hotel."

"Honey, it's nice of you to allow Desiree and my family to stay here at your—"

"That would be 'our' house."

"Okay, I'll get used to that. But it's nice to have everyone together again under one roof."

"My pleasure. I'm all set at the hotel, and I have some of my friends from law school and from the university coming in tonight. We'll swap some old stories and have some dinner."

"Don't eat too much. The banquet after the wedding is going to be outrageous!"

The couple walked back to the house where they were warmly greeted by Dominique's father, Jean Claude, her mother, Chantal and her siblings, Charlotte, Josephine and Thierry, all of whom had arrived the night before from Louisiana.

"Bonjour," said maid of honor Charlotte. "I'm so thrilled to be here and so happy that you and Dominique are together. You will be so good for her."

"Me good for her? Let me tell you. She's good for me! And thank you for coming to Maine. I'm sure that it's a little warmer back in Baton Rouge."

"That's for darn sure."

A sharp tap on the shoulder made Tyson quickly spin around.

"Desiree! I was wondering when you were coming into town. How was the trip?"

"Great. Thank you for making all of the arrangements to fly me up here."

"Please, compared to the arrangements that you made it was nothing."

"What arrangements are you talking about?"

"Arranging to get me and your mother together. I will always be in your debt for that. Thank you for being so insistent."

His warm hug suggested the sincerity of his words, words that later focused upon the amount of pride he had in her efforts at Georgetown.

"People are really impressed with you down there. From what my colleagues are telling me, you're doing a terrific job. Keep it up."

"Thank you, Professor."

"It's time to drop that 'Professor' tag."

"Okay, how's 'Dad'?"

"How's 'Tyson'?"

"That'll take some getting used to. Let's play it by ear, Tyson!"

After a long hug and a kiss on the cheek, Tyson announced that he was heading to the hotel. "I'll see everyone tomorrow. Have a good evening!"

After a few morning rain showers, the sunny afternoon the next day saw a rise in the temperatures, proving Reverend Stogel correct. Just as planned, at noon, a small boat was anchored a few feet off the shore of Sand Beach, with a gangplank leading to the beach.

As he waved to those in attendance—some seventy people—Tyson and his best man, Grady, walked up the wood planks onto the deck of the boat, where Stogel met them with a hearty handshake.

The organist continued to play as Charlotte emerged from inside the ship's cabin, then started playing *Here Comes the Bride*, signaling the emergence from the cabin of Jean Claude and Dominique, the latter attired in a flowing, white lace, button-up wedding dress, as flashes lit up on the dozens of cameras and cell phones in the audience. Removing his daughter's veil, the proud father kissed her on the cheek and told her, "All of your life you have made me so very proud, and today is as good as it gets. I love you so much."

"I love you, too, Dad. Thank you for everything."

Shaking Tyson's hand, Jean Claude said, "Welcome to the family, son. Treat my little girl well."

"I promise you I will—for the rest of my life."

Reverend Stogel began, "Please be seated. Dearly beloved, we are gathered today to witness the union of two of God's exceptional children, Dominique and Tyson. Though their paths began in different parts of the country, hers in Louisiana and his in New York, today God has brought them both to Maine to be wed. The wisdom of God has selected a marvelous day upon which we have gathered, knowing that our wishes are for these two individuals to become a joyous, loving married couple.

"Dominique, you have always acted with thoughts for the betterment of those in your life. Know that today God has you in His thoughts and has brought you here, rewarding you for all of the good that you have provided for others.

"Please hold hands. Do you, Dominique, promise to love Tyson with all of your heart and to respect God's will that you are still an individual but are now going to be one-half of a happily married couple?"

"I do." Dominique beamed.

"And Dominique, do you promise that the words that you are about to recite are yours and are from your heart?"

"Yes, I do," she smiled again.

"Then what saith you to Tyson?"

Dominique turned to her groom. "Tyson, meeting you and then falling in love with you has been the most wonderful time of my life.

You are such a magnificent, unique man whose love I cherish. Please know that with each passing day, I will love you more and more. I thank God for the wonderful man he has brought my way. I love you, Tyson. I really, really do."

The Reverend turned to the groom. "Tyson, do you promise to love Dominique with all of your heart and to respect God's will that you are still an individual but are now also one-half of a happily married couple?"

"I most certainly do!" Tyson boomed.

"And Tyson, do you promise that the words that you are about to recite are yours and are from your heart?"

"Yes, I do." His grin stretched from ear to ear.

"Then, what saith you to Dominique?"

Tyson took his bride's hands. "Dominique, after many years as a lawyer, as I began my teaching career, a seasoned veteran advised me, 'Listen to what your students have to say because several of them will be smarter than you.'" He turned to face Dominique's daughter. "Desiree, I listened to you about your mother. Thank you.

"Dominique, I will always remember the first time I saw you, as you walked toward my car. It was from that moment that I thought that you were the most beautiful woman that I had ever seen, one that I liked from the very moment we spoke. That 'liking' of you soon blossomed into love, one that I will keep in my heart until the day that I die.

"I will probably never be able to express the full extent of the love that I have for you, but I promise you, in front of family, friends, and God that I will never fail in my attempt to show you on a daily basis. Thank you for marrying me, Dominique. You have made my life complete. I love you so much."

Reverend Stogel nodded his head with approval. "May I please have the rings?"

Desiree handed her mother Tyson's ring and Dominique placed it on her fiancé's finger. "With this ring, I thee wed."

The Reverend asked for Dominique's ring. Grady handed a sparkling diamond ring to Tyson.

Reverend Stogel began, "Just as the first ring was offered from the hands of the daughter, Dominique, so too is the second ring offered from the arms of the son, Robert. Tyson, please give Dominique her ring." He watched as Tyson slid it onto his bride's finger. "Please hold hands. Do you, Dominique and Tyson, each promise to love, honor, and cherish each other for as long as you both shall live?"

"We do."

"And do you promise to respect each other, be faithful to each other and be willing to acknowledge your love for each other from this day forward?"

"We do." The couple beamed.

"And do you promise to love each other through joy and sorrow, both success and failure and through both sickness and through health?"

"We do." The bride and groom looked tenderly into each other's eyes.

"Finally, in the words of an old Apache blessing, 'Now you will feel no rain, for each of you will be shelter for the other. Now you will feel no cold, for each of you will be warmth to the other. Now there will be no loneliness, for each of you will be companion to the other. Now you are two persons, but there is only one life before you. May happiness be your companion and your days together be good and long upon the Earth.'[i]

"And so, with the powers vested to me by the great state of Maine, I do now and forever pronounce you, Tyson and Dominique, husband and wife. You may now kiss your spouse."

With those words the couple embraced and shared their first kiss as husband and wife. After their passionate exchange, they hugged Desiree, blew a kiss to Robert's grave, and thanked Reverend Stogel. With Grady and Charlotte leading the way, they walked down the gangplank, where they were mobbed by the adoring audience. After several minutes of congratulatory wishes, they walked toward the Lincoln Town Car, which, of course, was being driven by a dapperly dressed Kingsley and rode into their new life together.

---

i. An Apache First nations Blessing http://www.tmclark.com/JP/apache.html October 4, 2014

CHAPTER 49

The Unexpected Call

Studios of WGDC
Washington, D.C.
Saturday, July 17, 2021
11:27 A.M.

After four minutes of being on hold, Leah was starting to get annoyed. Then a voice came on the line.

"Hello, Leah, this is the president. I'm told that you had to speak to me and my secretary said that you couldn't take no for an answer."

"Yes, Madam President. First of all, thank you for taking my call. Just so you are aware, I'm taping this conversation."

"As am I, go ahead."

"Great. My sources indicate that you are privy to the information that President Faulkner received from President Wilson. Would you care to comment upon that?"

"Leah, James received a crap load of stuff in that capsule. Just what are you referring to?"

"Madam President, did you or did you not receive information, perhaps via President Hathaway, regarding the 1865 Land Confiscation Act, which had been kept secret for more than one hundred years?"

The silence on the other end of the phone indicated to Leah that she had struck a nerve. After a momentary silence, Martinez fired away, "Leah, the interview stops here. Turn off the recording device."

"I will turn it off, but I beg to differ, the conversation will have to continue until I get the answers that I want."

"Are you aware of whom you are talking to?"

"Madam President, I called you, remember. Of course I know whom I'm talking to. Now, back to my question, please."

"Again, I'm not sure what you're talking about."

"Madam President, you are not aware of the information that I possess, information that could be very damaging to your presidency?"

Another bout of silence followed, broken when the president asked, "We're still off the record?"

"Yes, I have turned off the recorder."

"Okay, Leah, tell me what you think that you know."

"I know a great deal, Madam President. My sources indicate the troubling details behind the 1865 law, suggesting that it could adversely affect millions of people and the land that they think that they own. Worse yet, the many occupants of the White House have sat upon this information for more than a century. Further, President Hathaway may have been killed due to his willingness to share the information with the public. Think I might have something here? Care to comment?"

"Still off the record?"

"We're off the damn record, Madam President, until you say we're back on it. Now, please answer the question."

"Suppose I were to tell you that there may be something in the works that is related to what you are talking about."

"Could you please be a little more specific, Madam President?"

"At this time I can't."

"I'm afraid that you are going to have to be. I've been sitting on this information for a long time, and I want to get it out there to the public. So, it's either coming from the leader of the nation, or it's coming from one of its leading newscasters. Which will it be, Madam President?"

"Remember who you're talking to."

"I don't need you, Madam President. I can launch this information on my own."

"I can see why people in the Beltway call you a bitch, Leah."

"In the eyes of many people I might be a bitch, Madam President, but I will never be *your* bitch. Now, what will it be?"

"Leah, I've had meetings with key members of my Cabinet, as well as with several Southern governors and some important members of

Congress. We're stymied on this, I tell you."

"My source has worked out a plan that is more than fair to all possible parties. It's a sensible approach, one that has some carefully conceived increments to it. My source ran it by me a few days ago, and I think it would work."

"Interesting. And just how soon were you going to act upon this information?"

"I'm ready now. I could go forward with the story tomorrow."

"Wait, you can't do that."

"Madam President, the operative word is 'could.' But there are two reasons why I won't."

"Those being?"

"First, believe it or not, out of respect for you and your office."

"Thank you for that, although it's hard to believe. And the second?"

"Second, although our solution is one that can preserve the peace and will likely keep a lid on things, it should be something about which the public learns from its leader, not from me."

President Martinez paused. "You'd be missing a golden story—a potential news bonanza, you know."

"If you were to mention that I was in on the talks, that would suffice."

"That's very magnanimous of you, I must say."

"I recall the mess in the 1970s from Daniel Ellsberg's disclosures. This would be much worse—you're talking about the homes and businesses of people. No, Madam President, you should carry the ball on this one."

"Is it that you're worried about your reputation?"

"Not at all. Some things are presidential in nature—this being a prime example."

"When can we talk in details, Leah?"

"Hmm, have your people call my people."

"Sounds great. Oh, one more thing! What if I chose not to cooperate with you?"

"Madam President, my network has been informed that I have a blockbuster announcement prepared for tomorrow night's newscast."

"Would you have gone through with it?"

"Like I said, they've been informed."

"After you and I talk details, can you give me a few weeks to discuss matters with my people?"

"How about a week after we talk? I'll tell my people at the network that I'm holding off."

"A freaking week? That's going to be tough."

"For crying out loud, you're President of the United States. Lean on a few people. And Madam President, one more thing?"

"Yes?"

"I get the exclusive interview with you. And by exclusive, I mean, 'exclusive.'"

CHAPTER 50

The Interview

The United States Penitentiary, Administrative Maximum Facility
Florence, Colorado
Tuesday, August 17, 2021
6:30 P.M.

Leah Manders adjusted her microphone one last time. "Good evening. It has been exactly seven months since the assassination of President Elgin Hathaway, and it is the day mandated by the judicial system that the gag order could be lifted. The self-confessed assassin, Pierce Allen, has agreed to have only one authorized interview, that being held earlier this afternoon with me.

"The plea bargain arrangement has the former Speaker of the House serving a sentence of life in prison without the possibility of parole. For my interview, I have traveled to The United States Penitentiary, Administrative Maximum Facility near Florence, Colorado, the home of male federal prisoners who are thought to be the most dangerous."

Manders looked grave, yet triumphant. "The conditions under which the interview was arranged were simple—no question was out of bounds. I could ask anything that I wanted." She turned to Pierce Allen, clad in an orange prison jumpsuit, a far cry from his well-cut expensive suits. "Speaker Allen, thank you for agreeing to speak with me on camera. There are many questions that I want to ask you, but, before we talk about the recent events that have sent you to this prison, I want to talk about the early years of your life, a time period that made you a legend in your native Kansas."

Allen's expression was unreadable. "Okay, whatever you want."

"Mr. Speaker, your story is one of so many early triumphs—high school and college All-American careers. Then, in your junior year, you left Wichita State, after leading them to an Elite Eight appearance, to go to fight in Vietnam, reportedly to avenge the death of your older brother, Kyle. What led to the decision to leave college?"

Allen's reply was terse. "I felt that the nation needed someone shooting Vietcong more than they needed someone shooting jump shots."

"Your leadership skills had you quickly rise in the ranks, quickly becoming a captain. Tell us about that fateful evening of April 11th."

"Not much to say about it. I threw two grenades back at the enemy; the third one blew me up in the air, tearing my leg from my body."

"Yes, by diving on a live grenade to protect injured soldiers in your unit."

"Yeah, something like that."

"Mr. Speaker, you saved the lives of several men that night, losing your leg and any hopes of what many thought was going to be a promising NBA career. Any regrets?"

Allen permitted himself a small smile. "Regrets? Never. Lives are more important than layups."

Manders guessed he'd delivered that line more than a few times. "You returned a hero, were elected to Congress from your district, and had a distinguished congressional career."

"Yeah, that was a good time."

"Your fellow representatives elected you Speaker of the House, a title that you held for several sessions. So how does a man considered to be the most trustworthy and respected person in Washington become an assassin of the president?"

Allen smirked. "Circumstances, I guess."

"Care to elaborate on the term 'circumstances'? I mean, you became a cold-blooded killer. Why?"

"It was something that had to be done." Allen folded his arms across his chest.

"Speaker Allen, Elgin Hathaway was the President of the United States. Many people across the nation disagreed with some of his views, but to kill him? What were these circumstances, and why in God's name did you have to kill him?"

"God had nothing to do with it. I had my reasons."

Manders remained calm; she expected the stonewalling. "America would like to know these reasons—in fact, they demand to know them."

"Hathaway had to be silenced, and I was the only one capable of doing it."

Manders looked aghast. "Silenced? Why? And why were you the only one capable of doing it?"

"He was about to reveal some information—information that needed to be kept silent."

"What right do you think that you have to determine what the president of the United States can say and when he can say it?"

"Leah, if I were to disclose the information, I'd be doing the job that I silenced Hathaway from doing. Let's move on."

"Was it racial?" Manders pressed. "Because he was black?"

"What?" Allen's expression was unreadable, but he seemed startled.

"You heard me. It's a simple question, Mr. Speaker. Was there a racial nature to your action?"

"No, not at all."

"My staff and I did some research into your family history. In the 1850s your family lived in Pottawatomie, Kansas—"

"My God, Leah. The 1850s? Really."

"Like I was saying, that was the location that during the lead up to the Civil War John Brown had his infamous raid that killed several pro-slavery forces, among them two of your ancestors. Was that the beginning of your family's hatred for people of color?"

"Family hatred? That's unsubstantiated dribble, Leah."

"Really? How about your grandfather, Howard Allen, and his brother Clarence who were both members of the Ku Klux Klan?"

"That might have been them, but it wasn't me!"

"Okay, so you would say that allegations concerning your voting record are inaccurate?"

"What about 'em?" Now Allen seemed a little indignant.

"The record shows that seldom did you ever vote to support bills that furthered the cause of minorities."

"I probably chose to side with financial caution, not wanting to spend like my Democratic counterparts."

"That's bull, Mr. Speaker. It's known that you sponsored many bills that called for major amounts of spending. Are you going to try to dance around this or live up to it?"

Allen appeared to be swallowing his anger. "This line of questioning is ridiculous. Move on."

"I will, but just one more question about it. You and President Faulkner were close friends. Rumors avail that he shared similar views to the ones to which I was just alluding."

"Is there a question in there, Leah?"

"I was getting to it. You were said to have been his closet political ally. Here's the question, Mr. Speaker. Could your attack upon President Hathaway, a man who was despised by Faulkner, be a result of some devious pact between Faulkner and yourself?"

"That's absurd, Leah. Faulkner had nothing to do with this!"

"Despite the six meetings you had with him in the two-week period that preceded his departure from the White House?"

"Look, he was about to die. I wanted to see my friend. It had nothing to do with Hathaway—nothing at all. I made that determination on my own."

"But Faulkner's record on civil rights, like yours, shall we say, is a little light on substance. Perhaps the two of you collaborated—"

"Coincidence, Leah. Mere coincidence."

"I don't think the public will agree."

"Damn the public."

"Let's go back to you wanting to keep Hathaway quiet. How did you learn about the information that you feared he would reveal?"

"Faulkner told me because he was pretty ill at the time and he wanted someone who he could trust to know about it."

"So, you two did discuss the information."

"Yes, but that has nothing to do with Hathaway!"

"Oh, no? Well, Mr. Speaker, I want to read part of a letter that was sent to me and to Professor Tyson Joseph of Columbia University from President Hathaway. ' . . . . I have put a great deal of thought into our conversations of the past and have chosen to reveal to the American people the gist of the law. In the end, the public has the right to know, a right that supersedes any consequences that might arise from its revealing. However, I am fearful that Faulkner has a couple of allies in D.C. who might want to keep me from bringing to light these potent ideas, and so I have chosen to deliver a speech about them on my last day in office, sort of like the list of pardons that my predecessors reveal as they're about to leave office. Think not of this as a shirking of my responsibilities, letting everything fall into the lap of Maria, but rather an admission that I don't have enough time to lead this cause to its end. After her inauguration, I will ask President Martinez to allow me to pursue a leadership position on the topic, but that will be up to her.

"'In the meantime, I am aware that Faulkner has had conversations with a couple of key members of Congress, alas, I don't know who, regarding this soon-to-be pressing issue. I have kept my eyes open, thinking that harm might come from almost any direction. If for some reason I am not around to champion this idea, Tyson, please be the one to spell out its historical background, and, Leah, please provide it a public forum, one that will be heard in all parts of the nation.'"

Manders peered over the top of the printout at Allen. "That letter was overnight mailed to me from the White House. I received it the afternoon after you killed President Hathaway. Are you, Mr. Speaker, one of those who conspired with President Faulkner to keep this information quiet, and was that the real reason for your killing of President Hathaway?"

"Leah, as for this letter that you have read from, how does anyone know that it's from the president?"

Manders smiled evenly. "It has been thoroughly authenticated. Now, answer my question."

"I have to give it to your man Hathaway; he died for what he believed in. But if you want me to implicate a great man like Jim Faulkner in your fictitious ring of conspirators, I will not."

Manders pounced. "Don't dance around it. You conspired with Faulkner to kill Hathaway because of land, didn't you?"

Allen almost rose up out of his chair, and then, after looking at the guards, appeared to think better of it. "Don't you dare throw that baseless garbage into the face of the American people!"

"It's not garbage, Mr. Speaker. And let me tell you, I will use every ounce of my strength to bring to light all of the facts. While you're here rotting in your cell, I and dozens of others will be piecing together the true nature of your hideous actions—changing them from allegations to realities. I promise you, long after you and I are gone from this Earth, the truth about this will be etched in minds of generations to come.

"John Wilkes Booth, Charles Guiteau, Leon Czolgosz, Lee Harvey Oswald, and you, all killers of presidents. You had it all: respect, leadership, and power. Now you'll be doomed to live with this act for as long as mankind has the ability to read. And I promise to be the one who writes your everlasting epitaph." Manders stood up. "Guard, come get him. We're done here."

Chapter 51

The President Comes Clean

WGDC Studios
Washington, D.C.
Thursday, August 19, 2021
8:03 P.M.

" . . . And after the president speaks," said Leah Manders to her audience, "I will return to explain the key role that WGDC played in the investigation of this matter. The next voice you hear will be that of the president."

President Martinez stepped up to the microphone. "My fellow Americans, in the last few days I have become aware of information that may have an impact upon so very many of you. This information has been provided to me by persons in the government and in the private sector. I have ascertained that this information is accurate, and therefore, due to the confluence of their efforts, I feel that I must share the details of it.

"Shortly afterward, I will share with you a detailed plan that will help our nation adjust to the impact that it will provide upon all of us, a plan that was created by many members of the Congress, as well as members of my Cabinet, several state governors and several others in the private sector. For your viewing pleasure, after my speech, the entire procedure will be available on the White House website.

"The information is most pertinent to people who reside in the following states: Alabama, Arkansas, Florida, Georgia, Louisiana, Mississippi, North Carolina, South Carolina, Tennessee, Texas, and Virginia, although the ramifications might apply to citizens all across our nation. And although I have recently learned about the information, it dates back to the 1860s and has been privy to only a select few."

Martinez leaned in toward the cameras. "To tell the entire history of the information, I must take you back to the administration of Abraham

Lincoln and the waning days of the Civil War. In early April of 1865, a group in the Congress, one with enough members to constitute a quorum, passed a bill that called for the confiscation of land owned by slaveholders. The law stipulated that the land would be given to the slaves and/or any person who could prove that he or she was a direct descendant of a slave who lived on that particular piece of property. What's more, the law stipulated that these descendants had up to two hundred years to make their claims.

"The bill became law on the day that Abraham Lincoln died, April 15, 1865. My fellow Americans, due to the desire to keep it quiet by presidential administrations of the late nineteenth century and early twentieth, the law has remained secret until now. Please do not misunderstand that statement, as although it has remained secret, it is still the law of the land. Thus, land in several of the Southern states is liable to the claims of slave descendants."

Martinez paused. "I have met with the governors, senators, and representatives of each of the aforementioned states to discuss a plan of action regarding future claims that will be made upon land within their respective borders. Property in the following states is not affected by this law; Delaware, Kentucky, Maryland, or Missouri. In fact, other than the first eleven states mentioned, there can be no claims made by anyone against lands within any other state.

"Also meeting with me was a team of esteemed historians and lawyers who I contacted to work out the litigious aspects of the law and the potential resolution of its implications.

"The proposed plan agreed to by all those consulted is a settlement that could keep all affected parties satisfied. Next week the proposed plan will be presented to the entire Congress. First, there will be no laws enacted to attempt to counteract the 1865 law; rather, the potential judicial solutions will be allowed time to run their course.

"Those people who are descendants of slaves from those states affected by the law, in order to make a claim, will have to follow the strict guidelines that will be presented on the website. A short summary of these guidelines includes the instituting of detailed genealogical linkages to named slaves and oneself—establishing, for our soon-to-be-created agency named DECADES (Department of Evaluation Claims Associated with Descendants of Emancipated Slaves) a proven unbroken line of family heritage. Without this proof, no claim will be recognized. In addition, all claims must provide proof from Federal Census records that said named slaves did reside on the properties in question."

Martinez directed viewers to the website for procedural information. "As for those Americans, both individual and corporate, against whom potential claims will be made, our commission has set up a list of defense strategies, as well as guidelines, which among them include local, county, state, and federal agencies that will be able to provide assistance once you receive notice that a claim has been made against your property.

"I am hopeful for a tranquil period of adjustment, as we shall rise from the potential crisis-causing legislation from one hundred fifty-seven years ago. We have provided a clear-cut path to help assure a peaceful transition. Please refer to our website to search for detailed information regarding this important topic. In two days there will be a press conference answering many questions that might arise."

Martinez permitted herself a brief smile. "Good evening, and, may God bless America."

CHAPTER 52

The Aftermath

WGDC Studios
Washington, D.C.
Thursday, October 14, 2021

" . . . For a full report, here is correspondent Tom Connors in Atlanta," said Leah Manders to her audience.

"Leah, if Atlanta wasn't already named 'Hot Lanta', let me tell you, from the events of the last few days it could have easily captured that moniker.

"Tempers are flaring, Leah, and I have witnessed several arrests as people on the long lines are not pleased with the new, or should I say old, law. Most of those arrests are of people who are defending their homes or businesses."

"Tom, what are most of the complaints about?"

"Despite the recent public statements by the president, and despite the phone hotlines, the website links, and the cable station dedicated to the potential questions, answers, and complaints that most people might have, most people are complaining that they've been blindsided by all of the legislative action.

"They're receiving registered letters that claim that their property is under consideration to be taken over by some other party, a result of the Confiscation Law of 1865. I spoke with Mr. Harold Bright, a longtime resident of Villa Rica, who earlier today said, 'This is a disgrace. A disgrace, I say. I've lived on this property for forty-five years—hell, it's been in my family for nearly two hundred years. I got a letter from someone named Wilson Collins who is attempting to take over the property. My God, he lives in some town in northern Michigan. He's probably never been to Georgia, let alone Villa Rica. And to top things off, I have to pay for his claims. What kind of crap is that?'

"Leah, that's just one of the dozens of people I've spoken with—all with similar situations. The problems really get going when a person who is defending his property is on line next to a person who is trying to gain ownership of a property. That's a certain source of fireworks!"

"That was Tom Connors in Atlanta. Meanwhile, Janice Warmbir is in Beaufort, South Carolina, the county seat of Beaufort County."

"Janice, describe the situation there in Beaufort."

"Leah, Beaufort is a small town of about fifteen thousand and is the second oldest town in the state. It's a town known for its tourism, its arts festivals, and its shrimp festival. It has been a filming location for such films as *Forrest Gump*, *The Big Chill*, and the *Great Santini*.

"The land clerk's office is hopping—a scene similar to the one found in many southern towns. However, the most interesting conversation that I have had is with ninety-two-year-old lifetime resident of Beaufort, John Boykin, who had much to say."

Boykin was taped sitting in a chair, with a straw hat keeping the sun from directly hitting his already highly wrinkled face, his soft voice and deep Southern drawl making subtitles necessary: "We in South Carolina had a long history of having the federal government trying to screw with us—going way back to that darned Andrew Jackson and our beloved John C. Calhoun in the 1830s. Yet, this is sumtin' new—the federal government from one hundred fifty years ago is trying to screw with us now! No wonder we tried to leave dem 'fore the war. It makes me madder than a mule chewin' on a bunch of bumblebees."

"Janice, is Mr. Boykin typical of your average person in Beaufort?"

"Besides his age, he certainly represents the sentiments of the town. They're all upset. Leah, just one more thing, when I asked Mr. Boykin about how upset the people in town are, he said, 'Mad enough that I heard the preacher cussing.' That sums up things here in Beaufort."

Leah continued, "But everything about his law isn't humorous. Here's an exclusive report from WGDC's Lois Felderman."

"Tallahassee has erupted into violence—at least six dead, hundreds injured. The National Guard has kept the recent rash of violence under control, but, despite their presence, there's an uneasiness that looms over the state's capital. The original violence broke out as a planned march of protesters against the law moved into close proximity to a group who support the law. Tempers erupted, bottles were flung, and then shots were fired. One of the dead is a Florida State trooper, whose name is presently being withheld pending notification of his family."

"Lois, do you sense things are out of control?"

"Leah, things are bad here, and with the rumor of more troops being sent into the fray, there has been diminished violence, but a sense of urgency prevails, one that has leaders all across the region concerned. President Martinez must be concerned with what is happening in her home state."

"Lois, be careful and thank you. There are reports of gathering crowds in the cities of Little Rock, Fayetteville, Baton Rouge, and Memphis, while there are reports of vandalism in dozens of other locations.

"President Martinez says that the nation will wait for the courts to rule, but that could take a great deal of time. The president says that no legislation is planned. One of the so-called victimized citizens of Mississippi is Congressman Victor Polk of Tupelo.

"Mr. Congressman, good morning. How have the people of Mississippi been handling the situation?"

"Leah, there have a few isolated incidents, but for the most part, things here have been fairly calm. I am told that all of the local authorities are prepared for the worst."

"Is it true that you have had your home claimed?"

"Yeah, I received the notice two days ago. Someone from Pennsylvania has made a claim. Leah, I'm concerned about the president's lack of action. It's times like this that we need a man, umm, a leader, who can take control of a situation like this. We need a proactive person to get us out of this situation. What is Martinez waiting for—a full-fledged war to develop in the streets of the nation? I can't imagine Harry Truman, L.B.J. or Ronald Reagan waiting around for a situation to take care of itself."

"Congressman Polk, you were on record as having opposed the election of President Martinez. Is your dissatisfaction personal in nature?"

"Personal? Personal you ask me? The potential exists for me and a bunch of my constituents to lose our homes and businesses, and you're asking me if it's personal? Miss Manders, I could deliver a list of more than one hundred people who are taking this personally."

"Thank you Congressman Polk, and good luck with your situation.

"So there you have it. Many people are complaining about the president's lack of action. Remember, it's not just homes, but businesses too. Several of the major corporations are located here in the South. Several Fortune 500 companies like The Home Depot, Wal-Mart, ExxonMobil, Bank of America, and Coca-Cola have had claims brought against their respective lands.

"Kaitlin Sheehan has a report."

"Leah, I have contacted the offices of twenty of the largest corporations in our nation—all located here in the South. Not a single one—not one—would go on the record concerning this matter, all claiming that they could not comment upon potential litigious matters. Off the record, at least three acknowledged their concerns for the potential loss of their properties, although one confident CEO claimed that his company was equipped to keep the matter in court to, and I quote, 'The next millennium, if necessary.' Leah, business seems concerned, but seems ready to defend what it owns.

"From Charlotte, this is Kaitlin Sheehan, WGDC News."

"Personally, I feel that governmental inaction will not be tolerated by these companies, as billions of dollars will be called into question. Although President Martinez has said that she will wait for the courts to take action, what about Congress? What are they waiting for?

"Do you see what is happening in the streets of Tallahassee? Do you have your eyes closed to the death and destruction there? This could be the very beginning of the action there, or, if action is taken immediately, this could be the end of it. What are you folks waiting for? It is disgraceful seeing nothing being done.

"Thank you for tuning in. This is Leah Manders."

Chapter 53

The Last Words

Several months later
Mount Kisco, New York
Saturday, February 12, 2022
9:45 P.M.

As Dominique walked back into the bedroom and slid under the sheets next to her husband, she heard Tyson say on the speakerphone. "Yes, I *am* aware that it's President Lincoln's real birthday."

Tyson's next comment made it all too clear to whom he was speaking. "It's yours, too, Madam President?" Tyson replied. "Well, I hope at the end of your administration that you're held with the same level of esteem and respect that his was. So far, everything has gone very smoothly. You've gained praises from your party and from some of the opposition and the public, too."

"Professor Joseph, thank you for your service to our country. We couldn't have gotten through the electoral crisis without you," said President Maria Martinez. "And your work on the land crisis was indispensable. Your devised plan for both landholders and slave descendants, well, it was brilliant. Please, once again, thank Dominique for her valuable contributions to the settlement."

Tyson looked up to find his wife grinning. "It's great to be appreciated," he told the president. "But we're sure that someone else would have stepped up to the plate and delivered. That's one of the great things about this nation; there's always someone who's willing to take the lead and get the job done. Anyway, it was our pleasure. How are you dealing with the fallout from your decision to go public with the 1865 law?"

"Land clerks are really busy, to say the least," replied President Martinez. "My public stance, as you know, is that, a law is a law, is a law. It's still early in the game. The judicial wheels have just started to turn, cases in Arkansas, North Carolina, and Texas are moving up the judicial ladder. We'll have to see. Look, I have to run; state business calls. It's always a pleasure speaking with you. I'll be in touch soon—hopefully not for a crisis."

"Madam President, you too. I hope that you are feeling better."

"Yeah, we're out of the flu epidemic, and now I'm coming down with something."

"Be safe, Madam President; a lot of people have been victimized by it this year."

"The CDC says more than one hundred thousand so far. It's been tough, but they say that we're beyond the peak; things should be slowing down."

"That's good news. It's hit our family hard."

"Yes, I was so sorry to hear about your son, Robert. Did you receive my—"

"I certainly did. It was appreciated. Thank you. Be safe, Madam President."

After hanging up the phone, the professor turned toward Dominique and wiggled his eyebrows. She offered him a wry smile and said, "It's a good thing that I'm not the jealous type. Ten minutes on the phone as I, your loving wife, have to lie here and listen to you be all nice to the most powerful woman in the world."

Tyson deadpanned, "Is being president more powerful than being a superintendent of schools? I don't think so!"

It was Dominique's turn to laugh. She hugged her husband, snuggled up to him, and said, "I agree, she might have the power to bomb other nations, but she could never dish out a five-day suspension, could she? That's real power!"

"Her administration's doing fine," Dominique said. "Martinez's selection of Senator Gwen Fredericks-Hillman of South Dakota as vice president was great. He's a complement to her—he's a well-seasoned veteran. He knows D.C. inside out. And he's well liked too. They're making a great team. But, I have to say that I'm surprised that Brook Rider didn't accept the position as Secretary of Health and Human Services. He would have been great at it—he's such a natural leader."

Smiling, Tyson replied, "Oh, I think that he's going to be too busy to take it."

"Busy? Why's that?"

"First of all, he's reopened his lucrative medical practice and besides, during his time at the White House, he was able to find some information that vindicated his late father. He's going to be spending much of his time putting together a book that reveals some of the cover-up that took place in Dallas when Kennedy was killed."

"And you know this—"

"He needed a lawyer and—"

"Wow, will I ever see you? Talk about busy. But, seriously, I'm sure that that book will set this town on edge."

For several minutes the couple discussed the political climate of the nation, agreeing that President Martinez had been, as the professor coined it, "a good shot in the arm" for the nation, a person who had brought life back to the presidency—literally.

"Honey, I want to ask you something about your friend, Elgin."

"Sure, go ahead."

"Do you think he was going to reveal the Radical's land law, like his letter said that he would?"

The professor took a deep breath and said, "Honey, Elgin Hathaway was the smartest man I've ever met. He knew just what he was doing. He was well aware that a segment of society had a rightful claim to land and that for more than one hundred years; they weren't allowed to even know about it. He chose to become their advocate. Remember, in the letter he told me that he didn't think that the claims would go far. He figured they might get shot down by the big-time lawyers of the major corporations caught in the crossfire."

"I'm no lawyer, honey, but I don't think the courts will allow people to just have their land confiscated without a trial. And now, several of the corporations have bonded together—"

"And suppose there is a trial, the descendants would need a great lawyer on their side, wouldn't they?"

"I could imagine so. They'd need . . . Hey, wait a minute, are you saying . . ."

"You got it. I promised Elgin that I would consider being the lead lawyer, or at least helping out. But after Leah started pressuring me, I decided to create the transformation tools we'd need. With your help, of course."

"With my . . . help?"

"Okay, through your leadership."

"I hope I'll be able to see you every now and then. But I still don't understand what Elgin was going to get out of this. He would have had to announce it prior to our findings."

Tyson smiled. "He wanted to do what he felt was right. But he also helped himself in a couple of ways. Instead of being the two-month president who would become a footnote in history, he'll be talked about for the next century, just like Truman will always be remembered as the only president to order the dropping of an atomic bomb. In a sense, Elgin wanted to drop his own bomb. But I had a surprise for him, something that my research uncovered. When you were in high school, do you remember reading about Sherman's March to the Sea?"

"Of course," Dominique said. "1864, General William Tecumseh Sherman and his Union troops marched from Atlanta to Savannah, wiping out everything in their path. I believe that they called it the scorched earth policy."

"Yep, and in the eyes of many southerners, he became one of the most vilified men in history."

"But what does this have to do with Elgin?"

"Everything! One of the wings of Sherman's attack was led by Oliver O. Howard, commander of the Army of the Tennessee. Although Sherman had ordered the scorched earth policy, Howard couldn't go through with it. Folks call him the "Christian General."[i] When he reached the Sutton Farm outside Milledgeville, outside Atlanta, he refused to follow orders."

"Why, honey?"

"Howard's troops had practically destroyed Sutton's Farm, in advance of the infantry, with mortar fire. When they arrived at the main house, they found a horrifying sight. The masters had lined up their slaves as human shields. There were dozens of dead slaves on the floor, as well as the dead bodies of the masters. The lone survivor was a four-month old slave baby they found in a crib."

"A baby?" Dominique cried. "That's incredible! What happened?"

"They renamed the baby boy Oliver Howard Hathaway, after the person who found him, Corporal Kevin Hathaway. Poor kid; the only survivor. His family was devastated. Thanks to Southern hostility toward blacks, World War I, the Spanish Flu, the rise of the KKK, World War II, and the Korean War, the Hathaway family dwindled away. Oliver was the only one of that generation who survived long enough to have kids. Strangely, none of his descendants had cousins. In fact, through my research, I found that Elgin was the only family member alive who could trace his roots back to Oliver."

"The only one? Wow, but then, that would mean that they would be the only ones who could—"

"You got it; make a claim on the original Sutton land."

"That's amazing! Did you find out if he could claim any land?"

"Yes, I did plenty of research. Elgin would have been able to make a legitimate claim."

"That's incredible. What's there now?"

"An Asian automobile company built a manufacturing plant there. The land is worth hundreds of millions of dollars."

"What? You're kidding, aren't you?"

"No. Elgin would have fainted."

Dominique gaped. "But wait a minute. If Elgin had survived, what would he have done with all of that land and the buildings?"

"Knowing him, he wouldn't have done anything with it. He'd leave it alone, just charge them rent."

"Rent?"

"Yeah, I would have suggested about one hundred thousand a year."

"What? People would have accused him of selling out for the cash!"

"Whoa, you're rushing to judgment, honey. Chances are that he wouldn't have collected a cent."

"What? You just told me—"

"I said that he *could* have charged a lot of money. I didn't say what he was doing with it."

"Okay, so then what would happen to the money?"

"Over the years, in our many conversations, one of the things that's upset both of us is the fact that the NCAA has cut scholarships to the sport of track and field. Elgin probably would have used the money to set up a college scholarship fund for deserving kids. I would have helped him set it up. And appoint a panel to oversee the applications."

"Wow. That would be great. One more question: And who's on this panel?"

"Right now, I've only come up with just you and me! But with your educational background, I know you'd get the right people involved."

"I'd like that a great deal, honey. But let me get back to Elgin. Now that he's dead, if the case holds up, it's going to be in litigation for years."

"My law firm will continue to fight for him and his will. I'll make sure any money is used for the scholarships."

"Unbelievable," said Dominique, "I just wish Elgin were around to see all the good his money would do." She smiled ruefully.

Tyson said, "Oh. While I was on the phone with the president, Desiree clicked in."

"What'd she want?"

"I don't know; I couldn't put the president on hold. But I bet it's about that constitutional law professor. That class has been giving her a hard time. I'm not worried; she'll work her way through it—she's smart, just like her mother. In fact, as soon as she graduates and passes the bar, I plan to offer her a job in my firm."

Dominique beamed. "You will? You are too good."

"Well, the litigation for the descendants will take a long while—maybe all the way to 2065. I will need someone I can trust to carry on my work."

"Honey, you're the most thoughtful person I know," Dominique said. "Helping out Desiree like that is great, and setting up Kingsley in his own limo business was a stroke of genius."

Tyson squeezed her hand. "He deserved it—I really don't need him that much anymore."

"Why not?"

Tyson looked into Dominique's eyes. "I don't want to be on the road as much—I'd miss you too much."

"I love you so much, Tyson. I'm so happy that we're together. By the way, honey, you're not the only one to do research. I've been very busy myself."

"You have? On what?"

"Well, first I had to see when Desiree's graduation date is."

"Wednesday, May 18th!"

"Correct. Then I called your law office to see what's on your calendar after that."

Tyson squinted at her. "Okay, what are you up to?"

"With everything going on, we never really had that honeymoon we talked about. So on June 1st we're going to see the doctor."

"The doctor? What are you talking about?"

"Dr. Adeleke. We're heading to Nigeria—you never got to go there because of the flu epidemic. So, you and I are hitting the road."

Giving Dominique a passionate hug, Tyson said, "Honey, you're too much. Thank you so very much—that's great."

As their lips met and the embrace became more passionate, Tyson gazed into his wife's beautiful eyes, thinking about the happiness that he had finally had in his life. He pushed away thoughts of the many lonely days and nights before meeting her.

Coming in for another kiss, he hummed to himself his favorite song, by his favorite singer. *You know it, Marvin Gaye*, he thought, *ain't nothing like the real thing.*

---

i. Wikipedia Article: Oliver O. Howard: https://en.wikipedia.org/wiki/Oliver_O._Howard October 5, 2014

36636230R00224

Made in the USA
Middletown, DE
06 November 2016